Praise for Lama Surya

AWAKENING TO THE SACRED

'Surya Das brings a reader the how and why, the tools and the inspiration, to live one's life with spiritual practice as the priority. With clarity and humour, through stories and practice, this book welcomes those of all spiritual traditions to the process of becoming fully alive'

Sharon Salzberg, author of *A Heart As Wide As the World*

'*Awakening to the Sacred* will bring great gifts into the lives of its readers. It is user friendly, filled with beautiful teachings, gracious stories, dozens of practices, humorous tales, and wise practical ways to invite our hearts to awaken to the highest wisdom in every part of our lives'

Jack Kornfield, author of *A Path with Heart*

'Lama Surya Das offers a fresh and invigorating approach to the perennial quest which gives natural spirituality its rightful place at the centre of things . . . It offers a helping hand and open heart to the beginner and the seasoned spiritual traveller alike'

Mitchell Kapor, founder of the Lotus Foundation

'*Awakening to the Sacred* is a book of profound beginnings on life's spiritual path. Written with tenderness and warmth, it is a wonderful companion on the way of the sacred in everyday life'

Ken Wilber, author of *The Marriage of Sense and Soul*

'Surya Das leads the way through the essential values – wisdom, ethics and meditation – spicing the lessons with details from his own spiritual road trip'

Los Angeles Times

'A warm, accessible, deep, brilliantly written exploration and adventure . . . A marvellous and enlightening book'

Jon Kabat-Sinn, Ph.D., author of *Wherever You Go, There You Are*

'Offering the reader fresh, authentic impressions that are clearly the result of his own spiritual work and reflection, Surya Das emerges here as a genial 'post-denominational' spiritual teacher, one whose straightforward approach to the esoteric deserves to reach a wide readership'

Publishers Weekly

◆

Books by Lama Surya Das

AWAKENING THE BUDDHA WITHIN

THE SNOW LION'S TURQUOISE MANE

NATURAL GREAT PERFECTION
(with Nyoshul Khenpo Rinpoche)

◆

Awakening to the Sacred

Creating a Spiritual Life from Scratch

◆

LAMA SURYA DAS

BANTAM BOOKS

LONDON · NEW YORK · TORONTO · SYDNEY · AUCKLAND

AWAKENING TO THE SACRED
A BANTAM BOOK: 0553 81295 5

First publication in Great Britain

PRINTING HISTORY
Bantam Books edition published 2000

1 3 5 7 9 10 8 6 4 2

Set in 12/14pt Bodoni
by Phoenix Typesetting, Ilkley, West Yorkshire

Bantam Books are published by Transworld Publishers,
61–63 Uxbridge Road, London W5 5SA,
a division of The Random House Group Ltd,
in Australia by Random House Australia (Pty) Ltd,
20 Alfred Street, Milsons Point, Sydney, NSW 2061, Australia,
in New Zealand by Random House New Zealand Ltd,
18 Poland Road, Glenfield, Auckland 10, New Zealand
and in South Africa by Random House (Pty) Ltd,
Endulini, 5a Jubilee Road, Parktown 2193, South Africa.

Reproduced, printed and bound in Great Britain by
Clays Ltd, St Ives plc.

This book is dedicated to
my dear Dharma friends and colleagues,
the best of companions on the Great Way

This is what you shall do: Love the earth and sun and the animals, despise riches, give alms to every one that asks, stand up for the stupid and crazy, devote your income and labor to others, hate tyrants, argue not concerning God, have patience and indulgence toward the people . . . re-examine all you have been told at school or church or in any book, dismiss what insults your very soul, and your very flesh shall become a great poem.

WALT WHITMAN

◆

Contents

◆

PART TWO

Acknowledgments

◆

It takes a village to create anything worthwhile, at least these days. Therefore I want to thank all the loving spiritual friends and students who assisted me in the process of writing this book: Charles Genoud, Branden Kennedy, Deb Bouvier, John Makransky, Joel Baehr, Lucy Duggan, Trudy Goodman, Roger Walsh, Josh Baran, Mitch Kapor, Bob Hildebrand, Sharon Salzberg, Jack Kornfield, Joseph Goldstein, Cheryl Richardson, Susan Anthony, Lewis Richmond, Judy Kennedy, John Halley, John Friedlander, Richard Borofsky, Brian Maguire, Michele Tempesta, and Sylvia San Miguel.

I also want to gratefully acknowledge my terrific literary agent, Susan Cohen; dear friends, Kathy Peterson and Julia Coopersmith; and my esteemed colleagues at Broadway Books: my dear editor Lauren Marino, creative book designer Roberto de Vicq de Cumptich, dynamic publicity director Trigg Robinson, supportive managing editor Rebecca Holland, and Bill Shinker, the innovative publisher of a house I am proud to be part of.

Finally my gratitude, respects, and appreciation to my living Tibetan mentors, Nyoshul Khenpo Rinpoche and Tulku Pema Wangyal, and to the late Neem Karoli Baba, all of whom remain a constant source of blessings, inspiration, and guidance.

May all peace, blessings, good fortune, and delight be theirs.

Introduction – Awakening to the Bigger Picture

◆

Let none turn over books, or roam the stars in quest of God, who sees him not in man.

JOHANN KASPAR LAVATER, Swiss poet (1741–1801)

If you have picked up this book, then in all probability you are a seeker. My dictionary has a simple definition of a seeker as 'one who seeks: a seeker of truth.' In practical terms, a seeker is a spiritual traveller or wayfarer, a pilgrim who has embarked on a quest to find and experience the sacred. Seekers are ubiquitous: They can be found in every nation; they can be part of any religious group or denomination. The search for truth and love – something beyond and bigger than ourselves – is the common element.

Seekers want to understand and explore themselves as well as the universe with all its mysteries, both known and unknowable. In their hearts, seekers believe that the universe makes sense and their lives have meaning. They believe not only that truth exists, but that it can indeed be found, and experienced.

When I was young, and even more foolish than I am today, I believed that one had to travel far and wide in order to seek truth, divine reality, or whatever you call it. I believed that truth would most likely be found in the world's so-called sacred places. Yet the fact is that truth is everywhere; it knows no religious, cultural, temporal, or ethnic bounds. Truth is the perfect circle. Its center is everywhere; its circumference stretches into infinite space. The land on which we stand is sacred, no matter where we stand.

The Tao Te Ching says:

> *Without going out of my door*
> *I can know all things on earth.*
> *Without looking out of my window*
> *I can know the ways of heaven.*

Each of us – you and me – stands at the center of his or her own truth. Throughout the ages, saints, sages, and holy men and women have all discovered the same thing – that truth is found by living truly. Awareness is the essential ingredient in a spiritual life. Seekers walk the spiritual path to enlightenment because they believe it will bring a true understanding of reality – an understanding of 'what is' and how things work. The spiritual path is best walked step by step, very mindfully, with as much consciousness and commitment as one can summon.

I firmly believe that we've all been touched by the sacred, no matter how fleetingly. We've known breakthroughs, epiphanies, and blessed times of grace, no matter how ephemeral. Often these vivid moments happen when we are children. People tell me that they remember times, albeit brief, when the smoky veils of illusion and delusion lifted, and they were literally able to 'see the light.' Others have related childhood memories that include relationships with angels. Still others say they have had no such otherworldly encounters, yet they remember experiencing a sense of cosmic divine love, a magical universe of goodness, interconnectedness, and belonging so profound that it inspired them for a lifetime.

As adults, we also have brief glimpses of a more sacred reality. Sometimes we find it in nature – on a solitary walk in the woods or along a sandy beach. Sometimes it happens when we come into contact with a person whose spiritual energy is inspirational. Sometimes it happens when we attend a worship service, a meditation session, a spiritual retreat, or even something as secular as a fine concert. We come away transported, momentarily transformed by what we've seen and heard. We feel different – more grounded, genuinely real, and 'alive,' as well as more connected to the divine. We feel as though we have finally come home. We want the feeling to continue, and we think to ourselves, *I must do this more often. This is something that should be part of my life – all the time.*

Like all things, these glorious seconds of illumination eventually vanish. And when they do, the lives and worlds we have constructed for ourselves come rushing back in like the relentless tide. Our habitual patterns return, and the sublime feelings evaporate. But we retain the memories of those moments that contained the essence of spirituality – true peace, love, freedom, and a sense of belonging. It makes sense that we want to revisit and re-create these spiritual memories. It makes sense that we want to move in and stay closer to the light.

I've spent most of my adult life in various Buddhist

monasteries, as well as ashrams and retreat centers, so I feel as though I have a fairly good idea of what it means to want to lead a more centered and sacred life. And I know how challenging it can be to take the first committed steps on such a path. When I give lectures or readings, almost inevitably one or more members of the audience comes up afterward to tell me how much he or she wants to become more committed to spiritual values in his or her life. They usually tell me how difficult it is to find specific day-by-day ways to do so. Often they go so far as to ask me whether I think they have to leave their lives, their jobs, and their mates so that they can do more than merely pay lip service to their spiritual inclinations. Some even ask me to recommend specific sites in the Himalayas.

These people all want personal transformation and direct religious experience. Isn't that what we all want? Don't we all want enlightenment? As a new century begins, the question is not *whether* we here in the West want enlightenment, but rather *how*. How can we find spiritual transformation? How can we find a renewed sense of life, purpose, and meaning – here and now?

One of the greatest challenges that Western seekers face is finding ways to integrate spiritual values and pragmatic and practical practices into whatever they do. As seekers, we intuitively believe that the visible world we live in is part of a greater spiritual universe. We aspire to somehow experience a more palpable connection with that sacred universe. We sincerely believe that it is possible to become part of that universe by actualizing the divine light or spirit that is found within each of us.

Like me, most of the people who attend my lectures

come from a religious tradition other than Buddhism – usually Christianity or Judaism, traditions that often stress service both to God and humanity. Typically, these people are drawn by various Buddhist practices, such as meditation, because they want to bring more mindfulness and serenity into their lives. They are hoping that mindfulness, in turn, will help them become more compassionate, loving, and caring; they are hoping that mindfulness will help them find ways to serve and contribute; they are hoping that mindfulness will help them get rid of old patterns and habits that have proven to be unwise. These people want to be and act in more highly evolved conscious and wise ways. They want their lives to reflect more noble and inclusive aspirations and concerns. They want to live up to who and what they are. They want to fulfill their spiritual potential. They want their lives to have spiritual purpose.

In the early 1970s, I was fortunate enough to be present when the Dalai Lama was teaching at Bodh Gaya, the town in northern India where the Buddha became enlightened. Tens of thousands of people came to hear the Dalai Lama speak. The majority of them were Tibetan and Himalayan, but there were also small clusters of Westerners, most of them like myself, hippies on the Overland Route from Turkey to the end of the road in Kathmandu, Nepal. When the Dalai Lama was finished, he asked if there were any questions, and one long-haired American guy stood to ask the Dalai Lama the following question: 'What is the meaning of life?'

The Dalai Lama answered, 'To be happy and to make others happy.'

At the time I thought this was sort of a superficial

answer. It seemed so simplistic. I was twenty-one and very much 'into' reading philosophers and novelists like Schopenhauer, Dostoevski, Camus, and Vonnegut. It was that era. I probably still wanted to hear that the meaning of life was complex and understandable only to twenty-one-year-old intellectual elitists such as myself. I just didn't get the Dalai Lama's answer, 'To be happy and to make others happy.' What did that mean? And wasn't it hedonistic as well, I wondered? In my confusion, happiness seemed like such an ordinary self-centered concern.

I pondered the Dalai Lama's words for a long time; I even wrote them down in the small notebook I always carried with me in those days. Years later I was reading over some ancient Tibetan texts, one of which summed up the purpose of the spiritual path in its entirety with two simple phrases: for the benefit of self and for the benefit of others. It was then that I realized that self-interest isn't always selfish. What the Dalai Lama had said was at one and the same time perfectly clear as well as totally profound.

It's been almost three decades since I stood in the all-day sun in the tiny village of Bodh Gaya in the middle of the desert to get my first glimpse of the compassionate Tibetan leader. Today I appreciate the wisdom of what the Dalai Lama said. I also more fully appreciate how difficult it is to act and think consistently in ways that make ourselves and others happy. Think of what it would mean if we were always able to be happy and to make others happy – truly happy and fulfilled, not just paying lip service to happiness and wearing a facile smile. If we were able to do that, we would be living without thoughts, words, or actions that make ourselves or anyone else unhappy. We would be able to stop being either hurtful or self-destructive. We would be living without internal contradictions or conflict. What an amazing goal! What amazing lives we would have! What amazing people we'd be! What amazing spirits we *are*.

Part One

◆

Matters of the Spirit

Great men are they who see that spiritual is stronger than any material force, that thoughts rule the world.

RALPH WALDO EMERSON

◆

Who is holy? What is sacred?

As spiritual wayfarers, what do we think about? What do we talk about? Divine Presence, God, spirit, soul, reality, truth, self-knowledge, mystical experience, inner peace, enlightenment. The spiritual life is concerned with issues such as these. And when we talk about our experiences of the divine, we don't all use the same vocabulary. Sometimes we use the same words and mean different things; sometimes we use different words and mean the same things.

We share an intuitive sense that we are on a journey and that we must search for real answers to our real questions. We do this even knowing that we may find out that the answer is that there is no ultimate answer; some things remain unknowable. And that answer may well be enough. Nonetheless, as seekers we choose to live out our questions. Infinity is open-ended. That's what Buddhists call 'sunyata,' or emptiness.

Whatever words we choose to use, spiritual matters concern themselves with the true bottom line, with those things that really matter in the long run. As spiritual seekers, we think about how we can learn to love more deeply, know ourselves more truly, and connect with the divine more fully.

We think about those things that are beyond the self; we think about the intangible as well as the tangible; we think about the visible and the invisible; we think about touching the palpable sweetness of spirit; we think about how we can find ourselves in the whole, the bigger picture, the universal 'mandala.'

Entering the Stream of Truth and Light

◆

Lead us from darkness to the light;
lead us from illusion to wisdom
lead us from death to the deathlessness.
Lead us from conflict and suffering to harmony, peace, and happiness.

This prayer is from the Upanishads, the mystical Hindu scriptures, first written down sometime around 900 B.C. In many ways I think of these four lines as the universal seeker's prayer. Since the beginning of recorded time, the quest for truth, love, and the highest good has been associated with the quest for light.

As seekers, you and I search for illumination and guidance. We want understanding – not only of our immediate problems but also of the great mysteries of the universe. We want to be able to move from murky illusion and confusion to wisdom, certainty, and clarity. We want to go from delusion to truth; we want the promise that we will be able to escape the darkness of the soul's infernal regions and make it to a place of infinite luminous peace, contentment, and divine unconditional love. We want to leave ignorance and unconscious as well as semiconscious behavior behind. We know that the antidote to ignorance isn't just more information. We know that our spiritual life depends on our being able to cultivate a higher consciousness – a mindful consciousness – as well as greater awareness. We know that our spiritual life depends on cultivating our own capacity to love.

There is an old Jewish saying: 'God is closest to those with broken hearts.' For most of us this is a true statement. At times of great sadness and personal crisis we feel more tenderhearted and closer to our soulful center. When we are most confused and buffeted about by the vagaries of life, we hunger intensely for spiritual guidance and wisdom. Hasn't that been true in your own life? As you seek to deepen your spirituality, you may be reacting to a pattern of ups and downs that has proven to be ultimately dissatisfying. You may feel inwardly empty and long for a deeper connection to meaning, purpose, and the sacred. You may feel spiritually hungry as well as alone.

Some of you may feel discouraged because you believe that you have already 'given way too much.' Or perhaps you feel as though you can't 'give' or don't know how to 'give' what life requires; some of you may actually freeze up when it comes to giving or receiving love or spiritual gifts. Many of you have come to see that you are responsible for your own fate, your own experience, your own karma. You want to help create a better world for others as well as yourself.

Difficulties and disappointments often help us find and strengthen our spiritual resolve. At this moment, life's confusions have aided you by making you wise enough to know that you don't have all the answers.

This awareness – this sliver of light – has made you conscious of the possibility of some form of inner radiance, clarity, or light. You can almost see the light – hear it, feel it. You want to be able to know it and be(come) it. This glimmer of awareness represents an epiphany or mini-enlightenment.

The joys and sorrows of your human life are presenting you with a tremendous opportunity. Taking the spiritual path to enlightenment implies some unconscious if not explicit belief in the possibility of deliverance, self-mastery, and transcendence. Others before you have plunged into the sea of spirit and bliss; others have found what they were seeking while drinking deeply of the immortal, elixir-like waters of enlightenment. Why should any of us spend our lives as onlookers at the seaside, nervously wading in the shallows? Life has a lot more to offer than that. Others have found freedom, satisfaction, and liberation. You can do it too. We can all do it. Together. The time has come to stride in and begin swimming in the deeper waters. Surf's up!

Cultivating Awareness of the Light Within

◆

The heart and mind can find peace and harmony by contemplating the transendental nature of the true self as supreme effulgent light.

From the *Yoga Sutra* of PATANJALI, second century B.C.

Patanjali is often called the father of yoga because he was the first person to codify and write down yogic practices. In this meditation instruction, he is telling us to let go of all distracting sights, smells, and sounds and meditate on our spiritual nature, our luminous true self. He is telling us to look inside and experience the radiance within.

All cultures, peoples, and religious groups through all times have talked about the phenomena of light in the context of the religious or mystical experience. Those who have seen visions of holy beings typically see them surrounded by white light. People have always described going to the light, finding the light, being called by the light, dissolving in the light. We read about light in *The Egyptian Book of the Dead* as well as *The Tibetan Book of the Dead*. Men, women, and children who have had classic near-death experiences vividly describe arriving in a place of white light; they speak of themselves and others as being bathed in white light.

Prior to being described as the light of any religion, light was just light. Light is a part of the primary source material. Later, as the history of mankind developed, the concept of light became institutionalized; it was then interpreted according to cultural and religious beliefs. Pure light thus became light of God, light of truth, light of Buddha, light of Jesus, cosmic light, and ocean of light depending upon where you were born and what you were taught. Light, however, is the constant. It is fundamental energy.

The New Testament, referring to John the Baptist, reads: 'He came for testimony, to bear witness to the light that all might believe through him.' Later Jesus says, 'Put your trust in the light while you have it so that you may become sons of light.' God appeared to Moses out of the firelight of the burning bush. When Ezekiel saw the glory of the Lord, according to the Old Testament, he said: 'I saw as it were the appearance of fire, and there was brightness round about him.'

British mystic George Fox, who founded the Quaker religion, used the term 'inner light' to describe our ability to personally experience God within ourselves. He himself had such an experience, which left him with the lifelong conviction that everyone can hear God's voice directly without mediation by priests or church ritual. This is the central tenet of the Society of Friends.

According to Buddhism, all beings are imbued with a spark of inner divine light. In describing our original Buddha-nature, we use phrases such as innate luminosity, primordial radiance, the unobscured clear natural mind, and the clear light of reality. Zen masters call this original-nature or your-face-before-your-parents-were-born. The Jewish mystics use similar words when they speak of the inner spark or the spark of God. The Koran, referring to man, talks about the little candle flame burning in a niche in the wall of God's temple.

In one of the most famous examples of religious transformation, St Paul found God on the road to Damascus. Those who were travelling with Paul could not hear God, but they all saw the light. The New Testament quotes Paul, 'And when I could not see because of the brightness of the light, I was led by the hand by those who were with me.'

Almost inevitably a spiritual search becomes a search for divine or sacred light. By cultivating our sacred core, we search for this light in ourselves as well as in the divine. This light is not always immediately visible. It's as though we are digging deep into the earth. At first we find earth on top of rock on top of shale, but if we were able to keep going, eventually we would hit the earth's luminous molten core. This same concept applies to the clear, luminous light that resides in each of us. This is our primordial nature, pure energy or spirit, without beginning or end; it is the fundamental ground of being.

In Tibetan Buddhism this clear light is called 'Rigpa' or Ground Luminosity. *The Tibetan Book of the Dead* teaches that at the time of death Ground Luminosity – innate Buddha-nature – naturally dawns for everyone. As all of our negative emotions and worldly concerns fall away, this natural mind is left, free of the darkness of ignorance; in this way the luminous nature of *being* surfaces and shines out.

Tibetan meditators are trained to be able to recognize

this luminosity when it occurs at the moment of death, for this is one shining moment when the possibility of liberation occurs. But the possibility of liberation also occurs at every moment of life. All we have to do is let go of the extraneous and recognize and follow the natural light of awareness and truth.

In nature, of course, light is essential for growth. Watch your houseplants and see how they turn toward the light for nourishment. In the same way, as seekers, we turn to divine light for nourishment because of a natural spiritual tropism. We can begin to train in divine light meditation by closing our eyes and looking into our own inner radiance. Anybody can do this. Close your eyes, press lightly on your eyeballs, and see the shimmering black light. Peer into that, and you'll discover that it's not as dark beyond your eyelids as you might think.

In his fine book *The Healing Power of Mind*, Tibetan teacher Tulku Thondup Rinpoche says:

'Meditations on light can be used to heal specific problems, or they can help generally to make us feel more open and spacious. As we meditate on light, we can imagine the light as expanding beyond our bodies and shining forth without end. We can see the whole world as touched, suffused, and transformed into pure and peaceful light. If we meditate on light in a very open way, we realize that light in infinite, without borders or the limits of time and space.'

Another way to train in inner light meditation is by practicing a simple candle-flame meditation. To do this:

Light a candle in a darkened room.
Move about two feet away from it and sit down,
facing the candle flame.

Get comfortable.
Then begin breathing in and out quietly through your nostrils.
Let your body relax. Let your breath relax.
Just concentrate on the candle flame.
Watch it for several minutes.
Don't think about anything in particular. Let your thoughts go; let them settle.
Watch the flame. Let your mind go into it.
Suddenly blow out the candle and close your eyes.
See the image that forms on the inside of your eyelids.
Meditate on that light.

Yet another simple way to become conscious of inner light is by closing your eyes and focusing on the point on your forehead that is located between your eyebrows and up about an inch. This is called your 'third eye.' In kundalini yoga this is known as the forehead 'chakra,' one of the seven essential energy points, or chakras, in the human body.

Become more aware of the light in the center of your forehead in the following way:

Get comfortable, close your eyes, and focus on the forehead chakra. Find the point of light and for a few minutes concentrate on that. This light is part of your own natural healing energy system. Try doing this in a darkened room.

For a moment, let go of your worldly concerns. These are the preoccupations that can limit your vision. Let the forehead chakra open up, and experience a more spacious, open sense of who you are. Relax. Don't get nervous about finding either a new place in the universe or a new sense of what's important. Don't be afraid to find your own inner light.

Thoughts About God

◆

Every day people are straying away from the church and going back to God.

LENNY BRUCE

God requires no synagogue – except in the heart.

HASIDIC SAYING

God has no religion.

MAHATMA GANDHI

The Ethiopians say that their gods are snub-nosed and black, the Thracians that theirs have light blue eyes and red hair.

XENOPHANES

If triangles had a god, he would have three sides.

CHARLES DE MONTESQUIEU

Nirvana is another word for God.

THICH NHAT HANH

The Kotzker Rabbi once asked several of his disciples: 'Where does God exist?'

'Everywhere,' the surprised disciples replied with alacrity.

'No,' said the wise Rebbe. 'God exists only where man lets him in.'

HASIDIC TALE

God and Buddha, in Form and Essence

◆

The truth is, God talks to everybody.

NEALE DONALD WALSCH, *Conversations with God*

There is probably no other word more open to interpretation, misinterpretation, debate, and argument than the word 'God.' That's why talk of religion, along with politics, is so often verboten at holiday gatherings in America. It's just too thorny to risk alienating your family and friends.

To at least some degree, your concept about who or what God is or isn't depends on what you were taught, and how you reacted to those teachings. Here in the West, the vast majority of us grew up with a cultural connection to the Judeo-Christian traditions and the God these religions espoused. And who did God look like? Probably an older white guy with a long beard, seated above or astride the clouds. Or maybe he was a dead ringer for George Burns.

Small pockets in southern India are predominantly Christian. The Jesus depicted in their art does not have light skin or hair. He looks Indian – a lot like the Indian god Krishna in fact, with dark hair and eyes. This is what Joseph Campbell called the God with the myriad faces. Or as Muslims say, Allah has a thousand names.

Despite all this talk of God, many of us in this multi-colored, pluralistic, multinational world we live in have either forgotten, or were never taught, the common origins of the concept of the one God. I know that I have spoken with many Western friends who know an amazing amount about Asian languages and religions, yet didn't seem to realize that the Christian God of the New Testament; Yahweh, the Jewish God of the Old Testament; and Allah, the Islamic God of the Koran, are one and the same – or that all three of these 'Western' religions evolved from the same source.

As young people here in the West, no matter what our religious affiliation or how we imagined God to be, we all heard a great deal about him – at home, in schools, as well as in places of worship. We went to movies that talked about and sometimes even showed God speaking down from the heavens. In our cities and towns, we regularly walked past churches and temples and heard the songs and prayers behind the closed doors. On Sundays, Christmas, and Easter we turned on television sets and saw cardinals and bishops, and sometimes even the pope, talking about God. During Hanukkah, Yom Kippur, and Passover, we heard about the relationship between the Jewish people and the God of the Old Testament, Jehovah or Yahweh.

A great many of us learned how to pray to God as children. Some of us grew up feeling very connected to the God we prayed to; others had no such attachment; still others remember being afraid of God and his wrath and judgment. It didn't always seem to be a very pretty picture. In short, we were all familiar with the concept of God, whether or not we ascribed to it.

In my family, for example, my father followed the religious traditions of Judaism. My mother, like many of her generation, was less religious and appeared more connected to the Jewish culture than to the religion. I remember my grandmother, however, telling me never to spell out the word 'God' because that would be using the name in vain; I would, she said, be tempting God's wrath. 'G-d,' she assured me, was the correct way to go. Later, I got into trouble on my grammar school papers and reports because I tried to insist on the spelling I had learned at home.

In Buddhist countries such as Tibet one hears little or no reference to the word 'God,' and yet one hears a great deal about the same concepts that Western religions associate with a belief in a divine presence: infinite wholeness and all-inclusive completeness; sanctuary, refuge, and protection; being at one with oneself and the universe; compassion; unconditional, deathless, divine love.

Buddhism, of course, is not a theistic religion. In theory, Buddhism does not deal with theology, or God as creator or eternal being. Yet the Asian belief system is inhabited with countless gods (small 'g') and goddesses, meditational deities, protectors, dakinis, and unseen spirits and forces. These are not, however, to be confused with what Westerners think of as God.

Buddha was not a god, and he claimed no special familial connection to any god. During his lifetime, the Buddha was asked whether or not God existed. On this question, the Buddha remained silent. In fact, the Buddha said that he didn't think intellectual speculation on the existence of God was particularly helpful. He did not assert or deny God; he simply left theology to the Brahmin and Hindu philosophers of his time.

The Buddha's teachings were concerned with finding the nirvanic peace and freedom of enlightenment, the end to all forms of suffering and delusion. He saw these goals as being determined by the cause and effect of individual behavior without divine intervention.

Some say that Buddha was an atheist; most consider that Buddha was not atheistic, but agnostic. There is at least one classical reference to Buddha talking about God. This is found in a small obscure 'sutra,' or Buddhist scripture. In it, the Buddha is speaking to a Brahmin sect in the south of India about the path to enlightenment. As Hindus, Brahmins, of course, believe in God with a capital 'G,' as well as many less powerful deities or gods. Over the centuries there has been much discussion and debate over why the Buddha would talk about God. The explanation often given is that one of Buddha's great gifts was his ability to speak to each individual in ways that he or she could understand. Thus when he spoke to the Brahmins, he used words that they would readily understand.

Around the world, there are countless different ideas and concepts of God. For some people God is a name ascribed to the Ultimate, the Creator, Absolute Cosmic Consciousness, or Divine Mind. Some people see God as transcendent spirit or energy. Some people speak of God as the personification of truth and love. Some people say God is Reality. Some people only think of God as being 'out there' somewhere beyond our human comprehension; others see God as being only 'in here' in the deepest parts of the human spirit or soul.

One of my Zen teachers, Sazaki Roshi, once gave me the following Zen riddle, or 'koan': 'How to realize God while driving car?' If he were in his native Japan, my teacher might have said, 'How to realize Buddha while chopping wood?' Yet in California, which is where we were at the time, this great Zen master thought it made perfect sense, when teaching a Westerner, to substitute God and cars for Buddha and wood. He had no problem with the word 'God,' because the primary riddle, or koan, had to do with the concept of realization. The form was different, but the essential riddle of life remains: How can we practice penetrating spirituality no matter what we do?

Some Hindu devotees say God and guru are one and that by worshiping the guru, one worships God. In Hinduism, one can even worship God by worshiping one's mate. Thus we see Shiva and Shakti, Ram and Sita, Krishna and Radha, all archetypical images personifying an androgynous God in a male and female, polarity – Mr and Mrs God, as it were.

I'm sure you have a belief of some kind. Everybody does. Even unbelievers have a belief. Nobody talks more about God than atheists and agnostics do. You may want to define what you believe, or you may prefer leaving it completely amorphous. You may be happiest thinking of God as a significantly larger than life male, female, or androgynous entity; or you may feel closer to the view of God as Divine Presence. I don't think we, as spiritual seekers today, need to be bound by any formal formulation of God. At the very fundamental level, the light is always there even in the darkness, for even shadows are filled with light.

If you look closely at the large colorful Tibetan mandalas, in the center you will see a representation of the Buddha. This is to remind people of the essence that is contained within the form. Form and essence/emptiness are inseparable.

On Form and Essence in Your Own Spiritual Practice

◆

Whenever I lead or attend a retreat in this country, I am struck by the very different spiritual backgrounds of the participants. Some were raised as Roman Catholics; some were raised as Protestants; some were raised as Jews – Orthodox, Conservative, and Reform. Some came from strictly observant families that were fundamentalist in their attitude; others attended church, temple, or synagogue once or twice a year at most. And these categories all contain subcategories and variations.

Whatever your own background might be, if you search it, you might well find religious and spiritual practices that had meaning for you. You might have loved singing at midnight services. You might have loved lighting candles for the Sabbath. You might have loved the feeling of being part of a spiritual congregation or group. You might have always been drawn to gospel music and spirituals, Gregorian chanting, incense, or Russian icons.

Here, in today's post-denominational West, many of us are trying to create a new and refreshed spirituality. That does not mean, however, that we have to toss out the old. As you try to create your spiritual life from scratch, think about the spare parts and tools that you already possess. You may already own a whole chest full of spiritual tools that fit your hands exactly. Check them out to see whether they can be part of your life.

Are there prayers that you already know by heart? Are there hymns and songs that speak to you as strongly now as they did when you were a child? Do you want to fast and pray for Yom Kippur? Do you want to go to church and be part of Good Friday and Easter? Don't hide from these impulses. No matter what your religious history, love is love; atonement is atonement; prayer is prayer; spiritual renewal is spiritual renewal.

Some people argue with this approach, calling it 'mix and match' spirituality, dismissing it as being too 'New Age.' Some of these critics worry that this is a religion-lite approach and will almost by definition end up being watered down, too easy, and convenient. I disagree. So many of us grew up in families, towns, and neighborhoods that can be described as 'mix and match' that a spirituality that combines elements of several traditions makes sense. It feels authentic and true to who we are. This is, after all, America – the great melting pot. Critics are often people who are threatened by change. A new spirituality that reflects the Western experience does not necessarily mean that serious practices and values will be left out or sacrificed because they appear too difficult.

Janine, a forty-five-year-old playwright, says that her parents were originally Greek Orthodox, but when the family moved to a small midwestern town, there was no Greek Orthodox church. So her mother attended services at the local Methodist church, while her father became a Catholic. The reason given at the time was that her mother felt the Roman Catholic mass was 'too formal' and her father found the Methodist service too 'loose.'

As a child, Janine went to mass with her father, but she attended Methodist Sunday school. At twenty, she married someone who was Jewish. She and her husband agreed that they would raise their children as Quakers because the couple was strongly drawn to a philosophy that emphasized peace. Now that the children are grown and she is divorced, Janine finds that she frequently attends Greek Orthodox or Catholic mass. Sometimes she experiences a deep hunger for the ritual. However, at this point in her life she says that she would never consider becoming more deeply involved with either religion. She doesn't agree with the Catholic church's attitude toward women, and, as a divorced person, she isn't even sure what her status would be.

Lately Janine has started a meditation practice; she also takes yoga class three times a week and is beginning to understand the spiritual dimensions of these practices. In the meantime, she continues to volunteer with fellow Quakers at a shelter for women. Janine describes herself as deeply committed to a spiritual way of life, but she doesn't see any reason why she should be bound by the confines of any one religious group.

Many of us, like Janine, have backgrounds that include elements of various religions. Some of us had little in the way of spiritual training; some of us don't have such great memories of the religious institutions of our childhood; some of us have married people of another faith; and some of us are products of these marriages.

In the West there is also another large category of

seeker: men and women who are strongly drawn to the spiritual experience even though they feel disconnected from the religions into which they were born. People like this sometimes develop a Buddhist practice and discover to their amazement that the spiritual experience brings them closer to the religions of their childhood or, indeed, to all spiritual practice. In some ways, this was my experience.

As I often say, I'm Jewish on my parents' side. Born in Brooklyn, the name I was given was Jeffrey Miller. After my birth, my family moved to Long Island where I had a typical childhood playing in Little League and going to YMCA camps, where I was formally introduced to Christianity when I attended Sunday services outdoors under towering pine trees. Otherwise my upbringing was culturally Jewish. I learned enough Hebrew to be bar mitzvahed at thirteen and accompanied my parents to the temple for religious holidays.

In college I encountered philosophy as well as theology, and began to explore my spiritual side. Soon after graduation I travelled to India. In India, I began to explore all of the religions of the East. My first guru, Neem Karoli Baba, gave me a new name – Surya Das, which is translated as 'disciple of the light'; I lived in an ashram and studied meditation with the great Vipassana teacher, Goenka. I lived in Japan for a year, studying Zen, and I lived in Korea where I studied Zen with a Korean Zen master. Most of the 1970s and 1980s, however, I spent in Tibetan monasteries. I was trained as a lama in my teachers' monasteries in Nepal, Sikkim, India, and southern France. I am an American lama in an ancient Tibetan Buddhist tradition. But of course I am also a Jewish American spiritual activist. In our highly mobile society today, we are all hyphenates – hybrids of one sort or another.

As Westerners, we live in a multicultural world. By definition, our spiritual tastes are going to be eclectic. It doesn't make sense to deny our experience or our feelings. This more open approach to matters of the spirit doesn't weaken either our commitment to a peaceful, compassionate way of life or our resolve to act ethically and appropriately. Moving from the outer forms and institutions of religion to the more essential principles of spirituality is a good and significant option.

In all truly sacred traditions there is an essential resolve to cherish life and treat others ethically and kindly. All these traditions encourage us to be open to divine presence, both within and without, and tell us 'to practice what we preach' without hypocrisy or sleight of hand. For many, this message is of essential importance no matter who is carrying it.

In her book, *That's Funny, You Don't Look Buddhist: On Being a Faithful Jew and a Passionate Buddhist*, my friend the Vipassana meditation teacher Sylvia Boorstein talks about attending a week-long course taught by the Dalai Lama. At the end of the week, the Dalai Lama told the participants that later in the day he would offer the Green Tara Initiation as part of the closing. The Green Tara is a female Tibetan deity who embodies loving protection and compassion. When the Dalai Lama offers this initiation, it is a special blessing meant to help the recipients awaken the compassion in their own hearts.

Sylvia says that when the Dalai Lama made this announcement, one of the participants raised his hand to ask a question. As a practicing Catholic, he was concerned whether or not he should be part of this initiation. At first the Dalai Lama said that he thought it would be all right, but if the participant was uncomfortable with any element in the ceremony, he simply shouldn't do it.

Later, as the Dalai Lama was preparing to perform the empowerment initiation, Sylvia writes, 'The Dalai Lama, in a conversational tone, said, "I've been thinking further about the question of doing the initiation if you belong to another spiritual tradition. I think you can do it." He gave a list of reasons, explaining slowly and carefully, saying essentially that "compassion is compassion" and "a blessing is a blessing."'

I think it's important that this remain a theme in our spiritual growth. So try to let go of any knee-jerk responses of antagonism toward spiritual practices that seem different, alien, or foreign. The thing to remember as you create your own daily practice is that compassion is compassion, a blessing is a blessing, and a good heart is a good heart.

Making Spiritual Choices

◆

If going away is what it is to be a monk
then coming back
really
really
is what it is to be a Buddha.

But surely you can only really come back
if you've really gone away?

KO UN

Last night, across the globe, millions of new parents were awakened by the sound of a crying baby. Around the world, these parents responded by groaning as they stood up and made their way to the baby's crib in order to do what had to be done. All of these parents were renouncing, giving up, or letting go of their much needed sleep because they cared more about the well-being of a little child. The child's needs were more important than their own. Their parental love was stronger than their attachment to their own sleep.

Renunciation, an important and recurring spiritual theme, is not that complicated to understand. Renunciation means sacrificing or giving up something that seems important as that moment in favor of something that we know ultimately has more meaning. Each time we do this, we are making a spiritual choice – a decision to go with the bigger picture. Making these spiritual decisions or selfless choices is not always as unselfish as it appears. Like the parents who respond to their children's cries, when we make these choices, we do so in order to satisfy our greater and deeper needs.

It's true: A spiritual journey almost inevitably begins with a decision to renounce a certain way of life. But that decision is less about changing your environment or letting go of people and things than it is about transforming your inner being – learning the inner meaning of letting go and letting be in order to find wise naturalness and authentic simplicity.

The classic renunciation story, told time and time again, is the story of how a young married prince named Siddhartha Gautama gave up his heritage in order to seek enlightenment and ultimately become the Buddha. Siddhartha was born the heir to a small but opulent kingdom in the foothills of the Himalayas, in what is now part of western Nepal. Just before his birth, local soothsayers had seen the omens and told his father that the child would be either a powerful monarch or an ascetic holy man, a prediction that was later confirmed by the royal astrologer.

Siddhartha's father, the king, was appalled at the idea of his son becoming a wandering mendicant and ascetic. There were many such men living in India at that time, and the image of his princely son wearing rags, carrying a begging bowl, and living and meditating along the side of a dusty road struck terror into the king's heart. To keep Siddhartha from finding out that such a choice was even a possibility, his father surrounded his son with luxuries and shielded him from the harsh realities of the world.

Siddhartha was twenty-eight before his manservant helped him venture outside the palace walls for the very first time. On the young prince's first glimpse of the greater world, he saw four things that would change his life, and ours: (1) A man suffering the pains of a serious illness; (2) a man suffering from the afflictions of old age; (3) a human corpse being taken for cremation, surrounded by mourners. These stirring examples of human suffering did not frighten Siddhartha so much as they awakened the latent compassion within his heart. Why were these people suffering so much pain, and what could he, Siddhartha, do to help? Then, as he was returning to his palace, full of questions about the human pain, suffering, and mortality he had witnessed, he saw (4) a man walking peacefully along the road, wearing the thin ochre robe of a wandering ascetic and carrying only a small begging bowl. This fourth sight would determine the course of his life from that point forward.

We are told that Siddhartha found his brief experience outside the palace walls so startling, as well as moving, that he – like the cotton-robed mendicant – was compelled to make a spiritual choice and become a seeker. That very evening, the prince left his family, and turned his back on the pleasure and comfort of his father's palace. Buddhist scriptures recount how the 'devas' – gods and angels – muffled the hoofbeats of the prince's horse so that the sleeping inhabitants of the palace would not be awakened and impede the prince's spiritual quest.

Siddhartha renounced the life he knew and let go of

his attachment to the people he loved because he aspired to something more important. Once he made his decision, Siddhartha didn't hesitate. There was no ambivalence. Once he was in the forest outside the palace, he cut off his long princely hair with his own sword; then, before departing alone into the jungle, the man who would become the Buddha exchanged his royal clothing for his charioteer's. Later, as he took his first determined steps on the spiritual path, he would fashion his own simple ochre garment from rags.

Many would say that these first steps represented the Buddha's renunciation. But when Siddhartha left his father's palace, that was just the beginning. The Buddha didn't realize enlightenment simply because he let go of his attachment to his family. The Buddha meditated and practiced Hindu yogas and philosophies of all kinds for six long years before becoming fully enlightened. During those years, he had to learn to let go of other attachments that were just as binding, if not more so. He would have to let go of attachment to his ego, opinions, concepts, beliefs, and self-centered concerns. He would have to stop holding back in order to achieve the ultimate spiritual realization and perfect awakened enlightenment of nirvana, perfect peace.

I think it's important that we don't make the mistake of thinking that Buddhism or other genuine spiritual paths encourage us to walk away from responsibilities, friends, or families. Spiritual renunciation goes much deeper than any such external symbolic gesture. Kabir, the fifteenth-century Indian poet-saint, said that he didn't wish to simply dye his clothes the saffron color of a holy order; he said that he wished to dye his heart with divine love.

Milarepa, the great eleventh-century Tibetan yogi, said 'Leaving one's homeland is to accomplish half the Dharma.' But Milarepa never moved away from his homeland. Milarepa did, however, radically revamp his lifestyle by going into the wilderness to meditate, practice yoga, and pray; but he didn't set foot outside of Tibet. 'Leaving one's homeland' has a larger meaning of stepping out of our ruts and habits in order to spiritually reinvent our lives, and ultimately ourselves.

Milarepa said that he wanted to live and die without regrets. He wanted to attain freedom from guilt and fear; he wanted to realize peace of mind and a loving heart. And he had much to regret. Today Milarepa is remembered as a poet, a saint, and a sage, but before he dedicated his life to meditation, he had been responsible for several deaths in a clan feud. Out of his intense remorse, guilt, and fear, Milarepa did a complete turnaround, and in so doing, he is said to have reached perfect enlightenment in that one lifetime. Milarepa renounced his behavior; he walked away from the messy life he was caught up in. We know that he didn't entirely renounce his family because his sister Peta helped him, and eventually became a yogi too.

A book that was very popular during the 1970s was *Be Here Now*, by Baba Ram Dass. Ram Dass had been a well-known Harvard professor of psychology known as Dr Richard Alpert. When he went to India to study in the Sixties, Ram Dass left behind a career as well as many possessions including a Mercedes, a motorcycle, an MG sportscar, and a Cessna airplane. I feel he knows something about what renunciation really means. He wrote:

'You may think of renunciation in terms of some

external act like a New Year's resolution, or leaving family and friends to go off to a cave. But renunciation is much more subtle than that – and much harder – and much more continuing. On the spiritual journey, renunciation means nonattachment.

'To become free of attachment means to break the link identifying you with your desires. The desires continue: They are part of the dance of nature. But a renunciate no longer thinks that he *is* his desires.'

Renunication, of course, implies some sacrifice. And sacrifice is not something we like to talk about these days. It seems old-fashioned and preachy. But if we are committed to changing our lives, then we have to talk about what stays and what goes. We make these choices in our own self-interest. In business, we would call this the bottom line.

Have you ever had the following thoughts:

'I just can't go on like this.'

'This situation has become intolerable; I must change it and myself, or just let it all go.'

'Nothing I do seems important; I want my life to have more purpose and meaning.'

'I'm filled with negative emotions; I want to learn how to love.'

'I have all these loving feelings toward others, but I don't know how to act on them. I need to learn how to express compassion.'

'I can no longer live a lie; I want authenticity; I want to feel comfortable with who I am.'

Thoughts such as these are signals that we are ready to make some spiritual choices; we are ready to renounce lifestyles and patterns of behavior that aren't working; we are ready to become the people we are meant to be.

None of us can afford to squander our days, our years, or our lives. We have too much to give; we have too much to live.

For most of us, renunciation is not a one-time thing. We're all covered with layers and layers of encrusted barnacles, sediment, bits of seaweed, and odds and ends from our karmic scrap heap. These need to be chipped off a little at a time. We've all accrued excess amounts of emotional baggage, which we usually are able to drop only a little bit at a time; we all have opinions and attitudes that have become hardened in place. These impacted, calcified habits and attitudes can only be softened over time. We do this by making thousands, perhaps millions, of spiritual choices, small and large. We do this day by day.

Only you know what you need to relinquish in your own life. We all need to work on our tendencies to be greedy, acquisitive, angry, jealous, manipulative, or overly dependent. Every little renunciation of every self-defeating habit or thought process makes the next one easier. We begin to feel lighter. We begin to feel energized. We begin to see more clearly. We begin to find what we are looking for. We actually feel different, and it's extremely satisfying.

There is another aspect of renunciation and letting go that is equally important, as well as spontaneous and challenging. Chogyam Trungpa Rinpoche probably said it best when he said: 'Renunciation means to let go of holding back.'

Twenty-five hundred years ago, when the Buddha saw the pain that existed outside his palace walls, he stopped holding back. He opened his compassionate heart. He didn't run from what he saw; he didn't pull the covers over his head and hide. He didn't follow the way of the ostrich, burying his head. He didn't hold back his feelings. He didn't avoid reality. He didn't try to insulate himself from the suffering around him. Instead he made a gigantic leap. The earth is still trembling from his landing.

I think this is an important issue for the spiritual seeker of today. We need to remember that renunciation is not just about giving up attachments. It is the arising of an inner certainty that there is more here than meets the eye, and that we need to open to it. How? By releasing our tight grip; by opening our eyes, ears, closed fists, and guarded hearts. We can open our arms to embrace what we see. In this way, like the Buddha, we begin to reclaim our spiritual heritage; we begin to come home to what we genuinely are. It is simple, but not easy, to just let go. The world today is probably more complicated than it was during the Buddha's lifetime. Because we have become quite complicated, the Path too has become a little more complicated. Yet there it remains, right beneath our feet.

Letting Go Is the Path to Freedom

◆

Ring out, wild bells, to the wild sky . . .
Ring out the old, ring in the new . . .
Ring out the false, ring in the true.

ALFRED LORD TENNYSON

The path to freedom and liberation is rich with lessons about nonattachment and letting go. These are the spiritual lessons that we almost automatically resist time and time again. We know it's wise to soften, loosen up, and relax our grip a bit. But it's oh-so-hard to do it. The lessons we need to learn are repeated time and time again. And each time we fail to let go, we get rope burns from hanging on.

One day last week I spoke to my friend Pamela, who was very upset about her ongoing computer problems. Whenever her desktop has a glitch, she becomes distraught. Suppose her hard drive crashes; suppose she can't access her e-mail and address book; suppose she loses her data; suppose her tech support isn't immediately available. Her computer has had so many problems that there are entire days when she is consumed by anxiety. Since she has redundant backup systems installed on her computer, it's unlikely that she will lose data; she has several technicians she can call, and because she has a successful business, she can afford to pay for the help. Nonetheless, each time her computer acts up, she installs a new piece of software designed to make sure she won't have this particular problem again, and each time the new software program creates a new and different problem. 'It's like I'm being given a message,' Pamela says. 'I'm always anxious about my possessions; maybe I shouldn't have a computer. Maybe I shouldn't own anything.'

I agree with Pamela. Maybe she is being given a message. But the message is not that she should renounce worldly goods including her computer, or her winter coat for that matter. Maybe what Pamela needs to do is loosen up so that she is less overwhelmed with anxiety. Learning to let go of her anxiety is the issue, not her computer.

It's like going to the doctor and hearing him say, 'You are allergic to chocolate.' It's up to you – and no one but you – to give up your attachment to those delectable treats. But how can you do it? Maybe you're accustomed to eating chocolate ice cream every night. It gives you pleasure even if it's giving you stomachaches. For example, I've just recently given up caffeine. I'm sure this is right for me, yet there are still times when I crave the energy burst. Still, I feel so much better overall that it hardly requires much willpower and discipline at all to stay away from the stuff. Who needs that black sludge gunking up my inner light-works!

My old friend Susan is also learning nonattachment, because she has decided that she must end a relationship that has become destructive. But will she be able to just let go? Mark, a successful doctor, is in a group practice with several other M.D.'s. As silly as it seems (even to him), he keeps arguing with his partners about the color of paint that the interior decorator chose for the office walls. It's too late – it's already painted, but Mark doesn't like the way the walls look, and he can't let it go, no matter how much everyone pleads, 'Mark, get off it. Please, let it go. It's just paint.' Yet it still matters to Mark.

We all know what it is to struggle to release obsessive thoughts that insist on swirling around in our heads almost as though they have a life of their own. When we try to relinquish old behavior patterns and habits, we can almost feel the physical pain or wrench. We are often so invested in what went before that we hang on at all costs. We get so foolishly stuck – in how we think and how we act. We keep repeating the same mistakes, day in and day out. Why can't we simply switch gears?

One of my favorite Sufi teaching tales revolves around that famous wise fool, Nasrudin. In the Islamic tradition, although stories about Nasrudin's foolishness abound, his behavior always serves to impart wisdom imbued with an uncommon common sense.

This particular story opens with a view of Nasrudin sitting in a sunny Middle Eastern marketplace. He appears so uncomfortable and unhappy that a crowd of shoppers gathers around him. Nasrudin's face is red, his eyes are filled with tears, and sweat is streaming off his brow. At first people wonder what's wrong, but then they notice the pile of hot peppers that Nasrudin is eating, one at a time. Each bite seems to increase his discomfort, but he keeps chewing nonetheless. Finally someone asks, 'Nasrudin, why are you doing this?'

And he replies, 'Because I'm looking for a sweet one.'

In life, don't we all behave a little bit like Nasrudin? We insist on doing things our own way, even if that way has already failed dozens of times. We think that we are going to beat the odds. We foolishly become committed to what we are doing as well as very attached to the stories we tell ourselves about our behavior. Nasrudin, for example, exemplifies the guy who is so attached to his opinions that he keeps looking for love (or sweet peppers) in all the wrong places. He doesn't seem to learn from experience. Most of us behave in similar ways. Attachment is the culprit. Yielding, letting go, and moving on is the answer.

I'm sure you have several patterns that don't work in your own life. We all do. Sometimes these attachments represent questionable habits like cigarettes, alcohol, or even working to excess. Sometimes these attachments are reflections of the stories we tell ourselves about the world and our place in it.

Buddhist teachings stress certain attachments that we could very well do without. These all reflect attitudes and behaviours that keep us from making progress on a spiritual path.

Here's a list of some of them:

- ***Attachment to Pleasure/Pain Principle***

Daniel's many external achievements are right out there for all to see: his high-powered job, his big house, his ski chalet in the mountains, his two cars, his three computers, his business and personal connections, his beautiful wife in her fashionable clothes, his adorable children playing with their many expensive toys. He really expects satisfaction and pleasure from all the beautiful things he owns. Yet the truth is he hardly has time to get up to his ski chalet or stay home and play with his children. He often wakes up, looks at all he owns, feels unhappy, and goes out and purchases yet another object that he hopes will bring him satisfaction.

Most of us are very attached to what feels good, looks good, and tastes good. We get intoxicated on sensual pleasure, beautiful objects, and fabulous food and wine. Whenever we feel upset, we look for something external to provide a quick fix. Bad day at work, buy a new pair of shoes; argument with a mate, eat some chocolate. Feel insecure, take a vacation, have a drink, or find a lover. The need for this kind of gratification can take over and assume a life of its own. We become so busy indulging our appetites that we never delve into the underlying causes for our constant need for stimulation and pleasure. We are at the mercy of our incessant desires and aversions. The caption for this cartoon is: 'I want what I want when and how I want it. And I don't want anything to get in the way!'

It's easy to understand why we are drawn to pleasure, but as the Buddha pointed out, some of us are just as attached to our negative feelings as we are to those that are positive – just as attached to our unhappiness and the victim stories we tell ourselves as we are to our highs. As painful as our low points may be, something about the drama associated with them gives us a sense of satisfaction. It fits in with a personal, and familiar, view of the world or our place in it. Often we indulge our feelings of self-pity; we cling to images of ourselves as victims; we ruminate on the details of our disappointments. We say to ourselves, 'If only . . .' and 'I just wish . . .'

◆ ***Attachment to Opinions and Ideas***

Who doesn't think that his or her political views are best? Who doesn't think that his or her opinions should be followed? Opinions are so much a part of who we think we are. Sometimes we even inherit our version of the world, like opinionated DNA: 'I'm a Democrat/Republican/Liberal/Marxist/Conservative because that's what I was brought up to be.' 'My mother and father ordered Chinese food for dinner every Sunday night, and so do I. Never do anything else. No way.' We all know people like that. Sometimes we're even people like that.

And not only do we have strong opinions, we also make judgments about people who disagree with our view of the world. People go to war over opinions; they fight with their best friends over their opinions; sometimes we even end marriages because we find it easier to shed a mate than to change or loosen up a point of view. Glen, for example, has been trying to get his wife to agree to move to a new city. His way of doing this is through nightly filibusters. Glen is very attached to his style of relating. It never works, but he keeps trying. True conversation and communication is impossible during such a harangue, but this does not stop Glen.

There is a well-known Zen story about an arrogant and pedantic professor. Let's call him Professor Know-It-All. One day the professor reads something about Buddhism in a college newspaper. It piques his interest, and although he is sure that no one can teach him anything, he decides to find out more about Eastern wisdom. He learns that in his college town, there is a venerable Zen master. So the professor calls and makes an appointment for tea at the Zen master's home.

On the day of the tea, the professor and the Zen master sit across from each other. And the Zen master begins to pour the professor a cup of tea. And he pours, and he pours. The cup overflows and tea is flowing everywhere – over the table and onto the floor. The professor says, 'Master, stop! Why do you keep pouring? The cup is full. Nothing more can fit in.' And the master replies, 'Just as you too are so full of all your learning and opinions. You have to empty yourself in order to receive.'

The message, of course, is that when we hang on to our opinions or judgments, there is no room for anything else. It's as though we have all our opinions and ideas written on little pieces of paper and glued on, like sticky yellow Post-its, over every inch of our being. They are so heavy that they weigh down our arms and legs. They cover our eyes as well as our ears. We become so wrapped and wrapped up in our versions of reality that very little light can either emerge or enter.

◆ ***Attachment to Rites and Rituals***

The Buddha, like religious reformers the world over, was very aware that some of his disciples too easily fell into ritualistic patterns. They put so much emphasis on the letter of the law that they lost touch with its spirit. Whenever we become overly attached to the form of a spiritual practice (or anything else for that matter) we risk losing the meaning of its essence. We end up eating shells and husks, while overlooking the nutritious kernels and grain within them.

Religious practices can sometimes appeal to our compulsive, obsessive tendencies – our proclivity to focus on form to help us feel secure. We think that if we meditate for enough hours or do thousands of prayers, bows, mantras, or offerings, something will automatically happen. Yet this is exactly the opposite of what the Buddha intended. He realized that what we do with our attention is more important than symbolic sounds and gestures.

We're all somewhat ritualized in our behavior. We wake up, walk the dog, take a shower, drink juice, drink tea, read the morning paper. What happens if we change the order of any of our little daily habits? If we allow our attachment to rituals to become too ingrained, these rituals can become addictive patterns and hang-ups. This will obscure the miraculous little spontaneous arisings that spring up like flowers along our way.

I recently spoke to someone who complained that her life felt empty and lonely; she spent so much time on her spiritual regimens that there was no time for friendship or personal relationships. So many hours of her day are taken up with meditation, shopping for her vegetarian diet, and doing yoga that there is no place for anything else. She readily acknowledges that she has become obsessively rigid about these activities, and in the process her life has become more and more narrow.

As soon as we become too ritualistic about anything, our priorities inevitably get all screwed up and form assumes more importance than essence. For example, instead of spending time with our children, we spend time nagging them to make sure that they and their rooms look a certain way. Openness, warmth, and love feel more sheltering and protective than mere spit and polish. In fact, as we get older, it seems to become increasingly obvious that, on all levels, it doesn't matter how things look from the outside.

◆ *Attachment to Ego*

For most of us, attachment to ego – self-preoccupation – is the overriding theme in our lives. Can there be any question about this? Sometimes we get so caught up in ourselves that there is little room for anyone else.

Not that long ago I walked into a store that specializes in Native American art and handicrafts. On one of the counters, I spotted a sculpture of the head of a very masculine looking Native American. The predominant feature on his face was a large nose that was bent almost entirely to one side. The head itself was resting in a large hand, the fingers curling up over the Native American's forehead. The sculpture was identified by a little tag that read 'Broken Nose in the Hand of the Creator.'

When I asked the store's owner about the piece, he told me that Broken Nose was an Iroquois shaman remembered for two reasons: (1) extraordinary shamanistic power and (2) an ego to match. It seems that Broken Nose was more than a little too impressed with himself.

One day, Broken Nose decided that his powers were

so awesome that he could take on anyone, including the Creator himself. So he challenged the Creator to a contest, a test of strength. With great assurance, Broken Nose stood in front of a mountain, took a deep breath, and then with remarkable ease moved the mountain at least a foot in one direction. Amazing! Broken Nose stood back and waited to see what the Creator could do.

The Creator didn't waste a moment picking the mountain up, moving so quickly that the actions of the Creator and the mountain itself were blurred like a movie projector on fast forward. And then the mountain disappeared because the Creator was taking the mountain around the world itself. Just as Broken Nose turned his head to see what happened, the mountain came flying back into place. It struck Broken Nose across the face – thus giving him the nickname for which he would always be remembered, as well as the lesson that reminds us all that despite his admirable powers, Broken Nose was simply human, just like everyone else . . . just like you and me.

There is a reason why so many cultures and religions teach us about the damaging effects of too much egotism. Often ego, arrogance, and pride (a sense that one is somehow special or exempt) become synonymous. The early Americans took the proverb 'Pride Goeth Before a Fall' so much to heart that they embroidered it on samplers. The ancient Greeks referred to pride as hubris. Anyone who has studied Greek mythology or drama remembers hearing about the lessons of the ancient family known as the House of Atreus. This was a family of great influence, power, and wealth, and its members murdered, seduced, impregnated, and betrayed each other with fearsome regularity. Sometimes they even feasted on each other. In so doing, of course, generation after generation experienced disaster after disaster. They were often accused of hubris, an overweening and tragic belief that any mortal can be above the laws of the universe.

Don't we all sometimes think that we are hot stuff? A little bit better, smarter, stronger, funnier than the people around us? I personally find that I have to keep dealing with ego and pride, and I keep getting stuck. It's humiliating to admit how much I struggle with this, but I do, and it's something that I've been aware of almost my whole life.

Probably my first lesson in ego attachment came when I was on a Little League baseball team. I think we used to call it the PeeWee farm team. I must have been about six; and it was probably my first year. At that time, I thought I was one of the world's greatest baseball hitters. I mean, I kept it in context. I knew I wasn't as good as the New York Yankees, but I thought I was pretty terrific.

I vividly remember riding home with other members of our team – the Cheyennes – in our coach's car, a large eight-cylinder Cadillac. I remember the car as being almost large enough for the whole team. We had lost the game, but we were still going out afterward for ice cream. I thought I had played a pretty good game – better than anybody else, in fact. I turned to the coach and commented on what little me perceived to be the large number of wimpy players on our team. With as much hubris as a six-year-old can summon, I remember asking, 'Why isn't everybody like me?' 'Because Jeffrey,' the coach replied, 'if everybody was like you, we'd have nine left-handed first basemen.' I actually got the point.

Whether you call it arrogance, pride, hubris, narcissism, or self-centeredness, ego attachment is what separates us from our fellow beings here on planet earth. We can't really connect with ourselves and each other until we are willing to meet on an equal I-thou footing, without ego-armor, moats, or barricades.

We all have a tendency to define and identify ourselves by our attachments – résumés, clothes, job title, social status, academic accomplishments. I'm a successful person because I own nice things; I'm a smart person because I read and think a lot and have informed opinions. We buy into the stories we (and others) tell about who we are based on our attachments. Often we take our first steps on the spiritual path because we realize that we don't want to do this any longer.

When we make a commitment to the spiritual path, we enter into an unspoken internal contract with ourselves. We agree that we will begin thinking about what our attachments cost us. We will begin thinking about the stories we tell ourselves about who we are and what's important.

We ask ourselves: Do we own our possessions or do they own us? Are we controlled by our desire for pleasure? Do our opinions so define us that our innate goodness gets lost in the rhetoric? Are we so driven by our need for personal rites and rituals, schedules, timetables, and set ways of doing things that our priorities are lost? Are we so attached to our ego that, like the shaman Broken Nose, we are accidents waiting to happen?

When we walk the spiritual path, we start relinquishing those attachments that aren't really important in the long run.

Every loss can make way for other gifts yet unimagined.

Barns burnt down
now
I can see the moon.

MASAHIDE

Some Simple Thoughts About Unadorned Simplicity

◆

A morning glory at my window satisfies me more than the metaphysics of books.

WALT WHITMAN

Just to be is a blessing. Just to live is holy.

RABBI ABRAHAM HERSCHEL

Einstein was a man who could ask immensely simple questions.

JACOB BRONOWSKI, *The Ascent of Man*

Be humble, for you are made of dung. Be noble, for you are made of stars.

SERBIAN PROVERB

Moving Closer to Pure Simplicity

◆

Simplicity, simplicity, simplicity! I say, let your affairs be as two or three, and not a hundred or a thousand; instead of a million count half a dozen, and keep your accounts on your thumbnail.

HENRY DAVID THOREAU

When we relinquish, or renounce, the extraneous, we are left with the essential, which can't be lost. When we stop clinging to ego attachments, we lighten our load and learn who we truly are. That's the magic of simplicity.

This approach is at the core of all Buddhist teachings.

We all agree: Simplicity is beautiful; simplicity is spiritual; simplicity is a blessing. Simplicity is where we want to be. Less is definitely more. We see this wisdom brought to life in the aesthetic elegance of Zen Buddhism. In Zen practice, for example, meditation is often called 'Zazen,' just sitting. But the real meaning of Zazen is staying in the moment and just *being*. Letting go of extraneous thought, movement, and speech. Just being. Pure presence.

In our own busy lives, we wish for simple elegance; we long for a return to purity, naturalness, and innocence.

But as much as we may yearn for a way of life that reflects simplicity, we usually don't live that way. As we pack our bags for a trip, or glance around our homes and work environments, many of us have stopped asking the question, 'Do I have everything I need?' Instead we wonder, Do I really need everything I have?'

What does it mean to simplify? When I lived in a monastery, I was quite content with a monk's robes and some flip-flops for my feet. Now that I'm again a citizen of Western society, I travel with almost as much paraphernalia and gear as anyone else, and I keep asking myself why.

When I first left Asia and moved back to this country in the early 1990s, I rode buses and trains between airports and retreat centers. After a couple of years of this, my father gave me his large brown, rear-wheel-drive 1981 Buick, 'the Batmobile,' as we called it. At one point I went to Nepal for six months, leaving it parked in my friend Tom's barn. When I returned and discovered what the bats who lived in the barn's eaves had wrought, the car's nickname took on a very literal meaning.

After some icy New England winters, I passed the Batmobile on to someone and bought a used red Plymouth with front-wheel drive. Soon thereafter, my teacher Lama Nyoshul Khenpo and his wife came to visit. We did a lot of driving about, and that car became affectionately known as the Lama-mobile. It was very serviceable; it got me where I was going, and I was quite content. Then, one day, while driving to my home in Cambridge, I skidded on some ice and fishtailed off the road. It was not a happy experience. In the aftermath of the skid, someone whispered the magic words –

'antilock brakes' – in my ear so I sold one car and moved up to a newer, but still small car. This one was blue and, yes, on icy roads, the car felt safer.

Then I moved to an even more rural area outside of Boston. It was again part of a wish to lead a simpler, quieter life. In the New England countryside, the words 'snowplow' and 'tow truck' took on new meaning. There was no way around it: My little car simply could not negotiate the mile-long wooded driveway to my house. I would arrive home from a retreat where I had been teaching, carrying a suitcase, a briefcase, a laptop, books, and assorted gear only to find that the driveway was buried under six or more feet of snow. Four-wheel drive was the only solution. I felt as though I had no choice. I bought a green Jeep.

This kind of progression has happened in so many other areas in my life. I would still be happy with the first computer I purchased, but tribal consciousness seems to be in charge. The hard drive wasn't large enough; the software wasn't smart enough; the modem wasn't fast enough. One thing after another. So I had to upgrade. 'Upgrade?' What does that really mean to the quality of our days?

Life is like that. Unpredictable, complicated, and as difficult to manage as a wild horse. By its very nature, life is not simple. We frequently find ourselves upgrading at times when what we would most want is to streamline and downsize. Just this morning, a friend called, bewailing the complexities of her life. A television news producer, she felt as though it was impossible to stay up to date with the new technology, including cameras, computers, and computer graphics, and still have a life. 'Why are they doing this to me?' she said, only half joking. She feels overwhelmed by the onslaught of details in this great over-information age. She has to know so much before she can even begin to do her job.

All the sages of all the ages have said the same thing in a million ways: We lose God, meaning, and our very selves in complexity. The one-in-many is the magical play of life. When we get caught up in the many, we lose the one. Amid the plethora of forms, we lose sight of the essence.

As spiritual seekers, we want to be able to see the simple core meaning of what we do. We want to be able to sort through the clutter on our desks, in our lives, in our hearts, and in our minds and find what we're looking for. Finding simple solutions in today's chaotic lifestyles requires a great deal of attention and self-mastery. I once read a quotation on a yellow sticky on someone's bulletin board that said, 'Out of chaos comes a dancing star.' It's sort of like sorting through clothing piled on a chair and finding that last clean shirt. ('I knew it was there!') We want to be able to do the same thing with our lives. We want to sort through the chaos, peel back the many onion skin layers, and find that dancing star. It may be buried in chaos, but we know it's there, don't we? We are the dancing stars. By our own lights, we'll find ourselves where we want to be. But first we have to simplify.

The concept of the holy fool or sacred madman is contained in all the world's wisdom traditions. The holy fool – and many have argued very persuasively that Buddha, Jesus Christ, and Muhammad all fall into this category – is able to look at the convoluted, disturbing complexities of the world, peel away its layers, and see the simple straightforward essential truths buried within. The *One* within the many.

Simplicity is also frequently connected with innocence and childlike wonder. J. M. Barrie, the author of *Peter Pan*, wrote, 'I'm not young enough to know everything.' Jesus said that you have to become like a child again to enter the kingdom of heaven. The Japanese poet Kitaro Nishido once wrote, 'If my heart can become pure and simple like that of a child, I think there probably can be no greater happiness than this.' In our heart of hearts, we remember when we were children; we remember a time when we approached the world with a certain clarity and intuitive understanding. We had so little excess baggage; we had yet to add numerous projections, preconceptions, habits, and attachments.

We strive for simplicity in our own lives by chipping away at layers and layers of barnacles that have become attached to us over the years, or possibly even lifetimes. We are all so weighed down and overburdened by the extraneous. A classic haiku that I've always liked carries a swift, Zen-like message:

How refreshing
the whinny of a pack horse
unloaded of everything!

Wouldn't it be marvelous to be able to put down our self-inflicted burdens and strip away the nonessential? On the spiritual path, simplicity can be addressed on three different levels.

Outer: We simplify our lives by loosening our grip on the multiple layers and configurations of people, plans, expectations, and objects in our lives. We opt for more spiritual choices, letting go of bad habits and dissatisfying behavior.

Inner: We simplify our lives by simplifying our minds. This is best done through self-inquiry and meditation practice.

Innate: When we have seen through all the layers and veils, we are left with ground luminosity. Innate Buddha-nature. Just Being – Authentic Presence.

Nothing more to figure out, understand, or achieve. We have arrived. It's all so simple.

Seeking Mystical Experience

◆

The most beautiful emotion we can experience is the mystical. It is the power of all true art and science. He to whom this emotion is a stranger, who can no longer wonder and stand rapt in awe, is as good as dead. To know that what is impenetrable to us really exists, manifesting itself as the highest wisdom and the most radiant beauty, which our dull faculties can comprehend only in their most primitive forms – this knowledge, this feeling, is at the center of true religiousness. In this sense, and in this sense only, I belong to the rank of devoutly religious men.

ALBERT EINSTEIN

In this postmodern era, people don't just want a belief or understanding of divinity. They want some kind of special spiritual event. They want the payoff of an enlightenment or mystical experience. They want to be able to touch, feel, weigh, and know for themselves.

This need to reinforce one's belief with tangible first-hand evidence is quite understandable. People the world over love to hear and tell stories of mysterious, unexplained phenomena. In Tibet, these stories frequently revolve around events that take place at death. Some Tibetan meditation masters, for example, are said to have achieved Rainbow Light Bodies at death. This is a phenomenon in which a highly advanced practitioner's body literally dissolves into elemental energy known as 'prana' and, in so doing, creates a rainbow-like light.

We are told that when this occurs, often there is little or nothing left of the body itself. Sometimes hair and fingernails are all that remain; disciples ceremonially put these remains in religious shrines for good karma and blessings. My teachers Kalu Rinpoche, Trungpa Rinpoche, and Dudjom Rinpoche all told their students they had themselves witnessed these occurrences, which they said were the fruit of long and arduous meditation and yoga practice.

Tibetan tales, like fish and bear tales the world over, have a way of growing larger with each retelling. These stories can get very extreme. Experienced tantric masters are expected to experience bliss, peace, and lightness; I've heard stories that some tantric yogis are so light that they can fly in the sky. We also hear that some meditation masters aren't able merely to hold their breath and concentrate for minutes, they do so for hours, days, weeks, and months. One of the most extreme examples of this kind of tale revolves around the legend – still told by some tour guides – that the ancient mystic and tantric Buddhist patriarch named Kukai has been sitting in 'samadhi' (total meditative absorption) in his walled-up cave on top of the holy mountain of Koyasan near Kobe, Japan, for the last twelve hundred years.

My own teacher, Nyoshul Khenpo, once told me that lamas of old would sleep in caves high up on the slopes of one mountain, and meditate across the valley on another. He said that these advanced practitioners would use yogic breath and psychic energy in order to travel from place to place. Each day, everybody in the valley would see levitating lamas riding the rays of the setting sun. I always loved the image of rush hour with the Himalayan sky full of commuting lamas.

One has to keep a sense of humor about these things. The stories told in Tibet about the extraordinary and miraculous are part of an oral tradition that has been passed down for generations. I learned to take many of these stories with a largish grain of sea salt. And yet, when I was in Nepal with learned lamas, things did happen that were extremely hard to explain. For instance, I was there when my old Tibetan yogi master breathed out, smiled peacefully, and died consciously in a meditative state. With my own eyes I saw that he remained sitting up in Clear Light Meditation for almost one week, without any physical deterioration. His body still felt warm and there was a pink glow to his face and chest.

Another of my root, or primary, gurus, the late Sixteenth Karmapa, clearly read my mind on several occasions, and occasionally made explicit predictions to myself and other disciples that had an uncanny way of coming true. Everyone considered him clairvoyant. I've known several lamas who seemed to never sleep. The explanation given for this is that these masters have purified the gross obscurations veiling and obstructing their innate awakened heart-minds. By doing this, they are releasing and opening to an inexhaustible and limitless sacred energy flow. They are accessing the deathless cosmic life principle, which can be called clear light, inner luminosity, or Buddha-nature.

I have witnessed enlightenment experiences and healings too numerous to recall. These things are not as rare as one might think; they do get more airtime, however, in the traditional East. I truly believe that profound 'Vajrayana' (Diamond Way) empowerments and prayers by certain highly realized and perhaps even enlightened lamas have extended the lives of people I know. I have also seen that these wise teachers have been able to provoke breakthroughs and sudden enlightenment experiences in dozens of my old Dharma friends along the way.

With all this, however, the greatest miracle that I have ever witnessed is the miracle of love: that unconditional divine love, compassion, and spiritually nurturing blessings that overflow from the hearts of those who, through Dharma wisdom and its practice, have actualized and fulfilled in themselves the fruits of the spiritual path. According to Buddhist Dharma there are two categories of miraculous powers, or 'siddhis,' as they are called. These are known as worldly powers and transcendent powers. Some examples of worldly powers are mind reading, levitation, fortune-telling, etc. Transcendent powers, which include divine love and enlightenment, are significantly more meaningful. In Tibetan Buddhism, spiritual maturation – as exemplified by love and truth – is revered above all, with or without magical or supernatural power.

When it comes to unexplained phenomena, Buddhists are not alone. Saints and sages in all denominations and religions have demonstrated miracles and healings, which are not as immediately accepted as one would think. The Roman Catholic church, for example, has even made a practice of authenticating miracles associated with Lourdes, the French pilgrimage site where St Bernadette saw a vision of Mary. The requirements for proof seem to be very stringent, and yet there are still healings for which no reasonable reason can be found. I found the cave and spring at Lourdes to be an extraordinary sacred place of great spiritual energy and power, and well worth visiting. I also have friends and students in this country who have visited healers, and they swear that something positive has happened. There is no question about it, there is a large amount of documentation for things that we can't explain by any method other than to say that they are in the realm of miracle.

Wanting to believe in the miraculous and the mysterious is very much part of the spiritual search. And yet this desire for supernatural explanation leaves us vulnerable to charlatans and fake soothsayers of every type. We can sometimes be as much manipulated by our wish to believe as we are uplifted.

The Buddha was asked many times why he didn't show his miraculous powers. He said they were secondary to wisdom and love, which are the true miracles. According to the sutras, however, he did on several occasions perform miracles. One of these scriptures describes a debate between some local sages and the Buddha, which ultimately evolved into a contest of miracles. One of the sages walked on water; another walked on fire; finally the Buddha filled the sky with thousands of Buddhas like himself, and everyone bowed down in respect for his awesome ability. This miracle at Sravasti is still found painted on the walls of many Buddhist temples.

A little later, some of the Buddha's disciples reminded him of the many times he said there was no point in showing miraculous powers unless it was going to help others. The Buddha said that in the case of the sky full of Buddhas, it was there to reveal that there was more to the Enlightened One than met the eye; this feat made it possible for doubters to see with their own eyes that which is usually hidden. Stories such as these are always told to inspire faith and devotion. And in so many cases over the centuries, they have functioned exactly in that way.

Many seekers begin meditation in order to have unique experiences. When I first started meditating in India with my teacher, S. N. Goenka, I remember how amazed I was by the kind of experiences one could have. Goenka led intense ten-day meditation retreats. The other students and I would follow monastic disciplines such as little sleep, no solid food each day from noon on, and total silence except for Goenka's instructions. It was shockingly different from anything I had known previously. I started to have incredible experiences of light, and feelings of physical bliss. At night I would have clear dreams and a sense of being blessed and empowered by the Buddhas. Several nights I had little or no sleep; even so the following day I still only needed a cat nap after our vegetarian lunch eaten off of leaf plates.

I would get very enthusiastic and rush to the teacher to tell him of my experience. He would just laugh and say, 'Good, good. Very good. Just keep meditating.' Later I talked to other students who had the same experience. Goenka would almost always give the same kind of answers, and yet we all walked away satisfied.

What were those events that my mind produced during and after meditation? All meditation teachers, like Goenka, have the same advice: Don't dwell on these experiences. Just notice them, feel them, be mindfully aware of whatever momentarily presents itself, and let these experiences go. Don't try to interpret them. Don't try to inhabit them, or own them. Don't try to develop them further or hold on to them. Just keep meditating.

When I was studying in Japan with Zen master Uchiyama Roshi, I asked him similar questions. He always emphatically said, 'It's all "makyo." Just watch the show.' ('Makyo' of course means illusion or phantasmagoria.)

My various meditation and yoga teachers often reminded us not to get caught up in fleeting appearances or mental states, no matter how lovely or vivid they might be. They would remind us that they were just distractions – as the Buddhist sutras say, like dreams, like bubbles on a passing stream. A precautionary Tibetan teaching tale describes what happened to a Tibetan yogi who died by drowning after pursuing illusory goddesses-visions he had conjured up after meditating all night on the shore of a lake,

Now, students come to me with many of the same kinds of experiences, plus some unique ones of their very own. There may be nothing new under the sun, but there are always new forms of illusion. For example, some Westerners tell me that meditation has led them to believe that they are reincarnations of important lamas. Many say that they have had visions of their past lives; some say they are convinced that they have karmic ties to people they meet – especially fascinating and attractive ones. Often they are excited and even elated by what they are experiencing. Several have told me that in a past life they were the seventh-century founder of Tibetan Buddhism, Guru Rinpoche. It's interesting, of course, that nobody ever remembers being someone's servant or, for that matter, someone's pet duck. And yet there are karmic reasons why these students have these experiences. If they serve no other purpose, they are reminders that there is more to reality than what we see with our obscured vision.

Today, of course, my advice to these seekers is very similar to the advice my teachers gave me: Just keep meditating. Keep your eyes peeled, your mind awake, and your heart open. What else is there to say? Sometimes makyo is just makyo and requires little or no dream interpretation. Don't get caught up in these experiences. Don't get caught up in what happened yesterday, even if it was a blessed visionary dream or a meditational breakthrough. What is of value will remain while the ephemera dissolves like morning dew. Why be elated or disappointed? Just stay with the Middle Way of balance. Don't search for proof that insights gained from your mystical experiences are real. If it is truly your karma, then those who are searching for reincarnate lamas or Romanov heirs will find you.

Sometimes our insights about paranormal experiences are valid; sometimes we're fooling ourselves. The genuine lessons we learn stay with us, but the special effects will quickly disappear. Whatever grows on Mt Fuji comes and goes, but the mountain remains. In short, don't get sidetracked from the main story. Keep on keepin' on. Ten thousand years, straight ahead. Right now.

Shadows Here, Shadows There

◆

The Shadow is a moral problem that challenges the whole ego-personality, for no one can become conscious of the shadow without considerable moral effort. To become conscious of it involves recognizing the dark aspect of the personality as present and real. This act is the essential condition for self-knowledge, and it therefore, as a rule, meets with considerable resistance.

CARL G. JUNG

Just as we are all born with innate luminosity, so too we are all born with a darker or shadow side. Just as there is no right without left, no up without down, no east without west, so too light without shadow is almost a contradiction in terms. Look at the play of light and dark that exists all around you. In the heavens themselves, there are brilliant stars, but there are also unexaminable black holes. Some say that God alone exists without shadow. But if God is pure light, some might also say that the world itself represents God's shadow side.

A spiritual life is often defined as a search for luminosity and light. But if that is the case, what do we do about the darkness that we all know exists? What do we do about our own personal shadows? How can we integrate the Dr Jekyll and Mr Hyde in each of us?

Most contemporary theologians and scholars say that it is foolish to believe we can simply transcend or deny the shadow element, arguing quite persuasively that the only way to deal with the shadow side is to confront it, recognize it for what it is, and work through the attached conflicts.

All seekers eventually discover that their own shadow elements present the major struggles of the spiritual life. The Buddha was no exception. On the final night before his enlightenment, he was confronted with darkness in the form of Mara, an archetypical deity of darkness, who is often seen as the embodiment of death itself; Mara's very name is defined as destruction. In order to sabotage the Buddha's quest for enlightenment, Mara arrived with an army of demons; like him, they represented darkness. But it was all for naught because the Buddha showed no fear of the dark. Finally Mara called for his loveliest daughter, instructing her to seduce the Buddha. But the Buddha was master of his desires; he didn't have to prove anything; he had worked through his ego attachments. As the Buddha impassively stared at Mara's daughter, she too turned back into a demon.

This legend of the Buddha's enlightenment is not that different from the scriptural telling of what happened to Jesus before he began his ministry. Like Buddha, Jesus went into the wilderness to fast, meditate, and pray. 'The devil took him to a very high mountain and showed him all the kingdoms of the world and their splendor, and he said to him, "All these I give you, if you will fall down and worship me." And Jesus said, "Away with you, Satan."' Although some theologians take these stories of the Buddha and Jesus very literally, others see them as brilliant allegories, clear examples of what we can expect to happen to all spiritual seekers.

If the Buddha found himself plagued by demons, how can we expect to avoid them? Each of us will have to face his or her own crew of darkness; each of us will have his or her very own 'dark nights of the soul.' These happen not because an actual Darth Vader-type being presents itself to us with an invitation to do physical battle. No, our struggles are more internal. The demons we face are all of our own creation. Some of them don't even appear scary. Like Mara's temptress daughter, at first glance many appear quite appealing.

According to Carl Jung, these shadowy figures can be defined as those repressed elements of the personality with which we choose not to be identified. The shadow is the underbelly of our bright public personas. It includes the parts of ourselves that we keep hidden, sometimes even from ourselves. And who doesn't have at least a few rattling skeletons stashed away in various closets of psyche and memory? Try to repress, suppress, and deny the shadow side of our own personality, and we run the risk of attracting these elements into our lives in other ways.

Don't make the mistake of believing that this doesn't have real meaning in your own life. 'The shadow' is not just a philosophical concept. As we go through our days, time and again we meet our shadows. They tempt us, and they toy with us. They frighten us, and they repulse us. They come in different shapes and sizes, and they present themselves in different ways, depending on who we are and what our lives are about. John, for example, meets his shadow each time he becomes so enraged by his wife or children that he can't control his temper. Margo meets her shadow each time she drinks too much. Dave comes face to face with his shadow each time he makes unreasonable personal compromises and fails to say what he believes. Carolyn finds her shadows in the co-dependent relationships to which she clings like ivy. In short, our shadows make us do and say things that we would prefer not to acknowledge.

We see shadows at work all around us. Newspapers and television are filled with stories of scandals and words of hypocrisy about and from leaders, both spiritual and political, who can't quite walk their talk. These leaders may appear to be wrapped in shiny stainless-steel psychological armor, and yet there are chinks in that armor; shadow elements keep oozing out.

I don't honestly believe the hypocrisy we witness all around us is intentional. We see it happening because often our leaders don't know themselves. They are so concerned with persona and the images they present to the world that they choose to deny and repress rather than confront and handle their shadow conflicts. This kind of denial brings with it its own hellish state of mind. They may be trying to project good, but it becomes obscured.

Shadows also show up in our lives as projections. We look at others, and the qualities that stick out are those that we don't like or have simply repressed or failed to acknowledge in ourselves. In fact, often we surround ourselves with people who have qualities that we find less than desirable. Timothy, for example, has numerous friends whose behavior might be viewed as being less than ideal. Timothy's friends are greedy, frivolous, and sometimes even amoral. Not like Timothy, who perceives himself as an ethical person. He sits in harsh judgment of those people with whom he likes to hang out. But why does he spend so much time in this environment?

We've all behaved a bit like Timothy, and the shadow explains why. Buried shadows drive us to places we might not wish to go. The less we are able to face our own personal darkness, our own personal demons, the more we are compelled to confront and experience them in other, less conscious ways. We look for our shadows in the faces of others; we attract them to us.

Our shadows can either become our allies and teachers or our assailants and opponents. The more aware we become of all that is within us, positive and negative, light and dark, the more we will be able to handle life in a balanced, sane, and spiritual way.

William James said, 'Our ordinary consciousness is but one form of consciousness. All round us lie infinite worlds, separated only by the thinnest veils.'

The depths of the unseen, unmanifest, and invisible worlds of darkness that we fear are simply expressions of an inner reality, the silent subconscious working of our unexplored minds. We discover what's there only through self-exploration – by reaching in and holding what we fear up to the light, just as the ocean only gives up its secrets when we are able to dive into its depths – far, far below the sparkling sunlit surface.

Our dark sides as well as our lighter facets are also there for our enrichment and nourishment. They are there so that we can learn and grow. The message is very clear: Explore yourself and transform yourself. Just as the Buddha met Mara before his awakening, often we come upon our darkest shadows just before light dawns.

St John of the Cross called it 'the dark night of the soul.' In Dzogchen we call it the dark moonless night, which is deeply luminous within – as distinct from a bright moonlit night. The full moon in a dark sky is symbolic of enlightenment, but it has arrived at this state after it has completed the cycle that begins with the sliver of light growing out of darkness.

What we must always keep in mind is that nothing is ever completely negative or hopeless, or ultimately to be despaired. We all know the old saying, 'Every cloud as a silver lining.' Things *can* be turned over. We *can* see the light. In this faith, we live and flourish.

When we come into a more holistic and complete vision of reality and totality, we see that shadows are also nothing but light. There is no such thing as darkness, actually, or cold, for that matter. These two terms are merely defined by us in relation to the amount of light, energy, and warmth that is present or lacking. This mirrors the spiritual principle that teaches us that there is only light or that everything is Tao-flow, pure energy – the natural state.

I have a little shadow who goes in and out with me,
and what can be the use of him is more than I can see.
He is very, very like me from the heels up to the head;
And I see him jump before me, when I jump into
my bed.

ROBERT LOUIS STEVENSON,
A Child's Garden of Verses

Bringing Death into the Light

◆

You've got to love livin' baby, 'cause it sure beats the hell out of dyin'.

FRANK SINATRA

Death, like life, is a process. It can even be said that we are all born dying. That we will die eventually is a certitude. When we deny the fact of death or keep it hidden in a dark, never-to-be-examined recess of our mind, we avoid thinking about life as much as death.

Frank Sinatra died. Princess Diana died. Mother Teresa died. Albert Einstein died. So did Albert Schweitzer. The most powerful, renowned, smartest, richest, most saintly, best-looking, most talented people in the world have died. We're all going to die, sometime, but who among us lives as though they truly believed it?

We Buddhists are taught to preserve life, to appreciate life, and, like Frank Sinatra, to love life. Yet thinking about death – reflecting on our mortality – is a fundamental Buddhist spiritual practice. Not wishing for death, not hoping for death, not doing anything to hasten death, but *thinking* about death. In fact, the Buddha said that death was his guru; death was his greatest teacher. This is an issue that deserves some explaining.

The Buddha is obviously not the only spiritual teacher who exhorted his followers to consider the facts about life and death. Others have certainly done likewise. Through the centuries, people often feel that religious doctrine frightens people by talking about things like hell, fire, and brimstone. I agree that it often seems unnecessarily scary, exaggerated, and even objectionable. And yet an awareness of death is often the propelling consideration for those on a spiritual path.

When I was in my first three-year cloistered meditation retreat, one of our intrepid little band of monks and nuns was a bit older than the rest of us. He lived in the cell next to mine and I couldn't help noticing that he practiced with an impressive amount of enthusiastic determination. This pure hearted and generous soul attributed his diligence to his awareness that he would be around to practice for fewer years than the rest of us. He wanted to make certain that by the time he died he would have achieved inner peace and some measure of enlightenment.

Contemplation of our own impermanence reminds us of the fleeting, tenuous nature of life; it thus provides essential lessons about living in the present moment. A human life is a great blessing. If we accept and internalize the fact of our own mortality, then, by definition, we have to deal with the essential questions of how we live and how we spend our allotted time. We have to stop procrastinating, pretending that we have forever to do what we want to do and be what we long to be. If we think that we want to become better and more loving human beings, we had better start moving in that direction right now. A remembrance of death brings us face to face with the fact that life is like a waterfall rushing over a cliff; it can't be postponed. Your life is here and now, in this very moment. What would you do today if you knew you were going to die tomorrow, or next month? Whom would you talk to? What would you want to do? What messages would you want to express? What unfinished heart-business remains to be completed?

Recently I heard a story about a man – let's call him Gordon – who was diagnosed with a very rare form of cancer. His doctor informed him that he had less than a month to live. This was all terribly surprising and sudden. Gordon was just fifty years old. He had expected to live for many more years; he thought he had lots of time. Gordon hadn't lived a particularly noble personal life. He had three ex-wives, all of whom were angry at him; some would not even speak to him any longer. He had several children, who were angry at him, as well as angry siblings. He had a current girlfriend – also angry. Gordon was even angry at himself.

As a scientist, Gordon quickly did some research into this particular form of cancer, and just as quickly came to the conclusion that his doctors had given him accurate information. He accepted the reality of his situation. So there he was with just a month to live.

Gordon was a complicated man. He often related to others as though everything was a battle that he had no intention of losing. He hadn't always been kind; in fact there had been times when he had caused others a great deal of emotional pain. Nonetheless, Gordon was very intelligent; he knew he didn't want to die surrounded by ill will. And he didn't want to die alone. Gordon was a man of action. Faced with his imminent demise, what action could he take?

Gordon finally did the only thing he could think of. He called all the important people in his life, informed them of his prognosis, and asked them if they could possibly let go of at least some of the resentment they carried. He asked them if they could focus on the good memories; and he asked them one by one if they could come to his house and help him die. And amazingly enough, they did. Ex-wives, girlfriends, siblings, children, former business partners, and former employees all took time out of their lives to be with him.

In the last weeks of his life, Gordon wanted to talk with his family and friends about their relationships, and the things he had done. He wanted to apologize for the times he had been insensitive and mean-spirited; he wanted to die with his emotional affairs in some kind of order. He even arranged for several catered dinners at his home so that everybody could get together.

At first this all seemed very odd and wacky to Gordon's ex-wives, assorted children, stepchildren, brothers, sisters, nieces, nephews, and former friends and colleagues. They weren't sure of what they could say to one another or to Gordon. But as they congregated in the large living room or kept Gordon company in his medically assisted bedroom, it began to make sense. They all began to remember what it was about Gordon that they had once loved or admired. At his best, he was a generous spirit with tremendous life-affirming energy. In this critical moment, facing his own death, Gordon became his best self. There were good memories to cherish as well as bad ones that needed to be put to rest. And something else happened. All these people who were alienated not only from Gordon, but also from one another, began to come together like the large modern extended family that they were.

When Gordon finally slipped into a coma in a hospital, his entire family, as well as several friends, were at his bedside. And they stayed there, a handful of people at a time, in shifts around the clock. When he died at 3 A.M., less than five weeks after his initial diagnosis, close to twenty people were assembled in his room, supporting one another as well as Gordon.

The story of Gordon's death is very unusual. It almost seems like fiction, and yet I know it's true. Gordon died exactly as his doctor said he would, but in that short time, he managed to completely change his emotional environment as well as the way he related to others. He wanted to improve his life and his relationships, and he did just that. Most of us live our lives as though we are going to be around forever. If you thought you had a limited amount of time left, what would you do?

In the West we rarely talk about how people die, but among the Buddhist practitioners of Tibet, it's a fairly common topic of conversation. Not that long ago I received an e-mail from a Western Dharma friend in Nepal with news about the death of an important lama. The e-mail said that although the lama had died a week earlier, he remained in a state of intense meditative absorption, and that the lama's skin tone remained the same. The body had neither become rigid, nor had it started to decompose.

Dudjom Rinpoche used to joke that 'death is when true practitioners can finally show off.' What he meant by that was that after a lifetime of keeping one's spiritual light under a bushel to mitigate pride, the death of serious practitioners is often accompanied by miraculous physical manifestations and weather omens. These physical signs mean a great deal to the faithful. Some of this is hard for Westerners to understand or believe.

Whenever I'm in Asia these days, and I meet with senior lamas and their wives, I often find myself in conversations with them about how people died. They are always curious about how death takes place for experienced Western practitioners. They often ask if there were signs or miracles. Did the practitioner die sitting up or meditating? Were there rainbows? Were there eagles flying overhead? Within a very short period of time, my Eastern mind is activated, and my normal Western skepticism is put aside. I usually have a little chuckle to myself, at myself. I don't actually think that my Eastern friends need to hear of miracles to reinforce their belief in Tibetan Buddhist traditions. But what they do seem to want to hear is that Western practitioners themselves stay with their practice, at this all-important time, long enough to get some kind of truly transcendent results.

One of my good friends from our three-year retreat center was an American woman named Terry Clifford. Terry was a bright New Yorker with a doctorate degree who first became interested in Buddhism in the late 1960s. She had written a book on Tibetan psychiatry and healing, and she had worked hard to help bring Tibetan lamas to the States to share their teachings with Westerners. She was about forty-five when she returned to the United States after a three-year retreat in France. Shortly thereafter, she began to complain of headaches, and a brain tumor was quickly diagnosed.

Terry began to fail very rapidly. I was still in retreat,

but I remember hearing that her teacher from Sikkim, Dodrup Rinpoche, had visited and given her several esoteric initiations and blessings. Although Terry was wasting away, everyone reported that she seemed to be in good spirits. Terry had really taken her Buddhist teachings to heart and had made peace with her life.

It's customary to have one's lama attend you at the time of death to chant and guide you through the 'bardos' (transitions) after death, and Terry's teacher Tulku Pema Wangyal called her and offered to fly to the States to do just that. But Terry said, 'Thank you, but it's not necessary.' I remember hearing this and thinking that it was amazing how far she had come in her devotions. She had reached a point where she honestly no longer needed that kind of solace and external, formal support. We were all proud of her.

Terry died within a short time of her diagnosis. When it came time for her to die, she did so sitting up in the manner of yogis. She was at her home in New York City being supported by the arms of her dear Dharma friend, Vivian. Vivian later told me that when Terry died she was sitting upright, lucid and meditating. Right before the moment of death, she whispered to Vivian, 'This is it.' Then she was gone.

This seemed to me to be a very inspiring end to such a spiritual life. It was a very American Buddhist way to go – in the arms of another compassionate American Dharma sister. After her death, the Nyingma Khenpo Brothers came and performed the prayers and rituals for her passing, and then again at her cremation.

The point is that she died with blessed certainty and peace of mind. She was able to face her death honestly, wisely, and wakefully. I felt that Terry had fulfilled her life's aim and purpose, and accomplished the fruit of spiritual practice. Still, I miss her. We had so many good times together, both at home and abroad.

Thinking about one's own death can be a troubling experience. Most of us feel a little like Woody Allen when he said, 'I'm not afraid to die. I just don't want to be there when it happens.' I think we can all relate to that. The idea of death can be frightening. Denial can seem to be a good solution.

We are afraid to die because we don't want to let go of who we think we are. Our greatest attachment is not to our loved ones, or our possessions. It's to ourselves. Nobody wants to die. The ego doesn't want to let go. That's why in Buddhism, ego death is called 'great death' and physical death is 'small death.' What we have trouble comprehending is how deadening egoic existence actually is. Spiritual rebirth through self-transendence and enlightenment liberates us into deathless bliss not unlike our Western concept of 'life eternal,' if not exactly the same thing. There is certainly much more here than meets the eye!

When the Buddha encouraged his followers to remember man's mortality and contemplate death, he wasn't telling them to become morbid or pessimistically fixated on darkness. He was simply reminding them that body parts age and change, and that they (and we) wouldn't always be able to count on worldly satisfactions, material security, or even mental clarity. The Buddha taught that the one thing we can all count on is our innate goodness, our essential Buddha-nature – our innate luminosity, the love-light within us all. The Buddha was telling people to focus on that light, which he knew existed from his own experience, and learn to live in it and from it, by learning to love all creatures just as we love ourselves.

> *Oh son/daughter of an enlightened family. Your innate wakefulness (rigpa) is inseperable luminosity and emptiness and dwells as a great expanse of light; beyond birth or death, it is in fact, the Buddha of Unchanging Light.*
>
> From *The Tibetan Book of the Dead*

Rebirth, Then and Now

◆

Tibetan Buddhism is particularly well known for teachings on rebirth, but rebirth is a much more universal belief than is ordinarily thought. Going through some old papers, I recently came across the following.

BEN FRANKLIN'S EPITAPH

The body of Benjamin Franklin, Printer,
Like the cover of an old book,
Its contents torn out and stripped of its lettering
and gilding,
Lies here,
Food for Worms;
But the work shall not be lost,
For it will (as he believed)
Appear once more
In a new and more elegant edition
Revised and corrected
by the Author.

BENJAMIN FRANKLIN

Benjamin Franklin was one of my boyhood heroes. During his lifetime, he seemed to be involved in everything of any importance that was going on in the world around him. Sure, I admired him for his aphorisms and witticisms. But what really thrilled me was the story of his attempting to fly a kite in a thunderstorm in order to learn more about electricity. Two centuries later, his intellectual curiosity still seemed exciting and admirable.

Growing up on Long Island, although I had heard quite a bit about Ben Franklin and the Liberty Bell in Philadelphia, I never heard anything about his views on reincarnation – or anyone else's for that matter. Only a few years later, of course, Shirley MacLaine began to write about her experiences, and everything changed, even in suburban Long Island.

As Ben Franklin's epitaph shows, a belief in reincarnation is not as strange and esoteric as one might imagine. Long before Benjamin Franklin – and Shirley MacLaine – people the world over believed in the concept of reincarnation. Most geometry students remember Pythagoras, who was born in ancient Greece in 582 B.C., for the neat mathematical logic of the Pythagorean theorem – $A^2 + B^2 = C^2$. But during Pythagoras' lifetime, he and his followers were also known for their belief in the transmigration of souls. There is even an old joke attributed to the period that has actually survived: 'Once they say that Pythagoras was passing by when a dog was being ill-treated and abused. "Stop," Pythagoras said, "don't hit it! It is the soul of a friend. I knew it the moment I heard its voice."'

Jews around the time of Jesus' birth also believed in reincarnation. So did a fair number of early Christians, until 325 A.D. when the church Council of Nicea officially deemed it heretical. Today as then, of course, a majority of the world's population, whether they be Hindu, Jain, Taoist, or Buddhist, accepts some form of reincarnation.

When Buddhist teachers are trying to be precise, however, they tend not to use the word 'reincarnation' and prefer instead the term 'rebirth.' Reincarnation is actually more of a Hindu than a Buddhist belief because it implies a constant, never-changing, eternal soul that is reborn time and again. This is often likened to a person changing clothes. Although each lifetime brings a new outer identity, the so-called eternal soul remains the same life after life until perfect (re)union with God is achieved.

Rebirth, the preferred Buddhist term, describes a belief in innate spirit, which constantly evolves and changes. This is often likened to ripples on the ocean. Although the ripples don't turn into anything but water, which is their essential nature, over the course of time they change quite a bit – becoming larger and smaller and moving at different speeds. In our analogy here, the water (Buddha-nature) passes through various manifestations or incarnations, like waves, forming and transforming one into another, life after life as well as day after day, hour after hour, and moment after moment. A traditional image is that of a water-wheel filling and emptying its buckets as it turns.

What one does in each moment (as well as in each lifetime) has the power to purify and alter one's innate luminous spirit. This subtle difference over whether there is an immortal soul or who or what is reborn again is one of the ways in which the Buddha broke with the ancient Hindu traditions of his time.

The Buddha, who believed that he had been born many times, said that when he attained enlightenment, he perceived all the karma and interlocking workings of cause and effect throughout his many previous lifetimes. The Buddha fully understood the whole program. He saw not just the beginning and ending of his lives; he saw the cycles and behavior patterns that created these lives; and he intuitively understood the principles of karmic causation, interconnection, interdependence, and interpenetration.

Westerners who come from traditions that emphasize both spirit and soul seem to have no difficulty in rolling the two concepts – reincarnation and rebirth – into one. Seekers typically don't focus on the subtle theological conflicts that have historically taken place. What they often relate to, however, is the current debate in contemporary modern Buddhism that revolves around whether or not one has to *believe* in rebirth in order to call oneself a Buddhist. At one time, such a belief was considered essential, but this has changed over time.

Many modern teachers now say that one of the wonderful things about Buddhism is that you don't have to believe in anything in order to progress on the path of awakened enlightenment. These teachers say that Buddhism is dependent on meditation, self-exploration, wisdom, loving-kindness, and an ethical approach to the world and all its creatures. In this approach, belief is secondary; direct experience is considered fundamental.

Much of the information given to Westerners about the subject of rebirth comes from what they have read or heard about the long line of Dalai Lamas, whom Tibetans accept as incarnations of the Bodhisattva Avalokitesvara, the Buddha of Compassion. The current Dalai Lama is the fourteenth of these spiritual leaders. In Tibet it is believed that when a great Buddhist master such as the Dalai Lama dies, he or she is able to intentionally choose to be reborn in a way that is conducive to their continuing mission.

When a Dalai Lama dies, his belongings are given to his closest advisors and followers who hold them until there are signs or omens that (a) tell them that the new Dalai Lama has been reborn and (b) give them some idea where the child can be found. The Dalai Lama is not elected or chosen; he is sought, found, and recognized, a process that is sometimes helped by indications from the deceased in the form of oral or written instructions.

As those who saw the movie *Kundun* know, the little child who is believed to be the Dalai Lama is usually tested to see if he has some memories from his previous life. The same kind of procedure is carried on for many of the major lamas of Tibet. This is known as the Tibetan 'tulku' system, and the incarnated lamas are known as 'tulkus.' The word 'tulku' can be translated literally as 'wisdom-embodiments' or 'Buddha-manifestations.'

Many of my original Tibetan teachers have died, but their tulkus, who carry the same name, are now growing up in various monasteries around the world. The wise and learned meditation master Kalu Rinpoche, for example, is believed to have been reborn as the child of a nephew who was his secretary as well as one of his closest disciples. This child currently lives in his monasteries in Darjeeling and Bhutan with his parents. My first Tibetan teacher was Lama Yeshe. His tulku is a Spanish-born teenager who now lives in southern India at the monastery there known as Sera, which was also the name of his very well known monastery in Tibet. There are also several Westerners who have been recognized as incarnations of Tibetan teachers. Some of these are women.

Just recently I returned from my teacher's Shechen Monastery in Nepal where I attended the traditional week-long enthronement of a little child, who is believed to be Dilgo Khyentse Rinpoche's tulku. These enthronements, as you can imagine, are particularly joyous occasions.

Since China now controls Tibet, there have been many problems surrounding some of the newest little Tibetan tulkus. The second highest ranking lama (after the Dalai Lama) has always been the Panchen Lama. Within the last few years, there has been a wealth of newspaper reports about finding the new Panchen Lama. The Dalai Lama recognized one little boy still living in Tibet as the Panchen Lama. The Chinese government, which wanted to have a Panchen Lama they would be able to control, chose another child. They then took the first little boy away to China, and he has not been heard from since. This is a matter of great importance to Tibetans, and trying to help the child who is believed to be in China is a priority to the Dalai Lama, who refers to this child as the world's youngest political prisoner. It's a real tragedy.

Within Tibet itself, probably the best known line of

reincarnated lamas after the Dalai Lama and Panchen Lama is the line of Karmapa Lamas, who are the oldest examples of the tulku system. The tulku system became a part of Tibetan culture during the twelfth century when the first Karmapa, who was the head of the Kagyu lineage, attained enlightenment. There is a legend concerning the first Karmapa's enlightenment that is accepted as gospel by Tibetans. It says that when this Karmapa attained enlightenment, the female deities known as 'dakinis' were so thrilled that they wanted to offer something special. Using hair from their own heads, they wove a black hat for the Karmapa which rests, symbolically, above his head wherever he goes. The Karmapa is therefore known as the Black Hat Lama. Centuries later, the emperor of China had a jeweled black crown made for the Fifth Karmapa. This material crown is often worn during ceremonies and initiations. Tibetans believe that anyone who sees the Karmapa wearing this crown will receive extra blessings and an assurance of eventual enlightenment.

Another legend says that during his lifetime, the Buddha predicted that there would someday be a lineage of enlightened teachers who would be called by the name Karmapa, and that they would spread the Dharma for the benefit of all until all would be enlightened. In fact, 'Karmapa' is translated as 'he who performs the work of a Buddha.' The Karmapas, who continue to be the oldest unbroken line of Tibetan tulkus, are said to be able to foresee their own deaths as well as their own rebirths. Consequently they usually leave instructions in the form of a prediction letter, about how and where they will be reborn.

The Sixteenth Karmapa was one of my most beloved

and close teachers. He was considered to be a living Buddha. Everyone who came in contact with the Gyalwa Karmapa seemed to know that they were in the presence of awe-inspiring spiritual greatness and power.

I met the Sixteenth Karmapa when I was at my teacher's monastery in Darjeeling. My first face-to-face meeting with him came about because a group of us were lined up to be blessed. When my turn came, I was suitably awed. He had enormous spiritual presence. One was always aware of his warm and brilliant spirit, and I was always greatly moved by his presence.

After that first meeting, my friends told me that my picture, with the Karmapa, was on display in a window in town. The next time I was in town, I saw the photograph they were referring to. The Karmapa was smiling at me. My head was turned, and only part of my face was visible. It was visible enough however for the photographer, whom I met later, to complain jokingly that I had spoiled his picture. He said he wanted to get the Karmapa's smiling face alone, but they couldn't remove my profile without destroying the shot. I still have a print of the photo. It's one of my most cherished physical remembrances.

The Karmapa, who made many teaching trips to the United States, had a hilltop monastery in Woodstock, New York. He died in a hospital in Chicago in 1981. Like most Tibetans, he was a firm believer in rebirth. The Sixteenth Gyalwa Karmapa was a great animal lover. When I knew him in Nepal, he had a pet black dog, as well as many rare tropical birds and parrots that he had trained to recite his name mantra, 'Karmapa chenno,' which translates as 'Lama, heed me.'

One of my favorite stories about the Karmapa was told to me by one of his attendants. When His Holiness was still a boy living in his monastery in Tibet, he had a servant named Yonga, who suddenly and mysteriously left in the dark of night, never to return. No one seemed to know where Yonga had gone. When Karmapa made psychic inquiries, he learned that no harm had befallen Yonga, and he decided to let the matter drop. Then a few years later, the Karmapa found out that Yonga had died. The youthful Karmapa, who had loved Yonga, was appropriately sad to hear the news; prayers and benedictions were made in Yonga's memory, and life went on.

Time passed. Then one day the still-teenage Karmapa and his followers were travelling by horse in the sparsely inhabited northern plains of eastern Tibet. When the party stopped to rest, the Karmapa wandered off in the steppe-like wilderness. A monk attendant followed not far behind.

Suddenly the Karmapa called out, 'Yonga, Yonga,' as he used to do when hailing his late servant. The attendant wondered what on earth was going on, but he continued to follow behind the Karmapa, sure that the Dharma protectors were protecting his master.

Karmapa continued wandering through the lonely deserted grassland, gently calling 'Yonga, Yonga.' Suddenly there appeared, mewling, a little Himalayan blue sheep. Fearlessly, the sheep walked up to the Karmapa and kneeled to lick his outstretched hand.

The Karmapa turned to his faithful attendant, smiled sweetly, and said, 'Now Yonga has come back to me.'

From that day on, I was told that the Great Dharma king, Karmapa, and his sheep were inseparable.

Buddha Dharma itself is now being reborn here in the Western hemisphere because of the spiritual work of a large group of dedicated Buddhist teachers from Asia who were kind enough to pass on what they knew to Westerners. At least part of the credit for the rebirth of the Dharma here in the West belongs to the Sixteenth Karmapa. The Karmapa was believed to be a living Buddha, and many considered him omniscient as well as prescient. Concerned about the intentions of Communist China, for example, the Karmapa actually left Tibet well before the communist takeover in 1959 and established a monastery with his followers in Sikkim.

Throughout his lifetime, the Sixteenth Karmapa worked to plant the seeds of Dharma throughout the world, making several long trips from his home monastery in Sikkim to Europe and America. He did so because he believed that carrying the Dharma out of Asia was absolutely necessary. The Karmapa was, of course, also very aware of the stunning predictions that had been made in the eighth century by the original founder of Tibetan Buddhism, Padma Sambhava. His now famous prophecy states, 'When the iron bird flies, and horses run on wheels, the Tibetan people will be scattered like ants across the World, and the Dharma will come to the land of red-faced people.' Many people have said that when the Sixteenth Karmapa chose to die in Chicago rather than in his own home, it sent out a clear message to Buddhists everywhere. The Dharma and Tibetan Buddhism had taken a giant leap. It was ready to be reborn in a new way, in the New World.

I think of Karmapa often and dream about him with

astonishing frequency. He told his students, 'Each of you will be in my heart through all my lifetimes. Listen to my voice within you, and you will know.' Nobody ever said he was learned; all said he was compassionate, powerful, omniscient, and clairvoyant. He was a great spiritual master.

When you are in the East with the many lamas, tulkus, monks, nuns, and ordinary Buddhists who believe 100 percent in rebirth, it is difficult not to feel the same way. When the Sixteenth Karmapa gave initiations and empowerments, amazing things happened. Spiritual dreams, energy eruptions, and visions of the Buddha and other deities were commonplace. So were other types of awakening experiences. Rebirth in that environment seemed as though it was perfectly rational. When a young tulku talks to you of his memories of his past life, as has happened to me, it seems absolutely credible. Here in the West, however, one is more apt to say, 'Who knows for sure?'

HERE-AND-NOW REBIRTH

So what does this ancient universal doctrine of rebirth and the recycling of ourselves have to do with our day-to-day lives? It helps if we keep in mind that the concept of rebirth applies to more than just individuals. Ideas can also be reborn; movements can be reborn; and yes, even the Dharma itself can be reborn. In fact it is being reborn, here and now, literally as we speak. It is being reborn in you, and me, and in anyone else who hears its call.

Personal individual rebirth applies not just to life

after life. It also means here-and-now, moment-to-moment rebirth. Every out breath we make is like a little death, and we are consequently reborn every instant. Each time we undergo even a small transformation and life change, we are reborn. We have the opportunity to reinvent ourselves continuously. And we do. Each cell in our body changes every seven years. I'm not making this up as I go along; it's considered scientific fact. Our mind is constantly changing. We are all works in progress, as I like to say, with almost infinite possibilities.

At one time or another, most of us have felt depressed and defeated. What we often wait for in those moments is a rebirth of hope. People who become alienated from each other and then reconcile often refer to a rebirth of love. Several people have pointed out to me that this concept of rebirth is not that far removed from the Christian idea of renewal as symbolized by Easter and the resurrection.

We all wonder and worry, don't we, about what's going to happen to us when we die. What's beyond the grave? Is it a better life or is it cold oblivion? The doctrine of rebirth helps us observe directly in our own lives how the process of change takes place. We let go of our childhood and our youth; we relinquish old relationships; we move through middle age and on to old age. The more skillfully we let go, the more gracefully we will be able to enjoy the next stage. The cup has to be a little emptied out of old preconceptions, opinions, and fixations in order to enjoy what comes next. Tibetan teachings on rebirth are all about applying the principles of living in the moment. It's about *conscious* living as well as dying.

Rebirth has yet another spiritual purpose. Like the Asian masters who agreed to teach Westerners the Dharma, we all have the capacity to become representatives of that which is good, wise, and mindful. In this way, we help wisdom, goodness, and mindfulness be reborn time and time again in others.

In the age of the nanosecond, rebirth, like everything else, seems to happen more quickly. One thought leads to another; an old thought is recycled; a new one is reborn. It all happens so quickly. In each life, we are presented with myriad opportunities for rebirth and glorious new beginnings. The more deeply we are in the present moment, the less resistant we are to the ebb and flow of change and evolution. If we are able to live in the here and now, we are able to move gracefully with the flow of events. When we take fixed positions and hang on, we get swept away, as everything eventually does – including large boulders and even continents. To get the full benefits of rebirth in this lifetime we must learn to let go, to not get stuck or fixated on our ideas or concepts. We stop resisting and let reality flow through us.

People throughout time have tried by various means to prolong life or find ways to control natural transformations. Everything from cryogenics to mummification has been employed. There is a dark side to all of this, and seekers should always be wary of facile claims in this area. The issues of birth and death are so large and so frightening that we are all sometimes inclined to want to grasp at any straws. There are those who have even chosen suicide as a way of avoiding natural transformations. I'm thinking of the people who killed themselves at Jonestown or the members of the Heaven's Gate cult.

We saw some of them on television. They seemed intelligent and educated. What were they thinking? What made them believe that they would be able to get a seat on a comet? Tibetan Buddhism teaches that it is a negative action to kill anyone, including yourself.

Understanding the true meaning of the wonderful concept of rebirth allows us to accept the inevitability of change. It teaches us to let go of those things we can't hang on to – in the larger sense, our bodies themselves; in a smaller sense, the wonderful taste of a sumptuous dessert; and in a very meaningful way, to the belief that we can control the uncontrollable. This practical application of rebirth reinforces our intention to live ethically, truly, and joyfully in the moment with the knowledge that all things are recycled and reborn.

It is no more surprising to be born twice than to be born once.

VOLTAIRE

Faith and Doubt

◆

Now faith is the assurance of things hoped for, the conviction of things not seen.

HEBREWS II:I

Life requires faith. It takes faith to brush your teeth, lay out your clothes, set the alarm clock, and go to bed every night. Before they went to sleep each night, the Kadampa masters in Tibet used to follow a deathbed custom by setting their teacups upside down. They did this to remind themselves that life is impermanent. There is no certainty that any of us will wake up. So when we tuck ourselves in and set the snooze buttons on our alarm clocks, we believe in something. We believe in a tomorrow that we haven't seen. This is faith.

It seems next to impossible to discuss contemporary spirituality without talking about the implications of faith. Every religion or belief system calls for a leap of faith of some sort. Jews have faith that they have received the word of God, the Messiah will come, and that all Jews will be reunited in Israel. A major theme in the Passover service is the rallying cry, 'Next year in Jerusalem.' Jews share this faith. Christians, of course, believe that the Messiah has come; they have faith in Jesus and his promise. In millions of churches around the world, each Sunday Roman Catholics chant their mystery of faith, 'Christ was born, Christ has risen, Christ will come again.' And Muslims have faith in the Prophet Muhammad and his words as coming directly from God.

However, since Buddhism is not really a religion in the traditional theistic sense, some scholars argue that faith has no place in a Buddhist practice. They stress, and I think rightly, the importance of practice. Thich Nhat Hanh has said, 'It is not a matter of faith. It is a matter of practice.' The Buddha himself took a very pragmatic approach to spiritual practice. 'Try it and see for yourself whether it works' is an oft-quoted piece of advice from the Buddha.

But stressing the practical should not discount the part faith plays in Buddhist practice. In fact, all Tibetan masters without exception say that faith and devotion are a major part of the path. There is a well-known song in the Mahamudra lineage that says: 'Renunciation is the feet of meditation practice; mindfulness and awareness is the heart; faith and devotion is the head. May we realize these spiritual qualities and progress on the path.'

Renunciation is likened to the feet because treading the spiritual path helps the seeker walk away from worldly values; awareness and mindfulness are at the center, the very heart of practice; faith and devotion are likened to the head because the head includes the eyes, which represent the vision to keep looking deeper.

Right after college, I travelled to Bodh Gaya, the site of the Buddha's enlightenment. There I was but one in an endless line of countless seekers and pilgrims. One of the things I remember best are the many times I stayed up long into the night discussing and debating issues of faith and spirit with my fellow wayfarers and travellers. We were a very mixed group. Some were Christian, some Jewish, some Buddhist, some Hindu; some were on Taoist, Sufi, Sikh, and Jain paths. There were dropouts from California on the road to Kathmandu, academics working on dissertations, linguists, world-class athletes, mountain climbers, ex-Green Berets who had served in Vietnam, traders, and smugglers, along with great numbers of monks and nuns, Catholic as well as Buddhist. There were those who were spending one night in an ashram, and there were those who had been there for decades. There were those who were devoted to one guru and those who had been with every guru. There were sages and schnooks, saints and sinners, and everything in between.

Bodh Gaya was filled with temples – Burmese, Tibetan, Zen, as well as Hindu. The Zen temple had an enormous bronze gong that had been brought by ship from Japan. At dawn and dusk, two monks would strike it several times, swinging at it with a huge log. We would wait for the sound, timing our days by the great, almost sonic, boom that could be heard echoing across the desert plains. At night as it began to get dark, thousands of Tibetans carrying butter lamps and lit candles would walk around the stupa monument. They would then set them reverently before the historical Buddha's gilded stone seat beneath the Bodhi Tree.

One couldn't help being aware of the amount of faith and devotion that was present in Bodh Gaya. But when we sat up late talking, it also became apparent that everyone had different views on what or whom to believe in. And yet all these people had to believe in something or else why would they be making such a pilgrimage?

There are many faithful in the world. We see them everywhere. Yet there is no one for whom faith is automatic and immediate; it doesn't always come easily. Faith has to be worked on. Yes, there are certainly those who find it easier to believe than others. I've always considered myself a bit of a cynic, and someone who questions everything. Here in the West, I meet many people who have belief systems that include guardian angels, astrology, crystals, spirit guides, and demons, as well as God and a large array of traditional household saints. But many others simply don't have it in them to believe in something they haven't experienced personally.

In fact, there are those who make fun of faith, likening it to superstition. But the truth is that faith is good for us. Medical study after medical study shows that people of faith live longer and recover from illnesses more quickly. All this proves is that what one person calls superstition, another calls science. Deep faith wipes away fear and gives one a sense of one's place in the universe. The late Catholic theologian Henri Nouwen said, 'Faith is the radical trust that home has always been there and always will be there.'

In the East, of course, there are vast numbers of deities that are worshiped, or 'believed in.' As Buddhism travelled out of India and was carried to the Himalays, Southeast Asia, China, Korea, Vietnam, and Japan, portions of the already existing religions in these countries were folded in. What evolved then were three separate branches of Buddhism – Zen, Theravadin, and Vajrayana. The infinite heart of the Dharma is timeless and not limited by the trappings of culture, language, or time. Nonetheless, there are differences in the various branches of Buddhism that reflect slight differences in belief.

In Tibet, for example, the indigenous religion that predated Buddhism was known as Bon, a shamanistic belief system with its own native pantheon of gods and demons. Some of the colorful rituals of the Bon tradition found their way into Tibetan Buddhism and exist still. These rituals resonate with some Westerners; others find them too 'exotic.' In the same way some are very comfortable with the simple spare elegance of Zen while others find it too stark. Many Western Buddhists tell me that they feel most at home with the modern Vipassana or Insight Meditation tradition, which probably has the least amount of rites and rituals.

Given these three traditions, a question I'm often asked is, 'Exactly what is it that Buddhists believe?' In fact, I often ask myself what it is that we have faith in. What beliefs, if any, are the essentials of bare bones Buddhism? I think there are several practices that reflect a core Buddhist belief system.

For example: *Buddhists have faith that we can all find a haven, a safe port in life's storms.*

We find this sanctuary in what is known as the Three Jewels: Buddha, Dharma, and Sangha. In all Buddhist traditions, a new practitioner becomes part of the community by taking part in an ancient rite known as the refuge ceremony. The refuge prayer or vow simply states:

> I take refuge in the Buddha, the enlightened teacher
> I take refuge in the Dharma, the spiritual teachings
> I take refuge in the Sangha, the spiritual community.

Taking refuge in the Triple Gem means that we trust and have faith in Buddha, as an awakened teacher, and in Buddhahood – the possibility of enlightenment for each and every one of us; it means that we have faith in the Dharma, the enlightened spiritual teachings and the reality of truth itself; it means that we have faith in the Sangha, the possibility that we can heal and be healed by the love and service found within the spiritual community. Whenever we seek spiritual solace and something we can rely on, we turn to Buddha, Dharma, and Sangha.

This belief has subtle and far-reaching implications. If the individual seeker, for example, is able to believe in (or even just be open to) her own possibility for enlightenment – her own innate Buddha-nature – she will, by definition, have faith in her own basic worthiness, in her own potential and innate capacity for goodness. The Dalai Lama once stunned a group of Western scholars by asking them to explain what was meant by the term 'low self-esteem' that Westerners so frequently discuss. His Holiness was unfamiliar with that concept even though he had been instructing Westerners in Buddhist theory and practice for decades.

In Tibet, there is no term that corresponds to low self-esteem. How could there be in a country where everyone is viewed as a potential Buddha? A certain degree of self-esteem or individual personal value and belonging is taken for granted. This belief in the value of one's own self then logically extends to a belief not only in one's own potential for awakened compassion, but also to everyone else's innate potential.

When we discuss faith, we also have to raise the issue of doubt – faith's flip or shadow side. Looking around at the world, there is certainly reason to feel doubt. In fact, there are those who say that doubt is one of contemporary man's greatest problems. T. S. Eliot wrote:

> *Between the conception,*
> *and the creation,*
> *Between the emotion,*
> *And the response,*
> *Falls the Shadow.*

That shadow represents doubt. What we need to understand is that it's hard to undertake anything without some doubt or uncertainty. Even a meditation session brings a certain amount of doubt. 'My mind is never quiet . . . I can't do this . . . I don't think I'm doing it right . . . I don't think I can last for twenty minutes.'

Experienced meditators, however, expect the mind to wander. They expect doubts and confusion and are prepared to cope with them. It comes as no surprise that doubt affected all the saints and sages, including the Buddha himself. Welcome to the club. Faith is what helps us continue on despite our doubts.

In my own life today, I have just moved. It's been a major undertaking involving furniture, clothing, dishes, odds and ends, and, of course, many books, tapes, Buddhist artifacts, and papers. These books are currently packed in cartons that are piled high in the farmhouse that will be my new home. As I look at these cartons, I honestly doubt that I will ever find my books or anything that I need, ever again. If I focus on the doubt, it only seems to grow deeper and become overwhelming; it might even turn into despair. Yet I have moved before, and I understand the process. Therefore I have faith that everything will emerge from the cartons sooner or later, and in reasonable condition. I have faith in the people who are helping me, and I have faith in my own ability to adjust and get through this interim period. This has been done before, and it is not rocket science.

On the spiritual path, one can expect to go through periods where faith escapes us and doubt, sometimes even despair, emerges. It can all seem chaotic, confusing, and filled with deep valleys beset with shadows. We begin to doubt the process; we begin to doubt the possibility of enlightenment itself. My Korean Zen master Ku San (Nine Mountains) used to say: 'Small doubt (and questioning) brings small enlightenment; great doubt (and questioning) brings great enlightenment!' He used to engage us in spirited dialogues called 'Dharma Combat,' playfully jousting with our deepest fears, questions, and issues.

Sometimes all we can do on the spiritual path is summon enough faith to hang on, realizing that everything is in transition. No matter how bad it gets, life guarantees that the situation will change. So wise men and women let go and have faith that things are simply passing through. When we feel despair about anything in life, we can always take a moment or a day off before starting again, for no point is the final end point; everything is in process. Even if we don't immediately see how to change a difficult situation, we can renew, recharge, and re-empower ourselves, trusting that things are impermanent, transforming and metamorphosing right before our eyes. There is an ancient meditative technique that is taught for those times that a meditation session becomes difficult: Stop, take a breath of fresh air, relax, refresh yourself, and start again. The same is true in life. When something isn't working out, or you can't face a painful situation, take some time and then start again. This is timeless wisdom and timely advice. Try it. To be able to do this implies faith.

This kind of faith comes with the conviction that we can be open to the wisdom of allowing our lives to unfold. This faith in the future is the exact opposite of trying to control our lives or the lives of those around us. Faith is the underlying theme of the famous Buddhist maxim of 'letting go,' which really implies *letting be.* When we have faith we are more authentically open to dancing with life in whatever form it presents itself. This kind of faith brings greater joy and engagement and less fear, hesitation, and aversion as we think about what tomorrow will bring. It allows us to experience more awe toward the mysteries of life, and less concern.

THE AVOWAL

As swimmers dare
to lie face to the sky
and water bears them,
as hawks rest upon air
and air sustains them, so I would learn to attain
freefall and float
into Creator Spirit's deep embrace,
knowing no effort earns
that all surrounding grace.

DENISE LEVERTOV

Karma:
Truth and Consequences

◆

Do not overlook tiny good actions, thinking they are of no benefit; even tiny drops of water in the end will fill a huge vessel.

Do not overlook negative actions merely because they are small; however small a spark may be, it can burn down a haystack as big as a mountain.

THE BUDDHA

All major spiritual traditions rest on the belief that the universe has a moral dimension and that there is some form of personal accountability for our actions. Starting with the banishment of Adam and Eve from the Garden of Eden, the Judeo-Christian tradition, for example, describes a God who hates evil and loves good. In theistic traditions, virtue and righteousness are ultimately rewarded by divine grace.

In nontheistic Buddhism there is no God who rewards good and punishes evil. Thus there is no outside intervention. Instead Buddhism depends upon a notion of universal law and responsibility. This is called 'karma' or the law of cause and effect. We look to no other creator as a first cause or moving principle of the universe. The law of causality is explained like basic physics: For every action, there is a reaction. As we sow, so shall we reap. Drop a glass, it's going to break; drop a ball, it's going to bounce; pull a thread, the hem unravels; giving a friendly dog a pat, receive a tail wag in return; feed a crying baby, the baby thrives; help a neighbor move, gain confidence in your ability to give. The more you give, the more you get back.

The law of karma teaches that we can have faith in our ability to affect our own lives and the lives of others. Buddhism believes that by doing good we accumulate merits that affect our destiny, creating a sort of karmic bank account. This understanding is firmly rooted in a recognition of the interconnectedness and interdependence of all things. On this subject, the Dalai Lama has written, 'Buddha's teaching is that you are your own master; everything depends on yourself. This means that pleasure and pain arise from virtuous and nonvirtuous actions which come not from outside but from within yourself.'

Because teaching takes me around the country, I spend a number of nights in hotels where guests receive complimentary copies of *USA Today*. I think of it as 'the traveller's newspaper.' Just this morning I opened the paper to an article on the front page of the sports section about major league baseball playoffs, and I saw these words: 'Each series has its special karma.' It made me smile to myself. These days talk about karma seems to be just about everywhere, even on the sports pages! Even so, we Westerners often tend to be a little bit confused about exactly what karma is. I've certainly heard more than one person say, 'I don't know what I did in my last life to deserve this.' The 'this' is usually a difficult relationship, a hard job, or a particularly bad run of 'luck.' The problem with this kind of thinking is that it tends to be fatalistic and negates taking into account all the things that the person might have done – or not done – in *this* life; it negates taking into account all the things we could do *today* to change what we will experience tomorrow.

The three most common errors we make about the ancient, timeless, cosmic, and yet oh-so-practical teachings of karma are as follows: (1) to assume that our karma is somehow fated or predestined; (2) to believe that we have a fixed future and that our karma is scripted or written in concrete; (3) to feel helpless in the face of karma.

To understand karma, we need to recognize that in Buddhism the facticity of impermanence, contingency, and flow precludes the notion of any real eternal heaven or hell. Instead Buddhists say that karma is the operative law of reality. The universe is viewed almost as a karma machine. Karma creates the world, our life, and our experience. Collective karma shapes our world; individual karma shapes our personal destiny. Karma is the creator.

Buddhist morality is not based on any ideas of absolute good or absolute evil. Instead Buddhism talks about skillful and unskillful action, wholesome and unwholesome words, thoughts, and deeds. How we handle ourselves in a cause-and-effect operated universe determines our karmic fate or destiny. When we act in ways that are virtuous, these karmas or actions are considered skillful; the opposite, of course, is also true – nonvirtuous behavior is considered unskillful. This is the sole basis of Buddhist ethics and morality; the bottom line of wise and foolish, skillful and unskillful – the compassionate logic of benefit and harm.

Skillful action is cultivated and encouraged because it helps lay the groundwork for good karma. Remember, karma is cause and effect, or, as I like to say, truth and consequences. When we behave in ways that reflect wisdom, sanity, and compassion, we open the doors to a better life – and better karma. In short, when we start acting and reacting differently, we get different results. Our karma becomes our Dharma – our destiny, our duty, our expression of truth as we know and experience it.

The Buddhist masters say that those who understand causation and contingency, in the context of emptiness, understand reality. Everything in Buddhism circles back to understanding how things appear and how they actually *are*. The underlying reason for meditating, for example, is that meditation helps us develop a clearer, more mirrorlike awareness of reality and what's taking place around us. Cultivating this kind of awareness means that we are less likely to be victimized either by outer circumstances or our own semi-conscious responses; we are able to see through, and stand free from, karmic conditioning. We are able to skillfully handle our karma instead of foolishly trying to avoid, deny, or elude it.

Mirrorlike awareness is a sane response to any kind of situation or stimuli. It improves our karma, almost by definition, because it opens us up and gives us the space and clarity to view things objectively before we react. In this way, our responses to life become more intentional and skillful. We realize that we have choices; we become better able to let go of our conditioned knee-jerk responses.

The laws of karma are actually very empowering. We may always be aware of strong emotional and psychological winds blowing from past events and experiences, but even so, how we sail through these winds can make all the difference. No matter how strongly we've been conditioned, we don't have to go through life perpetuating old patterns.

We often hear people saying, 'I've been down that street before, and I don't want to go there.' Sometimes, they shorten it and simply say, 'I don't want to go there.' When we use this expression, we are saying that we don't want to be part of the same old tape loop continuously spinning round and round. We are proclaiming that we have choices. This is a matter of conscious awareness. Building new patterns is the best way to work with karma.

An important thing for seekers to remember is always to approach the laws of karma with a sense of balance. Don't use karma like a weapon to blame yourself, fate, or anyone else for everything that goes wrong. It doesn't make sense to go so far in one direction that we are constantly overcome by feelings of guilt and shame; nor is it helpful to go overboard in the other direction and develop a nihilistic approach as if nothing matters. As the Buddha said, stay balanced in all things.

I'm often asked various versions of the following question: 'Do you think the reason I'm having so many problems with my relationships (with my mother, my father, my child, Frank, Joan, James, Jane – fill in the blank) is because we are karmically connected from a previous life?' My honest answer to these questions is always the same: 'Possibly; I don't know. You must have *some* karma from the past to be going through this together now.' That much I know. What I don't know is whether the past karma was created yesterday or several hundred years ago.

The most important lessons that seekers can take away from the Buddhist teachings about karma is that new karma is created all the time. We engage with others in the *now*. If you and your mate are arguing over who should be doing the dishes or grocery shopping, it probably doesn't help to consult soothsayers about ties from the past. Padma Sambhava said, 'If you want to know your past life, look into your present condition; if you want to know your future life, look at your present actions.'

Dharma wisdom consistently reminds us to stay in the present and deal with naked truth as it is happening right now. In the New Testament, Jesus reminded his followers to deal with today by saying, 'So do not worry about tomorrow, for tomorrow will bring worries of its own. Today's trouble is enough for today.' I once heard the Dalai Lama interviewed on a television talk show. Someone asked him if he remembered his past lives. He deflected the question by answering, 'I can't always remember what happened yesterday.'

Since we accumulate karma from this life, as well as from any past life, we can make sincere efforts to create good karma for the future by keeping our dealings balanced, straightforward, and fair. Causality is always very much in evidence. Today's uncooperative act in the family kitchen, for example, can provide the fuel for tomorrow's seemingly unrelated argument in the family car.

Since karma is a fundamental causative law, it affects everything and everybody. Plants, animals, nations, groups, and the world itself are part of the interwoven karmic process. Vietnamese Zen master and poet Thich Nhat Hanh calls it 'interbeing.' We see karmic results very directly in the environment. In the early nineteenth century, people didn't see any harm in dumping waste into the oceans. Now we all pay the karmic consequences for such shortsighted, disconnected thinking. Buddhist wisdom points out that there are no accidents. Global warming, for example, is no accident; we all have a hand in it.

On the other hand, the universe is a mysterious place. The enlightened Buddha himself said that although he knew five hundred of his past lives, only someone with complete omniscience could understand every karmic concatenation or causal link. To emphasize this, he pointed out the uniqueness of peacock's tails, each with its own wondrous pattern and color, saying that it would take an omniscient one to understand in precise detail exactly how every little tail feather had come about. Who can know what combinations of events conspired to bring about everything that happens – both good and bad?

Buddhism does, however, teach that no matter what we did in the past, we determine our own future, and can do so with more conscious intentionality. The wisdom traditions are filled with stories about men and women who were able to overcome and purify even the worst kind of actions and their karmic consequences. Although karma is inexorable, it can be worked with; it can be altered, and it can be transcended. Tibetans say negative karma has one redeeming feature: It can be purified and transformed.

Of course it's difficult to change our own karmically

conditioned patterns and habits. No one said it was supposed to be easy. We become so frozen and accustomed to our own way of living and relating that we fall into ruts, neurotic and otherwise, and forget that there are numerous other ways of acting and being. Our opinions become so ingrained that it's hard to step out of the old tracks and grooves. The strongest habits, of course, are addictions, which are excellent examples of karmic conditioning. Each time we act on our habits we reinforce the impulse. Addiction is karma hardened like Krazy Glue until it seems frozen in place. But even addictions can be reconditioned and eventually deconditioned.

I have a friend, for example, who feels that she is addicted to chocolate, which makes her put on weight and causes her face to break out. She tries very hard to resist the temptation, but every now and then she gives in to the chocolate impulse; then she feels as though she can't stop. She says that when that happens, she has to start all over; even a tiny piece of chocolate makes it that much harder to say 'no' to the next one. I feel that way about ice cream, which I try to avoid.

If giving up chocolate and ice cream is difficult, consider how hard it is to give up caffeine, alcohol, drugs, or tobacco. How about the many reflexive behavior patterns and ego-coping strategies that we are accustomed to falling back on? I know someone who has a difficult time controlling his temper. Based on the advice of a therapist, he is wearing rubber bands around his wrist to help his practice of self-observation. Whenever he feels like yelling at someone, he snaps the bands to remind him to stop and think about whether getting angry is something he really wants to do. In this way, he is struggling to recondition and retrain himself. Good for him!

Anyone who has ever tried to alter behavior knows firsthand how difficult it is. Successful behavior modification, no matter what the behavior, requires positive intentions combined with determination, will, strength, perseverance, awareness, and character. Yet many people are strong enough to behave differently, and in so doing, they create new karma. In the best cases, they finally find the freedom and fulfillment they have always been looking for.

If we want to direct ourselves to a better future, perhaps the best thing we can do is to start trying to cultivate greater awareness of how we can create better karmic fortune in our lives. We can do this as individuals or as groups. People working together can create better karma for the entire group. The women's movement, for example, started changing karma for all women. The dedicated men and women who are working to save the rain forests, the oceans, and wildlife are working to create better karma for all mankind. The simple basic law of karma: From apple seeds come apple trees.

Ask yourself, what can I do today to change my karma tomorrow? Pick out one thing about your life that is less than ideal and start working on it. Karma comes in many forms – physical karma, emotional karma, family karma, communal karma, gender karma, societal karma, national karma. You can change the karma of your relationships with loved ones by acting differently; at lunch today, you can change your physical karma by eating differently.

Here are some simple examples of people who are changing their karma.

Last year, Annie saw a doctor and discovered that even though she was only in her mid-forties, she was courting a heart attack. Her cholesterol was through the roof; ditto her blood pressure. She started taking medication and immediately began an exercise and diet regime, which has given her remarkable results. She looks better and feels better. The improvements in her life extend beyond the physical. She says that feeling better about herself has made her a better parent and improved the way she relates to her children. This will ultimately help their karma as well as hers.

David has alienated most of the important people in his life with his frugality. After years of listening to complaints from his wife, David has finally acknowledged that there is something wrong with his attitude toward money, and he has entered individual as well as family therapy. It's only been a few months, but David has made some major compromises with his family about how family money should be spent. Again, everyone's karma is changing due to his new behavior.

Janette, who lives in New York City, has always dreamed of being able to drive into the country on weekends. Her big problem was that she didn't know how to drive. Last year, Janette made a major sustained effort and learned how to drive. This year, Janette is renting cars and beginning to take small excursions. She says that driving has changed her life. It's so much fun! It has also changed her karma.

My Tibetan teachers often said that the best way to improve karma was to cherish, preserve, and protect life in all its forms. Doing so cultivates gentleness, nobility, and generosity of heart. Recently one of my students told me that when she was walking in a little garden, she heard a tiny rustling coming from under some leaves. Turning the leaves over, she discovered a moth that had become entangled in a piece of vine. Gently, she helped the moth get free. As it fluttered away, she immediately felt better about the world and herself. It was a positive burst of instant good karma. We improve our karma whenever we restrain our unwholesome or bad habits; we improve our karma every time we are materially, emotionally, or spiritually generous with others; we improve our karma every time we cherish and preserve life. We feel the results immediately by the way we feel about ourselves.

Buddhist practices such as mindfulness help us pay closer attention to the implications and results of our actions; this in turn will loosen the knots, tangles, and chains of repetitive karma. The next time you find yourself caught in one of those repetitive tape loops that come around time and time again like recurrent dreams, catch yourself before you get caught up in the tape. Name what is happening. Is your karmic tape filled with self-doubt, self-recrimination, guilt, anxiety over something you can't control, anger, dependency? Is your tape filled with addictive urges? Whatever is on your tape, say to yourself, *There's that tape again.* And change it.

Don't get tripped up; don't reach for your familiar, fundamentally unsatisfying, habitual coping behavior. Don't just drop like a couch potato into the rut of your comfort zone. Instead walk to the window, relax, breathe a little, and smile if you can. Breathe in, calming and relaxing the mind. Breathe out, letting go and smiling. Count ten easy breaths.

Inhale, exhale . . . one
Inhale, exhale . . . two

Now get up and go about your day. Hopefully you've changed that inner tape, and with it, your karma.

The Buddha pronounced this round of Causes and Effects, this universal chain where never was a beginning, to be the Law.

From *The Path of Purification*, by
BUDDHAGOSHA, second-century master

The Search for Reality and Truth

◆

Things are not what they seem to be, nor are they otherwise.

LANKAVATARA SUTRA

What is meant by 'reality'? It would seem to be something very erratic, very undependable – now to be found in a dusty road, now in a scrap of newspaper in the street, now in a daffodil in the sun. It lights up a group in a room and stamps some casual saying. It overwhelms one walking home beneath the stars and makes the silent world more real than the world of speech – and then there it is again in an omnibus in the uproar of Picadilly. Sometimes, too, it seems to dwell in shapes too far away for us to discern what their nature is. But whatever it touches, it fixes and makes permanent. That is what remains over when the skin of the day has been cast into the hedge; that is what is left of past time and of our loves and hates.

VIRGINIA WOOLF, *A Room of One's Own*

Reality is that which, when you stop believing in it, doesn't go away.

PHILIP K. DICK

Reality leaves a lot to the imagination.

JOHN LENNON

Since things neither exist nor don't exist,
are neither real nor unreal,
are utterly beyond adopting and rejecting – one might as well burst out laughing.

LONGCHENPA, fourteenth-century Tibetan master

Living in Truth/Embodying Dharma

◆

The wise are never arbitrary when leading others into harmony with the truth. Wise, they are guarded by truth, for they act in accord with the Dharma.

THE BUDDHA

Truth is sometimes defined as the agreement or congruence of the mind with reality. For centuries, theologians, as well as philosophers, have tried to define exactly what truth is. The idea of truth is so important to philosophy that early philosophers almost inevitably capitalize the 'T.' It thus becomes Truth, with a capital 'T.'

Back in the fifth century, the Christian church father St Augustine wondered how he could tell whether or not the scriptures were true. How could he know, for example, whether or not Moses was telling the truth? He wrote, 'And if I did know it, would it be from him that I knew it? No . . . but within me, in the inner retreat of my mind, the Truth, which is neither Hebrew nor Greek, nor Latin nor Barbarian, would tell me, without lips or tongue or sounded syllables: "He speaks the truth."'

Most of us believe truth exists, otherwise we would stop our questioning; we continue our probing of the world we live in because we believe that if we search deeply enough, we will find the answers we seek. The remarkable thing about the search for truth is that it is an ongoing quest. It is part of the process of life itself. The poet Rainer Maria Rilke once wrote, 'Live in the question, rather than settling for an easy answer.' That's a good answer; even so, we sometimes become so frustrated with our quest that we feel like Gertrude Stein, who once wrote:

> There ain't no answer,
> There ain't going to be any answer
> There never has been an answer.
> That's the answer.

Around the world, the terms 'spiritual seekers' and 'seekers of Truth' have always been used interchangeably. The great Indian spiritual leader, Mahatma Gandhi, titled his autobiography *The Story of My Experiments with Truth.* His spiritual practice as he defined it was truth seeking. As a concept, Truth resonates with all seekers everywhere. Here in the West we often hear the phrase, 'God is love, God is Truth.' So even if we don't relate to the notion of God as supreme being, we relate to the idea of universal truth.

In the East, when we talk about universal truth, we most often use the word 'Dharma.' Dharma is a comprehensive term with multiple meanings. In the largest sense, Dharma refers to any teaching that reflects essential and universal truths. The Dharma is anything that is in profound accord with reality, whether that anything be spiritual, religious, philosophical, moral, or even scientific. Thus when we talk about Buddhist teachings, we call it Dharma.

Buddhism points out that although it may be hard to define truth, we can define reality. Reality is simply 'things just as they are,' undistorted by our own projections and illusions. Reality is *what is*. Buddhists sometimes call this 'suchness,' as in 'such as it is,' or plain 'isness.' And it is a Buddhist ideal. When we are able to live and act in profound accord with reality, we are embodying truth; we are embodying wisdom; we are embodying Dharma.

In some ways, of course, reality also has its relative or conditional aspect. Thus reality has form and function as well as essence. The essence reflects 'isness' or 'things just as they are,' while form relates to 'how things work.' We might, for example, refer to an object as a real table or a real book, knowing that it could just as easily be called real wood or real paper. To the human being, a glass of water is just a drink, but to a fish, water is home and the universe itself. We recognize the 'isness' of water; we also recognize the various roles it plays and 'how it works.'

Knowing this, we realize that a search for truth and reality has to go beyond any superficial assumptions and concepts about ourselves, others, or the world we live in. As we seek truth, we realize that we need to learn not to be deceived either by mere appearances or by our own projections.

At this point, the seeker of truth might be tempted to say, 'Get real, Surya, cut to the chase.' The seeker's question might be: 'In practical terms, how does this apply to the spiritual path?' The answer is that the spiritual seeker is concerned with truth in two primary and very practical ways.

- ***Cultivating Clear Vision*** – being able to see reality – the truth of what is and how things work

- ***Cultivating Personal Authenticity*** – being able to 'be real' and live truly

CULTIVATING CLEAR VISION

The Buddha once said:

> *Regard this fleeting world like this:*
> *Like stars fading and vanishing at dawn,*
> *like bubbles on a fast-moving stream,*
> *like morning dewdrops evaporating on blades of grass,*
> *like a candle flickering in a strong wind,*
> *echoes, mirages, and phantoms, hallucinations,*
> *and like a dream.*

Has there ever been a time in the history of mankind when we have been more in need of clear seeing? On an outer level, whenever we turn on our television sets, we are bombarded by people telling us what to buy, what to wear, what to eat, and what to think – in short, what to value. In the United States, there are politicians, religious leaders, pundits, advertisers, talk show hosts, as well as hundreds of lobbyists for special interest groups. All of these people with vested interests seem to want us to view the world the same way they do. They all claim that they speak the 'truth.' Everywhere we turn, someone is 'putting a spin' on reality. There is even a new profession; people who practice it are called spin doctors.

On an inner level, we also 'put a spin' on our own lives. Fantasy is very appealing, and we use it to tell ourselves stories about what we're doing; we tell ourselves what we want to hear. Sometimes we tell ourselves that we are successful and happy; sometimes we tell ourselves that we are miserable failures. Sometimes we tell ourselves that we have all the answers; sometimes we convince ourselves that we have no answers. We tell ourselves stories about our personal history and our present as well as our future. The fact is that we are all subject to some degree of denial and self-deception.

Sometimes what we humans tell ourselves corresponds to what we are hearing from others. Many smokers, for example, chose to believe the tobacco lobby when it said that smoking wasn't all that harmful to one's health; many consumers think life isn't worth living if they can't afford the newest styles; many voters accept at face value politicians' explanations as to why it isn't economically feasible to follow ecologically sound policies.

One of the great principles on which Buddha Dharma rests is that of 'wisdom,' which we define as 'clear seeing' or 'clear vision.' All of the Buddha's teachings concern themselves with helping seekers develop clear vision. Buddhists talk a great deal about what it means to open the third eye, the wisdom eye of clear seeing and penetrating awareness. In fact, one of the Dalai Lama's first books was called *Opening of the Wisdom-Eye*.

Here's why: When we are able to see 'what is,' we are able to approach the world fully conscious and awake.

We are then able to see through and beyond all the false messages and false messengers; we are able to recognize and see past what attracts us or repels us; we are able to get beyond our own prejudices, projections, and biases. We see why we accept one person's point of view and reject another's. In this way, our distortions and delusions begin to lose their hold over us, and we become better able to recognize what's important and meaningful. On an individual level, this can have tremendous implications. Wisdom – clear vision – means that as we become wise, we are less controlled by circumstances, people, or unfulfilling and questionable habits.

Buddhists believe that when we are finally able to open the wisdom eye, or the eye of Dharma, we will be able to shed our dualistic view of the world. Wisdom gives us the vision to see the bigger picture, and in this way to go beyond our ordinary isolationist egocentric point of view; instead we will connect to others from our real common ground. There is an ancient saying that the 'Truth remains for those whose eyes remain unclouded by longing.' What this means, of course, is that we can begin to find truth only after we have started to loosen and remove our own biases and attachments.

CULTIVATING PERSONAL AUTHENTICITY

If I had my life to live over, I would start barefoot earlier in the spring and stay that way later in the fall. I would go to more dances. I would ride more merry-go-rounds. I would pick more daisies.

Octogenarian NADINE STAIR

We could all afford to be a little more genuine, a little more authentic, couldn't we? Why is it that we need to grow old and wise before we realize that the inner child is still there, alive and well, ready to play? Why is it that we need to grow old before we understand how much joy there is to be found in doing the simple things that reflect and embrace our essential joy and goodness?

Shakespeare said, 'To thine own self be true.' The ancient inscription on the Oracle of Apollo at Delphi, Greece, read, 'Know thyself.' Gandhi wrote, 'Turn the spotlight inward.' But how many of us know or even remember ourselves? We spend so much of our time living in a world of 'shoulds,' trying to fulfill the expectations that are placed on us – by ourselves as well as others – that we fail to be authentic. We fail to be true to ourselves.

Some of us carry so much shame that we pretend even to ourselves that some of our memories don't exist. We put these memories in secret rooms and throw away the keys. There are things we don't want to see or know. Some of us feel as though we spend too much time playing roles, hiding ourselves behind the masks we put on in order to face the world. We wear special clothing to create an image; we create personalities to match the images we want to create. With all the roles we play, we sometimes realize that we're not who we think we are. But then who are we really? The 'Who am I?' question is an important one. In life we ask this question again and again in so many ways, looking for the right answer, seeking our true identity. Perhaps the answer is that there is no answer.

What would happen to us if we were to start peeling off the various layers of persona? If we peeled off the clothing, the facial expressions, the goals, plans, ambitions, the socialized behavior, the roles we play, and the feelings that have become frozen in place . . . what would remain? If we were able to keep peeling and peeling, at the deepest level, what would we be left with? Christians might say that we are left with our eternal soul, the reflection of the kingdom of God. Buddhism says that if we go deep enough, what we are left with is our unborn, undying, original, unprocessed natural state, our genuine being. That is Buddha-nature, our true nature – our own share of heaven within, or nirvana. The whole purpose of meditation practice is to help us connect to reality and the truth. Meditation is so simple, so direct, so honest, natural, and straightforward. Naturalness is Buddha-ness.

We all admire people who are able to combine holiness with a natural down-to-earth quality, people who are genuinely in touch with others as well as with their own true nature. In Tibet when we want to refer to somebody as a holy person, a wise and compassionate practitioner, the term we use is 'cheuba,' which is literally translated as a 'Dharma-doer,' a spiritual practitioner, or an embodiment or practitioner of truth.

We admire practitioners of truth, but how can we ourselves live that way? Tibetans pray regularly, 'Bless us that our heart-minds may become one with the Dharma. May our lives mingle with the truth.' Here in the West, we might pray that our hearts and minds become one with the truth and that we walk in the light of truth.

Once in days of old, there was a monk who was practicing a walking meditation as he circumambulated the ancient Petring Monastery. His distinguished teacher

Geshe Tempa, who was also out for a walk, saw the monk and said, 'It's good to circle holy places, but it is much better to practice the sublime Dharma.'

Chastened, the monk began to study, memorize, and recite dozens of ancient Buddhist sutras. One day as he sat poring over the holy Sanskrit and Tibetan texts, his teacher came upon him again. 'It's worthwhile to study scriptures and accomplish virtuous acts like memorizing and copying scriptures,' Geshe Tempa told the monk, 'but it is far better to practice the noble Dharma.'

The monk was now very confused, but he gave his teacher's admonitions the serious thought they deserved. What he finally decided was that he needed to begin an intense meditation practice, and he began to meditate in earnest, hour after hour, day after day. The next time Geshe Tempa found the monk, he was sitting in a corner with a concentrated stare. 'Meditation is a very good practice,' Geshe Tempa said, 'but genuine Dharma practice would be even better.'

By now the monk, as you can imagine, didn't know what to do next. There was nothing he hadn't tried, and yet his beloved teacher still hadn't approved of his efforts. 'Most venerable sir,' the monk pleaded, 'I want to practice Dharma, but what is it that I should do?'

'Simply stop clinging,' Geshe Tempa replied before quietly continuing on his way.

Often the deepest truths are the most simple and direct. We practice Dharma when we stop clinging to our preconceived notions about what we should do and achieve. We find truth when we learn to 'let go,' accept, see things as they are, and just be. We find truth by discovering our inner light, our inner value and values, our authenticity and genuineness. This is living truly.

* * *

Tibetan Buddhism includes a remarkable practice of self-inquiry and analysis that addresses the timeless 'Who am I?' question. It is designed to help seekers gain understanding and insight and get at the truth of what we are, as opposed to what we appear to be and what we would like to be – what we tell ourselves we are. The practice is called 'rushen,' which is literally translated as 'discerning the difference between.' The practice of rushen takes the question of 'Who am I . . . What am I?' to a new and deeper level.

I think rushen is absolutely one of the very best and most effective ways for Westerners to meditate since it so skillfully uses the analytical mental faculty to help us go beyond the self. This trenchant analysis helps us delve deeply and plumb beneath and beyond intellectual processes; it helps us break free from illusions and misconceptions about ourselves.

RUSHEN 'WHO AM I' ANALYTICAL MEDITATION

The purpose of rushen is to help you peel away the layers and layers of persona and conditioned behavior covering up your inner light, your luminescent Buddha-nature. Rushen will actually help you discern, or differentiate, the real from the unreal – your real nature from your persona.

Begin this meditation by asking yourself, 'Who or what am I?'

Then begin to examine one by one all the labels that you or someone else might apply. Take the time to consider and answer each question. Don't limit yourself to these questions; create others that reflect your life.

Who am I?
Am I really just me? Really, and only, me?
What is my name?
Am I a man? Am I woman?
Am I anything else?
Am I a father, mother, sister, brother, child, aunt, uncle, niece, cousin?
Am I a teacher, carpenter, plumber, lawyer, social worker, student? (Name your own occupation.)
Am I a member of a community, a committee member, churchgoer, meditator, sangha member?
Am I a voter? Am I a Democrat, Republican, Conservative, Liberal, Independent?
Am I someone's friend? Am I someone's enemy?
Am I the image I project to the world? Am I a casual dresser, a spiffy dresser? Am I neat? Am I sloppy?
Am I someone who drives a big car, small car, truck?
Am I anything else?
What are the labels I use to describe myself?
Who am I, really?

Now take this exercise deeper.
Who or what is asking these questions?
What am I experiencing at the present moment? Am I bored, tired, curious, confused, happy?
Why am I feeling what I feel right now?
What do I feel?
What sounds do I hear right now in the present moment?
What sights do I see?

Take whatever presents itself in your field of awareness – whether it be a sight, a sound, or a physical sensation, and take it apart, a little at a time. *What is that sound?* for example. *Is it outside of myself? Is it in my ear? Is it in my mind?* Or is it an interaction between all three – the perceiver, the object, and the interaction among them?

Where is my experience occurring? Is it in the head, the gut, the heart, the mind, the body?

We know that having ears alone isn't enough to hear. You also need auditory consciousness. After all, a corpse can't hear even though it has ears. As we pull back the well-placed defensive ego layers, some thick and some thin, we eventually arrive at the point where we realize that consciousness is the most fundamental, lowest primary denominator.

Ask yourself if you can experience something before it arises, before you conceptualize and label it. Can you, for example, hear a sound before you name it? Can you reach deeply enough into who you are so that you have the barest, most direct perception of sound without labels or thoughts? Just pure sound, unmediated by thoughts, concepts, or judgments.

What we are doing is trying to look into the nature of perception and knowing. Who is doing the labeling? Who is thinking 'I like it,' or 'I don't like it'? How do we know, feel, and think? Notice through direct self-observation how impulses, volitional activity, will, and the like arise and drive us around.

Ask yourself, *What do I think of myself? What are the labels I apply to me, here and now in the present moment? Do I see myself as competent, incompetent, unworthy, or so deserving that I'm positively entitled? Do I see myself as a victim?* Ask yourself, *Is this all I am? Is there nothing more to me than meets the eye?*

Are any of these labels remainders from past experiences? Ask yourself why you are holding on to these labels or images. What are the effects of holding on to old tapes – audio and video recordings from the past?

Who or what am I? In a nutshell, who or what is experiencing my experience right now? Sense it directly.

Discernment is a key facet of wisdom and spiritual intelligence. As we practice rushen, we try to find and get down to authentic presence – our own truth, our own reality. This is a profound Tibetan Dharma practice of the Dzogchen tradition, part of the masters' introduction to the nature of mind. This intensive self-inquiry asks us to employ our discriminating awareness through a process of elimination – not this, not just that – to recognize all the things we are not. By so doing we get closer to our inner light and what we truly are.

Many people who do this meditation say: 'But I didn't find anything.' In fact, this is the usual response. This is the bad news, but it's also the good news! If we can strip away enough, we arrive at a new beginning. Sometimes this sense that nothing is there lasts only a moment, but even that can be enough to get a renewed sense of freedom, openness, and truth. This is how we can begin the transformation process from the old notions of self that we drag around with us like so much extra baggage. This is one of the best Dharma practices for delving deeply into the conundrum of self and not self. In this way, we can experience our transpersonal nature – our *Authentic Being*. That's greater than any of those bits and pieces that we usually identify with as being the self.

There's a lot of freedom and delight in that, I assure you. This is a way to be a born-again Buddha – or Authentic You-dah.

Look deeply within yourself. I think you might like what you find.

The mind is by nature luminous, pure, and perfect.

THE BUDDHA

Enlightenment by Many Names

◆

To start from the self and try to understand all things is delusion. To let the self be awakened by all things is enlightenment. To be enlightened about delusion is to be a Buddha. To be deluded in the midst of enlightenment is to be an ordinary person.

JAPANESE ZEN MASTER DOGEN

Master Dogen lived in the thirteenth century. When he was only three years old, his father died; then, a few years later he lost his mother as well. Eihei Dogen was only eight years old, and he loved his mother dearly. Despite his age and his deep sense of loss, the young child wanted to make sense of his mother's death. Dogen stood with other mourners in the temple, staring at the smoke coming from the sticks of burning incense. As he watched the smoke rise and curl upward, an ash fell from the top of the incense. Dogen later wrote that, at that instant, his body and mind dropped away. He perceived naked reality and realized the transitory nature of life. This was his first enlightenment experience. It would stay with him throughout his life.

Students sometimes ask me what the difference is between a mystical experience and an enlightenment experience. And there is a distinction. Although mystical experiences bring with them an awareness of the sacred – a confirmation that there is something beyond self and the world we see – they don't necessarily bring wisdom, insight, or transformation. In short, mystical experiences are not necessarily enlightening. Mystical and religious experiences do not necessarily bring about a religious or spiritual life.

Enlightenment experiences, on the other hand, are awakening experiences. They bring an awareness of reality, just as it is. These experiences are inevitably accompanied by wisdom and indelible insights. This is what it means to wake up from the dreamlike trance of illusion and delusion. Of course, enlightenment experiences don't have to last for more than a few moments. And they often provide only mini-awakenings lasting just long enough for the seeker to say 'Aha' or 'Why didn't I see that before?' In fact enlightenment experiences often bring the sense of 'It was always there, why didn't I see it?'

One of the most difficult things for seekers to grasp is that enlightenment is not necessarily an otherworldly event. Enlightenment is about reality – things just as they are. By opening the wisdom-eye, we see what's there; we don't get to choose what's there. Years ago, a Zen master wrote: 'Before I came to Zen, mountains were only mountains, rivers were only rivers, trees only trees. After I got into Zen, mountains were no longer mountains, rivers no longer rivers, trees no longer trees. But when enlightenment happened, mountains were again only mountains, rivers again only rivers, trees again only trees.'

Buddhists draw a distinction between total perfect

enlightenment as experienced by the Buddha and the many smaller variations of awakening. The Buddha's enlightenment brought with it a complete understanding of reality: The Buddha's wisdom-eye was fully opened; he achieved perfect understanding of the laws of karma and rebirth; he understood ignorance, attachment, and desire. Remember that the Buddha is said to have remembered five hundred of his own past lives and understood in great detail his own path to awakening. It is also said that he was able to 'see' the past lives of others, and thus be able to help others by shedding light on their karma.

The Buddha's perfect enlightenment is sometimes described as occurring in one sudden earthshaking event. However, the path leading up to it was filled, as all spiritual paths are, with stumbling blocks to be overcome as well as smaller awakenings that prepared the ground. Struggling to remember his past lives was no mere parlor game for the Buddha. He wanted to fully understand the karmic cause-and-effect reasons behind his current life and path to enlightenment. In his lifetime Buddha gave up a great deal in order to spend years in meditation and self-examination, and he told his followers of still other lifetimes in which he had devoted himself to helping others. He had traversed every inch of the spiritual path, but in so doing, he had proved an important point. Like the first time a jet plane broke the sound barrier, the Buddha's awakening demonstrated that it could be done. When the Buddha became enlightened, the message he gave to all of us was that we could do it too. Anyone can become as awake, enlightened, wise, unselfish, serene, and compassionate as the Buddha. Enlightenment is our spiritual birthright.

Enlightenment spells out an end to delusion and ignorance. But going from ignorance to awakened awareness and understanding takes time. Classical Buddhist teachings, which lay out the progressive stages of insight, state that there are ten 'fetters' that bind us to the unawakened state. They are:

1. Self-illusion
2. Doubt and skepticism
3. Attachment to mere rule and ritual
4. Lust
5. Ill will
6. Craving for a rich material existence
7. Craving for supernormal experiences
8. Pride
9. Restlessness
10. Ignorance

Seekers who have had their first glimpse of reality are known as 'stream-enterers'; they are getting their feet wet in the stream of reality. They are touching nirvana, however briefly. It is taught that stream-enterers are able to get beyond the first three fetters – self-illusion, skepticism, and attachment to mere rule and ritual. After this first view of reality or 'what is,' the seeker, of course, has much more inner work to do before he/she can be considered fully enlightened or awakened.

Walking the path to enlightenment helps us learn to

uproot and discard all ten of these fetters. In very rare instances the fetters may be dropped all at once through a shattering transformative breakthrough, but for the most part they are shed one by one, a little at a time. Seekers should understand that it is unrealistic to expect that any of them will drop away without some degree of effort and struggle. We may, for example, be able to uproot ill will, but we still find traces of pride. Uprooting all traces of any one of the fetters can be likened to emptying a perfume bottle: Long after the liquid is gone, a slight scent remains. Eventually, if we do our spiritual work and maintain our spiritual practices, the power these fetters hold over us is weakened until they can finally be uprooted. When this happens the veils of illusion and delusion that surround us all fall away, and we can reach reality, truth. This is enlightenment.

The Buddha used to respectfully address others individually, as 'child of a noble family.' He did this even with people of the same age or older. He recognized that his students and disciples hadn't matured yet spiritually; they were still like children. He sometimes referred to his teachings as toys that could be used to lure children out of the burning houses of suffering, ignorance, and confusion they inhabited.

According to enlightened vision, we all resemble unconscious children in a benighted world – sleepwalkers who continue to create and perpetuate our problems. It's foolish for any one of us to believe that our difficulties can be solved simply by rearranging the personnel and furniture of our daytime dreams. The wisest and most direct way to resolve our difficulties is to awaken from our dreamlike states. And we can all do just that. The basic underlying premise in Buddhism is the promise that we can all awaken from unhappy dreams of illusion and delusion. I think it's a good idea to remind ourselves regularly that the name Buddha simply means 'awakened one.' American philosopher and psychologist William James once said that we are all only about half as awake as we could be.

Although we are acutely concerned about a better world, one of the greatest services we can each perform for mankind is to wake up and help dispel the ignorance and deluded behavior in our own lives. This would be a real service, a contribution to one and all. In altruistic Mahayana Buddhism we strive for enlightenment, not just for ourselves but for all beings. A Mahayana prayer that I often use is:

May all beings everywhere
with whom we are inseparably interconnected,
be fulfilled, awakened, liberated, and free.
May there be peace in this world
and throughout the entire universe,
and may we all together complete the spiritual journey.

In order to help us fulfill this spiritual journey of awakening, all of the schools of Buddhism have developed a series of practices – skillful means, devices, and even little tricks. All of these are designed to help us become conscious and awake. Buddha Dharma is a panacea that comes in different flavors and styles.

Zen Buddhism, for example, has a technique that has been used for centuries to help a seeker have a breakthrough, eureka-like experience – an 'aha' awareness of reality. This technique is known as koan practice. A koan, which is often described as a mind-breaker or conundrum, is typically used in the following way.

The student commits him- or herself to attending an intense meditation retreat with a Zen master. These retreats, known as 'sesshins,' typically last at least five to seven days and often go on for three months or longer. The participants spend long hours meditating and chanting and then doing some physical work such as dishwashing or sweeping to round it out. Spiritual practice is broken only by short periods in which to rest, eat, or sleep. Each day, the individual student has as many as three or four private interviews with the master, during which time the student is given a koan. Over the days of the sesshin the master continues to confront the student with this koan or mind bender again and again, demanding an answer. The koan is really a crazy-making question, an existential riddle that the master uses to drive the student to a deeper, more profound understanding of reality, and in this way to provoke an enlightenment or 'satori' experience.

Some classic koans or riddles are: 'Does a dog have Buddha-nature or not?' 'What is the sound of one hand clapping?' 'What did your face look like before your parents were born?' It is up to the student to provide the answer. Once in ancient times, when a Zen master who was holding a wooden bowl was asked the following koan, 'What is the holy Buddha?' he replied, 'This wooden bowl.' But, I ask you, how is holy Buddha a bowl?! Another master, when asked the same question, answered, 'Toilet paper.'

Each student at a sesshin is given a specific riddle which he/she is supposed to ponder and work on for the rest of the sesshin. Most of us remember those huge balls of chewing gum or hard candy that we used to call jawbreakers. Well, that's why koans are often known as mind-breakers. We just chew them over time and time again until our mental teeth and jaws, and eventually even our heads, wear down. *Yesss!*

My Korean Zen master had a favorite koan. It was 'What is it?' No matter what was happening, we were supposed to focus on that koan. Let's assume, for example, that a student is sitting down and she becomes aware of a plane overhead. She repeats the koan, 'What is it?' Now what is it? Is it the sound the airplane engine makes? Is it a flash of shining metal in the sky? Is it the memory of a photograph of an aircraft she saw in a recent newspaper? Is it nothing more than a mental mirror that shows the student her projections? Is it three hundred-plus people cramped together watching a bad movie while chewing honey-roasted peanuts? What is it? What the hell is it? What is real? Is anything real?

The student who attends a Zen sesshin can expect to be goaded by the master, who typically tries to apply spiritual shock tactics (hopefully lovingly administered) to break through the student's personal shell of ignorance. Sometimes a student hears the same koan so many times that he doesn't know what to say. Sometimes a student goes in to see the master for a private interview, and the master, sensing that the student has no answer, rings the bell to end the interview before it even begins. The master is simply trying to startle the student into a new awareness. My friend, the Zen master Robert Aitkin Roshi, says that through koan practice, he can drive almost anyone, even novice meditators, to have a satori experience. I have personally seen Zen masters who have consistently been able to help drive their students to euphoric epiphanies or enlightenment experiences.

There are many stories in Zen about people who had sudden and unexpected satori experiences. One nun, long ago, was carrying a bucket of water across a field on a moonlit night. Suddenly the bottom of the bucket fell out, and she had an enlightenment experience. What did she see to provoke her experience? The water in the bucket had been reflecting the moon. As the water dropped away so did the reflection. She could see nothing. When the bottom fell out, perhaps she saw her ego drop as well. There was no inside or out, no dualism, no moon, no sun, no nothing – which is really something!

There is a story about another Zen monk who was sweeping some tiles on an outdoor path. One was loose and as the broom hit it, it flew away and hit a bamboo stalk, making a sharp 'clack.' The sharply reverberating sound of bamboo and tile striking together precipitated his satori awakening. Why should a mysterious 'clack' precipitate an awakening? Of course, both the nun and the monk were spiritually ripened and mature from the years they had already spent in spiritual practice. And they would spend many more years deepening and stabilizing their awakening experiences.

Not everybody can expect to have sudden sharp glimpses of reality. In Buddhism there is an age-old debate about the value of sudden versus gradual awakening. For most people, it's probably a bit of both. Just as the fruit falls when it is ripe, so too students become aware only when they are ready. Unless we are ripe for an awakening experience, the moment is going to pass unnoticed.

In Tibetan and other schools of Buddhism, there are

other ways of precipitating awakening experiences. Chanting, meditation, fasting, good works, and ritual music or dance are some examples. When we practice self-inquiry, for example, asking ourselves time and time again, 'Who or what am I?', we do so in order to wake up and break through to direct perception of absolute reality. In Tibetan Buddhism there are secret whispered teachings and shock tactics as well as ancient esoteric empowerments and initiations to help seekers reach spiritual maturity and self-realization. My Dzogchen masters used to startle us by shouting 'Phat!' in the middle of our meditation. If we didn't awaken, at least we had a good laugh.

A unique practice in Tibetan Buddhism is known as 'phowa' or consciousness transference, which is another way of being catapulted into the awakened state. In this practice, the spiritual practitioner learns to intentionally transform his or her ordinary state of mind into enlightened mind. In phowa, we learn to gather our mind and collect our energy, and then project it out through the fontanel, the crown chakra at the top of the head, and then project it into the heart of Amitabha, the Buddha of Infinite Light, in his Western Buddhafield of Infinite Bliss. Phowa practitioners are typically initiated into the practice by a qualified master. This is a practice that many Tibetans rely on at the time of death to be assured of spiritual direction and a better rebirth, raising consciousness into higher states from which awakening can be more easily accessed.

Some practitioners train over their lifetime until they are proficient at casting their finite conceptual minds into the radiant incandescent expanse of naked awareness. They do this so that they are also prepared at the moment of death, even without the help of their lama or teacher. Of course, the ultimate phowa experience is the great realization that the heart of Buddha-mind is here and now within our own mind.

There is one Tibetan lama who is renowned the world over as the phowa lama. His name is Ayang Rinpoche, and he is said to be particularly skillful at helping students catapult themselves into an enlightened state of mind. This new awareness may last only a few seconds or more, but for many this glimpse of awakening is enough to transform them for life. There is a word that Ayang Rinpoche and phowa practitioners traditionally shout at the moment when we try to make the great leap through the crown chakra. The word is 'hic.' Say the word 'hiccup,' and notice how the body reacts when we accidentally hiccup. The shoulders and energy go upward. I like to think of the 'hic' as helping us make the hike up to the peak of awakening. 'Hic,' really more of an exclamation than a word, is used like a hook to grab hold of energy and consciousness, like an exclamation, like shouting 'hey.' It doesn't have a meaning, but it arrests your attention.

Here is a Phowa Meditation you might want to try on your own.

Invoke, and visualize in the form of a luminous light, the highest, most sacred being you can imagine. It might be Buddha, Jesus, Tara, the Virgin Mary, or a favorite saint. If you feel no attachment to any such image, visualize a sphere of sacred light, filled with light and blessings, streaming out to you. Place this visualization directly in front of you and slightly above your head.

Now visualize your own heart-mind and all your

energies as a sphere of light. Gather up all your energies from the energy centers in your body until you can see and feel the ball of light.

Take three or four deep breaths in and out; then hold your breath and visualize this ball of energy being pulled up through the body and out the head through the crown chakra. As it is bursting out of the crown chakra, shout forcefully, '*Hic.*' Imagine the light that is your spirit merging with the sacred light. Think, *My mind and divine mind, Buddha-mind, are one.*

I often do this practice at night as I am about to go to sleep. I imagine myself laying my head in the lap of the loving luminescent Buddha, but you might prefer Tara or Jesus. This is a great way to rest our weary hearts and souls and prepare for resting our heads in the lap of the divine at the moment of death.

There are many other practices that help bring us closer to awakening. Greater self-awareness in any form can help bring about breakthroughs and deepen inner wisdom. Some say that meditation alone, watching the breath, can bring about enlightenment. Simple mindfulness practices help us strip life down to its very barest essentials. We do nothing but breathe, in and out, again and again. As we do this and watch what comes up in our heads, and our bodies too, we become able to see how much we add on. We see the excess baggage, the projections, stories, and fantasies, we see how we ourselves define and thus create so much of our own experience. When we practice mindfulness of breathing, we notice the extraneous complications we add on to basic *being*; we see what we do to create the snarls and twists in our lives. This awareness helps us learn to return to a simpler, less exhausting way of being and knowing.

Many people, for example, aren't aware of the obsessive nature of their thoughts until they try to meditate and discover that they can't slow down or let go of thinking. Too often they are thinking about the same thing over and over again. Meditators frequently discover that understanding their thought processes, biases, projections, and interpretations in itself can be a breakthrough experience.

Try the following exercises in awareness.

- Practice eye gazing by looking into your own eyes in a mirror and noticing whatever comes up in the mirror of your own internal awareness. Can you look at your own sense of identity? Can you see what you are thinking – watch your own inner dialogue? The eyes are said to be mirrors of the soul. Just observe what comes up, minding the mind. Up the ante by holding another small mirror behind your ear and look into your many reflected eyes. Go into the myriad reflections, you and you re-reflected and re-reflected; lose yourself in the experience. Then look into who you really are.

- Try the same practice with a trusted loved one by looking into each other's eyes. Agree before you start that neither of you will react or communicate in any way – no words, actions, or facial expressions. Just bare attention – eye gazing – just looking, not reacting or interacting. See how the addition of another ego brings up your own ego and your own need to alter, control, or change the moment. As we look into another's eyes, most of us feel as though we should do something. So even though you feel as though a grin might be nice, stick to your agreement not to communicate. You can talk about it later. This is a self-awareness practice. Give yourself and your partner too the gift of a nonjudgmental, noninterfering, nonreactive moment of heart-to-heart, soul-to-soul transpersonal communication.

- Imagine yourself as a sphere of light with no role or gender, just a luminous cloud or transparent sphere. See what can be observed from this vantage point. Try experiencing your own mind as completely transparent, like a pure crystal that undistortedly reflects whatever is placed next to it. One of my teachers, the great Tibetan master, Dilgo Khyentse, used to hold up a crystal during Tantric initiation and shake it, exclaiming loudly, 'What is mind?' In this way he would try to shock students into new awareness. 'The nature of mind,' he used to teach us, 'is clear lucency.' He used this shock technique to remind us that the nature of mind is clear, lucid, infinite, and radiant.

The thing to remember about enlightenment is it doesn't happen overnight. It's a steady process of spiritual maturation that we go through. I like to think of it as being somewhat like the pickling process. Just putting a green cucumber in vinegar for one moment or one day doesn't make a pickle. It has to stay in there for a good while. If you pickle a cucumber for six months or a year, then it gets totally pickled. If you just dunk it in and out, it's still a cucumber. But if the cucumber sits around long enough with the vinegar and the spices, it gets totally pickled. It can never go back to being just a cucumber.

This is true even if you've had an enlightenment experience of some kind. As wonderful as an enlightenment experience can be, it still usually means that although you've had a glimpse of a better and saner reality, you're still a humble cucumber – so don't be too proud! Satori is not the end of the path, but the beginning. As I always say, it seems easier today to get enlightened than it does to stay enlightened.

Enlightenment is not what we think it is, and transformation is rarely a once-and-for-all experience. So it's not the actual enlightenment experience alone that counts, but the living of it, embodying it, stabilizing it, and working out its implications in everyday life. That's what matters. If enlightenment doesn't show up in daily life, what good is it? True spiritual realization manifests as enlightened activity – as Buddha activity. Not just epiphanies. Enlightenment is as enlightenment does. It's where and how you live, not just what you believe in. It's who you are and can be, not just who you imagine you are. In the meantime, stay awake to what you are experiencing right now. It's the best show in town.

When he was fifty years old, and a few years from his death, the enlightened master Dogen wrote a poem that I think says a great deal about what it means to view the world from an enlightened perspective.

> *Fresh, clear spirit covers old mountain man this autumn.*
> *Donkey stares at the ceiling sky; glowing white moon floats.*
> *Nothing approaches. Nothing else included.*

Buoyant, I let myself go – filled with gruel, filled with rice.
Lively flapping from head to tail,
Sky above, sky beneath, cloud self, water origin.

◆

Since I received enlightenment in the infinite wonders of truth I have always been cheerful and laughing.

HUNG CH'ENG-CH'OU

Opening the Heart: Learning to Love

◆

This is my commandment, that you love one another.
JESUS, quoted in John 15:12

I once heard a story about a group of recently departed men and women who found themselves standing in line before the proverbial pearly gates. Anticipating divine judgment about their lives, they all began to question themselves about their earthly behavior. 'Was I a good parent?' 'Did I accomplish something of value in my life?' 'Did I attend religious services on the Sabbath?' 'Did I donate enough to the needy?' And when they finally reached the gate, all these souls were asked only one question, 'How well did you love?'

It is possible that there is only one question that seekers need ask themselves about their spiritual progress and that is, 'How well do I love?'

Since the beginning of time, men and women with great, noble, and tender hearts have urged humanity to love one another. The Dalai Lama has told his followers, 'If you want others to be happy, practice compassion. If you want to be happy, practice compassion.' Mother Teresa once said, 'It is not how much we do, but how much love we put into the doing. It is not how much we give, but how much love we put into the giving.'

Learning how to love is the goal and the purpose of spiritual life – not learning how to develop psychic powers, not learning how to bow, chant, do yoga, or even meditate, but learning to love. Love is the truth. Love is the light.

What do you think of when you think about love? Do you think about the people you love – your children, your romantic partner, your parents, your friends? Do you think about your pets – your dog, your cat, your oh-so-smart and talkative gray parrot? Do you think of the things you love – enjoying nature, fishing, sitting in your garden, swimming in a lake on a brilliant summer day? Do you think about Prince or Princess Charming, and the love you hope someday to feel? Do you think about love of God, love of your community, love of music, sports, or reading? How about love of justice or freedom? Do you extend your love to yourself; do you consider your own level and degree of self-love, self-esteem, and self-acceptance?

When we talk about the love we have in our lives, often we are describing an appreciation for something that is beautiful, or at least beautiful and moving to us. When we say we love something or somebody, what we often really mean is that we love the way that something or somebody makes us feel. We might say we love a specific person, but if we look into it, what are we really loving? Our thoughts frequently reflect an attitude of 'I love how I feel when I am with you – most of the time.' Or, 'I love my work, but I can't wait for the weekend.' So what does that mean? That we don't love this person or job when he, she, or it fails to produce a good buzz?

As we walk the spiritual path, we're trying to come to a better understanding of what love means; we're learning to open our hearts and cultivate a deeper, less self-centered, more reliable, and all-inclusive brand of love.

My first guru in India was the amazing Hindu saint, Maharaji Neem Karoli Baba. His whole teaching reflected a passionate love of God combined with a loving service to mankind. As a Hindu 'bhakta' (devotee), he devoted his entire spiritual practice to finding union with God; as a teacher, he opened his heart and taught his students that the divine love-light shines in and through everyone. A translator-attendant often walked beside him. Even so Neem Karoli Baba, whom we called Maharaji, which means great king, spoke few words and gave even fewer lectures or speeches. All his teachings seemed to be contained in the radiant love with which he embraced us, his disciples and followers.

After Maharaji died some of us were given pages from the diary that he wrote in every day. I remember hoping to receive such a token of his legacy and anticipated reading these pages, for I somehow imagined that they would contain notes about his life and thought. I hoped and expected that they would perhaps shed some light on or reveal to me something about this mysterious saint, whom for a period of my life I saw almost every day, but who seemed to most of us to be perfectly incomprehensible. When the pages were handed out, we all saw what Maharaji had been writing. On each page, there was a new date, and then the only other word written down again and again, in red ink, was 'Ram, Ram, Ram,' which is another way of saying God. This was Maharaji's mantra, and this love of the divine was his legacy.

I remember one day at Maharaji's ashram, he was sitting on his bed on the porch, and about twenty of us were sitting in front of him. He surprised all of us by asking through his translator, 'How did Christ meditate?' We were all dumbstruck. We had never thought about Christ and meditation. Then Maharaji answered his own question, by exclaiming, 'He was lost in love, lost in love, lost in love . . . lost in love.' And then he was silent.

Plato explained love by saying, 'Love is a kind of madness, a divine madness.' How can one define or explain a holy madman? Who can understand the God-intoxication of St Francis, Rumi, or other such 'fools for God'? The great Tibetan yogi Milarepa once sang, 'Craziness is the characteristic of my lineage: crazed with devotion, crazed by truth, crazy for Dharma.' Neem Karoli Baba's life exemplified that kind of loving madness. His passionate love of the sacred glowed through him and cascaded over whoever was near. When you were with him, you felt as though there was simply nowhere else to be. His main teaching to us was to love, serve, and remember God by loving, serving, and remembering humanity – serving God through serving man.

When I met him, Neem Karoli Baba was already well into his eighties, or perhaps even nineties; no one could help noticing that he treated everyone equally – people he had known for fifty years as well as people who had just walked up the road that morning. He was a great inspiration. In his ashram, various holy men would often read and tell us stories from the Ramayana, the ancient Sanskrit epic. The Ramayana, which Hindus consider sacred, tells the story of Ram, an incarnation of the God Vishnu, and his divine mate Sita. In India, God is imaged in both male and female forms. Ram and Sita thus represent and personify Mr and Mrs God.

The Ramayana is an allegorical, mystical work chock full of both good and evil spirits. Throughout its pages, Ram and Sita face many trials; in these they are aided by the sacred monkey king Hanuman, whose unique capacity for passionate love and service is reflected in the devotion he feels for Ram and Sita.

The stories of Hanuman are among my all-time favorites. At first, like most Westerners, I didn't understand the concept of a monkey god. What was this, I wondered. *A monkey?!!* Then as it was further explained and clarified, the secret began to reveal itself in all its profundity and relevance to my own life.

I always remember the complete devotion that the monkey, Hanuman, feels for Ram and Sita. He loves them with all his heart and wants desperately to be with them all the time, night and day. Finally Sita comes and tells him, 'Hanuman, when the Lord and I are alone at night you can't be with us.'

'Why, why, why?' he wails.

Sita patiently tries explaining it to him. 'Hanuman,' she says, 'do you see this red mark, the tilak, on my forehead? That means that I am married to God and only I can be with him day and night.' (For in India, that red tilak forehead mark is like a wedding ring on the fourth finger.)

Thus Hanuman stops asking *why* he can't be with Ram and Sita and instead – like a good seeker – begins to focus on *how* he too can unite with the sacred – with God. In this way, he jump-starts himself onto his own spiritual path. In India, the color red represents God and divinity. So Hanuman, jumping to a logical conclusion for a brilliant monkey, goes to the marketplace bazaar by night and pilfers a whole bag of powdered red dye. He uses this to dye his whole body and soul the color of the divine so he can be with his God figures, Ram and Sita, wherever they go. Ever since then, as the story goes, Hanuman has never been apart from them. His time is completely absorbed with serving the divine.

Hanuman represents man's wish to be with God; his animal nature represents the animal nature in all of us. Yet Hanuman's animal nature is transformed by a life of service to the divine. He embodies the idea that if we dedicate our lives to service and love, then we too become godlike or saintly. That's why Hanuman is called a monkey god. Just as Charles Darwin found out, we evolved from monkey-like beings into higher and more conscious beings – a knowledge incorporated into mythology around the world centuries before Darwin.

In the religious art of India, Hanuman is often depicted tearing his breast apart. Buried deep in his open chest and heart is a picture of Ram and Sita, standing together hand in hand, as couples do for a marriage ceremony, amid a garland of flowers. Through his deeds and service, Hanuman was able to internalize the sacred and find it in his own heart. He exemplifies the path to God through devotion, unselfish service, and unconditional love.

Once, at our ashram, while we were all listening to a mendicant or holy man, known as a 'saddhu,' read from the poetic Ramayana, Maharaji became so overcome with emotion at the recounting of Hanuman's love and devotion that he jumped up from where he was sitting, tears streaming down his face, and hurried into his room.

He just couldn't contain himself at hearing of the love that was expressed in this epic tale he had certainly heard thousands of times before. Whenever I feel spiritually dry or complacent, I think of Maharaji and remember the monkey's tale and smile to myself, always.

Maharaji died near one of his ashrams in India at the exact time of the full moon of September 1973. When the huge procession of followers accompanied his body through the ancient holy city of Brindavan, tens of thousands of mourners lined the street to throw flowers at the bier. In his memory there were spiritual songs, music, and chants, as well as charitable feeding of the people of that city for days.

In Maharaji's temple there is a huge reddish-pink marble statue of the beloved, saintly, and heroic monkey Hanuman. Everyone tells me that on the day of Neem Karoli Baba's cremation, tears were seen rolling down the marble monkey's cheek. Maharaji's teachings of serving God by serving humankind were really heart opening. It's been more than twenty-five years since his death, and I think often of his great love of God and man.

All religious and spiritual traditions have holy men and women who inspire love because of their capacity for love. Mother Teresa, the Dalai Lama, St Francis of Assisi, Albert Schweitzer, Baal Shem Tov, Rumi, Kabir, St Theresa of Avila, Hildegard von Bingen. In every culture, in every time, and in every place, there have been spiritual giants who walked among us. Some may never have been recognized or canonized by any formal religious groups, but their behavior spelled out sainthood nonetheless. And the quality that these spiritual giants embodied was love.

People sometimes tell me that they were fortunate enough to grow up with loving spiritual role models. They have memories of grandmothers, grandfathers, uncles, aunts, and parents who seemed always to be kind and loving – free of negative emotions or behavior. These role models emanated goodness, compassion, and caring. In Tibet, these anonymous unheralded spiritual giants are even given a name; they are known as hidden yogis.

During the late 1960s and early 1970s, a number of Westerners went to Asia to study Buddhism. Most of those who stayed did so because they were fortunate enough to find teachers and gurus who accepted them as students and embodied love daily as generous benefactors and mentors. These teachers had a great deal to teach us about meditation, but they had even more to teach us about love and what it means to be good, kind, compassionate, and joyous.

We all throw the word 'love' around as though we all know what we're talking about and we're all talking about the same thing. However, there are really at least three separate and distinct kinds of love:

1. ***Instinctive love***

   This is the love that many people call 'chemistry.' Instinctive love happens when we are drawn toward another human being by a combination of karma, powerful pheromones, and subtle energy. We sometimes call it romance, lust, or passion; I prefer the term 'instinctive love.' Instinctive love sometimes provides the basis for a deeper, more emotional love – sometimes not.

2. ***Emotional love***

Emotional love makes us feel connected and bonded. We feel this kind of love for our parents, mates, children, and friends. With some people we feel so connected that we use the expression 'soul mates.' Emotional love often starts with a sense of liking someone; from that, love builds and grows deeper over time as we learn to trust and open our hearts.

3. ***Conscious love***

We often refer to conscious love as unconditional love or divine love. Of all types of love this is the hardest to cultivate. Conscious love describes the ability to love without reservations or agendas. I use the term 'conscious' because this love rests on a firm foundation of intentionality. It's no accident; it doesn't evolve from lust, fantasy, or need; we don't expect anything in return beyond the radiant joy of simply loving.

Walking the spiritual path means that we are trying to learn to love consciously. We put a certain emphasis on the word 'trying' because that's what we are doing – loving to the best of our ability. I think that seekers sometimes tend to beat themselves up because they haven't fully mastered unconditional love. I've actually heard people say, 'I'm not good enough. It's not really love until I can love like God loves.' But who is able to love like God loves?! We're human beings trying to understand and cultivate what it means to feel divine love. We have to start with small, realistic goals.

Those individuals who teach us the most about love often do so by their capacity to express love daily in dozens of small ways. Mother Teresa said, 'We cannot do great things. We can only do small things with great love.' Mother Teresa stood less than five feet tall yet she was a spiritual giant. She also said, 'What we are doing is just a drop in the ocean. But if that drop was not in the ocean, I think the ocean would be less because of that missing drop.'

I think it helps if we try to take Mother Teresa's words very literally and focus on the small hourly happenings. We need to make our intentions real by finding small, concrete ways to show our love to the beings who cross our paths. As we try to increase our capacity for love, we have to *practice* loving. It's like a muscle that needs regular workouts in order to be most effective.

But how do we *practice* loving? Love is a huge concept. To get a handle on the practice of love, let's break it down into some of its interrelated components; in this way, love becomes a more manageable goal.

• ***The Practice of Forgiveness*** We live in a world filled with injustices. Some of these seem to be directed straight at us individually, and we frequently respond by taking them very personally. 'Someone did something mean to me!' 'Frank forgot Valentine's Day!' 'Marla is so insensitive; she left me waiting in the rain . . . again.' 'Ted left me for somebody else . . .'

Don't we all know people who have caused so much pain that forgiveness seems too much to ask of us? Some experiences seem designed to leave us with small pieces of bitterness, pieces that we can't let go of, pieces that become frozen in our hearts.

And how about the large-scale injustices in this world – so horrific that they are difficult to imagine?

Whenever I talk about love and forgiveness, inevitably someone raises a hand to ask about the Holocaust and Hitler. I have to admit that I have no ready answers. Some events are so indescribable that, as the expression goes, 'even God hides his face.'

If you were born in Algeria, can you really be expected to forgive what was done to your brothers, sisters, parents, and children? How about if members of your family were murdered in the Holocaust, or if you come from Rwanda, Bosnia, or Cambodia, or a dozen other places where hatred has ruled and prevailed? How can you ever forgive genocide? How can you forgive apartheid? How does the Dalai Lama manage to forgive the Red Chinese for what has happened to the Tibetan people? And yet I know he does. This is the powerful spiritual magic of the wise and loving heart.

Forgiveness and forebearance in the face of evil is a difficult subject. Who can grasp the incredible displays of cruelty that go on around us every day? The Dalai Lama himself has told me that he's not totally beyond anger. But he has learned to work with it; he has learned to deepen his own compassion and sense of forgiveness. Each act of forgiveness is, of course, an act of love. It is also an act of liberating wisdom; it frees the heart and mind from excessive burdens and leaves us free to experience anew the present moment, beyond past and future considerations. This is an internal miracle that each of us has the power to bring about, I assure you.

When we fall short of forgiveness, it reverberates back on ourselves. We pay a terrible price for bitterness, anger, resentment, and hatred. It can affect our physical as well as emotional health. We all need to be able to forgive. Yet it's important to understand that we can forgive without forgetting. Thomas Szasz once wrote, 'The stupid neither forgive nor forget; the naive forgive and forget; the wise forgive, but do not forget.' If we are hurt by a person or a situation, wisdom and common sense tell us to avoid similar situations. Wisdom and love are always connected.

When we forget the past, when we deny pain, our own or anyone else's, we deny our memory, and as Elie Weisel so movingly points out, we deny healing, and we deny hope. It's difficult to forgive an Adolf Hitler, a Pol Pot, or an Idi Amin, but we work at forgiving a human race that has allowed the hate that's found in Nazism, racism, or any other form of hatred to flourish. We have to forgive our own part in this even as we vow to resist hatred. If we can't do this, then there is no hope for the future.

Remembering the many injustices and cruelties of this world helps us become more conscious of our own behavior and thoughts. If we really revile and detest man's inhumanity to man, as we say we do, then we have to painstakingly root all forms of hate and prejudice out of our own hearts and minds. This is absolutely necessary for our peace of mind and well-being, as well as to further peace in the world. This is part of loving.

Perhaps one of the most important things seekers need to keep in mind about forgiveness is that we sometimes need to start by forgiving ourselves. We each need to make peace with our own memories. We have all done things that make us flinch. We've all done things that we feel need forgiveness. But can we do it? My friend Gail gains weight easily; when she eats even one calorie too many, she can't forgive herself. Last week, Alan lost his temper with his children; he really yelled at them. He feels so guilty that he can't forgive himself; he feels like a bad parent. Dorothy put her aging mother who has Alzheimer's into a nursing home; even though Dorothy feels as though she had no choice, she can't forgive herself, and wishes it could be otherwise, Barbie lost her employer's briefcase, filled with important papers. Her employer forgave her and told her to let it go, but she can't forgive herself. Dennis feels as though he broke his girlfriend's heart; he just can't seem to forgive himself. Whenever Daniel makes a work-related mistake, the people in his office hear him reprimanding himself. 'That was really stupid,' he says in a tone of total disgust. Sometimes he even hits himself on the head using the palm of his hand. 'Idiot!' he exclaims. What on earth could Daniel be doing or thinking that deserves so much condemnation? Why is he so hard on himself?

Often we need to begin our practice of forgiveness by simply becoming more gentle with ourselves. Saint Francis de Sales once wrote: 'Be patient with everyone, but above all, with yourself . . . Do not be disheartened by your imperfections. How are we to be patient in dealing with our neighbor's faults if we are impatient in dealing with our own?'

Something to keep in mind is that even the IRS has a statute of limitations.

◆ ***The Practice of Acceptance and Understanding***

There is a lot of talk in spiritual circles about tolerance and unconditional acceptance, but it's difficult to accept others unless we start with some basic understanding that all beings pretty much want the same thing. We all want to be happy. That's how we start out – all of us, without exception. Along the way, things get twisted.

A few weeks ago, my editor attended a Sunday service at a Protestant church in her neighborhood. Part of the service is called Joys and Sorrows, and parishioners who wish to do so stand and share some of their experiences and need for support and prayer. A woman named Andetrie Smith stood up and said that she had just had an experience on the New York subway. She was riding in a train when someone came in collecting money for two children because their father, in a moment of terrible rage, had set fire to the family home, and the children were burned.

The woman riding next to Andetrie became visibly upset. 'That's just horrible,' she said, 'I think people like that should be killed. He should go to the electric chair!'

'What to you think?' she turned and asked Andetrie.

As Andetrie described this experience, she said that she wouldn't have said anything except that the woman asked for her opinion so she gave it.

'No,' Andetrie said. 'I agree that this person did a terrible thing, but I don't think we help anything in this world by hating and wishing anyone dead. I think we have to try to understand what made him do this and try to love, accept, and understand the person, even though we hate the act.'

'Well,' the woman said, 'I don't see how that can be done. I'm Jewish and people hate the Jews, for example.'

Andetrie, a black woman who was raised in the South when it was still a segregated environment, said, 'Well I don't hate Jewish people. And I certainly understand what it is to feel hate and discrimination. I think we all just have to try to find ways to understand one another.' She pointed out to the woman that even Malcolm X, for example, changed his views in his last years of life before he was killed.

Andetrie Smith says she believes that love is treating others as she would want to be treated. And she would always want to be treated with understanding, honesty, and respect. When she spoke to this woman, she was trying to be honest. As she left the subway train, Andetrie said that she felt bad because of the hateful story she had heard about the man and his children, but she also felt positive about the experience because she felt that she had really communicated with this woman in the train and could see that she was thinking about what Andetrie said.

I love this story because it provides a concrete example of how we can all reach out and try to enlarge the circle of understanding. Andetrie didn't give up in the face of her fellow subway rider's anger; she didn't just reflexively and self-righteously form a judgment about this woman's inability to love and accept. Instead she tried to understand her fellow subway rider's point of view, empathizing with her as she tried to spread the value of greater love and understanding. Every little bit helps.

Accepting and understanding what others feel – 'where they are coming from' – may be one of the most demanding things that love asks of us. On the spiritual path we try to recognize that we can abhor someone's action without abhorring the person. We judge the action, not the person. In this way we begin to drop some of the burdens that are weighing us down. We begin to loosen the burdens of anger, of bitterness, or resentment. We all carry some resentment, of course. Many people, for example, resent their own parents. Then when they become parents themselves, their perspective on parents changes somewhat. They see that no matter how hard they try to be great parents, they still inflict things on their own children. They realize that their own parents were just human. Often forgiveness and tenderness creep back in. It's a circle, a wheel of being and becoming that revolves 'round and round.' We are all being recycled continuously, like a daisy chain.

In Buddhism, when we talk about the heart of love, the word we use is 'Bodhicitta.' The term 'Bodhicitta' is literally translated as 'awakened mind' or 'the mind of enlightenment.' When we cultivate Bodhicitta, or the mind of enlightenment, what we are cultivating is an open heart filled with love and concern for the welfare of all beings. As we awaken to the sacred, we work at opening our hearts until they are large enough to embrace all beings, as well as all opinions, even those that are different from our own.

The Buddha said, 'When you see yourself as not different than others, when you feel what they feel, whom then can you harm?'

◆ ***The Practice of Nonviolence and Cherishing Life*** Perhaps the first principle of spirituality the world over is nonviolence. A primary commandment is *Thou Shalt Not Kill*. The Buddha said that his entire forty-five-year teaching career could be summed up in four lines:

> *To do no harm,*
> *to cultivate the good and wholesome*
> *to purify heart and mind*
> *This is the teaching of the Enlightened One.*

In Sanskrit, the word 'ahimsa' means nonviolence, a radical turning away from harming others in any way. This was the first principle of Mahatma Gandhi, whose power of truth coupled with nonviolent, passive resistance broke the back of British military imperialism in India. It was Gandhi who said that he did not hate the British, he only condemned what they did in ruling his country. In receiving the Nobel Peace Prize for his nonviolent resistance to the military oppression of his countrymen in Tibet, and for preaching nonviolent resistance to universal human rights abuses around the globe, the Dalai Lama follows in the footsteps of Gandhi and Martin Luther King.

When we talk about cherishing life, we have to also talk about doing everything we can to create a more just, fair, and equitable world. Gandhi once said that the greatest violence was poverty. So it's not enough to pay lip service to spiritual values and ignore the real human issues of our time. We cherish life by cultivating a giving and generous spirit; we cherish life by doing whatever we can to save the planet and the beings on it.

In Buddhism as we try to cherish life, we recognize that there are many kinds of creatures and all kinds of beings, seen and unseen. We start with ourselves by cherishing our own lives and appreciating and valuing the wonderful opportunities we each have. We then extend this to the people we love most, recognizing that of course we cherish these lives. Then we reach out so that the circle becomes larger, and we begin to think about what it means to cherish the lives of strangers, and even those we don't like. We keep our love reaching outward, and in this way the circle grows larger. Eventually we are able to reach out further and further and include more and more beings in our circle of love. We include our pets, and our friends' pets too. Over time, we are able to extend our love so far that we include beings that we think of as insignificant: bugs, ants, mice, snakes, and yes, even cockroaches. Can we cherish these lives – can we cherish all life? For all forms of life are sacred, sacrosanct, and inviolable. Just like us, no one wants to die, suffer, be ill, or lose loved ones.

It's so easy to say, 'I don't kill. I'm a good person. I'm a pacifist.' But what about the subtle killings? The times we've squashed bugs without thinking? Or even the times we've squashed another person's spirit? When I was in the first grade, I remember taking a shortcut home from school through a parking lot behind a supermarket. There were some boxes and crates and there was a wounded and dying baby bird under the crates. Well I'm ashamed to say that I finished the job. Part of me really was thinking of putting it out of its misery. But what was the rest of me thinking? Perhaps I had seen *King Kong* the week before on TV. I ended up feeling so ashamed. I am still ashamed. I was acting out something that had been imprinted in me – by war movies perhaps.

I felt such intense remorse and shame because of what I did that I never told anybody until many years later. Thinking about that event eventually made me vow to never do anything like that again. I can no longer kill mosquitoes, for example. We all have personalized internal rap sheets to remind us of times that we failed to be sensitive, that we failed to love and cherish all life. Acknowledging our transgressions, repenting, and vowing never to do it again is a way of helping our karma and helping ourselves. It turns us around, and redirects us on a finer, more noble life course.

Mother Teresa is a role model because she was able to love and care for the forgotten, the sick, and the diseased. Her mission to care for the most poverty stricken, the sick, and the dying began in the 1940s when she came upon a dying woman outside the walls of her Calcutta convent. Mother Teresa had a profound realization that this woman's plight was not unusual, and she vowed that she would do everything she could to help those who were suffering alone. When she walked through the streets of India, to her compassionate loving gaze, no one was insignificant. She was able to extend her love to people whom others might think of as repulsive or worthless. Someone else might have walked through those streets and turned away rather than see the suffering, but Mother Teresa chose instead to try to care for these souls whom others had forgotten.

We cherish life whenever we put our energies into furthering harmony, peace, and reconciliation among all beings. The monks in Asia are very careful about where they walk so as not to step on insects. They do what they can to keep from killing any form of life, especially when travelling or digging in the earth. When I first witnessed this behavior I thought it was charming, but at first I didn't quite get it.

Last year I was visiting friends in the New England countryside and walking along a road after a rainstorm. Many little snails were crawling across the road where they could get smashed by cars, and I spontaneously found myself moving little snails across the road in the direction in which they were heading. As I thought about what I was doing, I realized that I had certainly come a long way. But I also began to think about why saving small creatures whenever possible is a *practice.* It helps us cultivate a mind of love – an awareness that all life is precious. It was the most beautiful part of my day.

◆ ***The Practice of Compassion and Empathy*** To be compassionate is to be able to have a profound awareness of what others are suffering. Modern psychological research on altruism has shown that we each have an inherent desire to help built into us at a fundamental level. There is more basic goodness in us than we might normally believe possible. Moreover, it has been shown that compassion and altruism is good for us. It improves mental as well as physical health; it brings about good karma. Chogyam Trungpa Rinpoche always used to call Buddha-nature 'basic goodness.' This translation was not literal, but it was his understanding of what it really means. We have innate goodness; human nature is basically kind and good at heart.

One of the practical ways to develop compassion is to remove the barriers to it. Many of us have become hard-nosed, thick-skinned, insulated by layers of ego-defense mechanisms acquired through countless skirmishes along the road of life. Spiritual practice can be likened to meat tenderizer, just to be light about this. Without using a mallet or other rough techniques, a little daily sprinkling of it can help us activate our tender hearts.

Being aware of suffering – whether it be our own or others' – helps us soften up. It can touch us, move us, and make us more loving by making us more open-hearted. The experience of a severe illness, tragedy, or even a broken heart caused by a failed romance can foster open-heartedness. Crisis and tragedy can have the effect of spiritual open-heart surgery. St Francis of Assisi was a teenaged rake and rich kid gone wild, but a severe illness laid him low, and after some months lying in bed he emerged as someone with great compassion and sensitivity to the poor, the miserable, the helpless, and the ill. St Francis' compassion and ability to identify and communicate with others, including wild animals and birds, has made him one of the beloved saints. We always see stone garden statues of him with birds sitting on his hands and shoulders while other wild creatures rest near his feet.

We can all use our own life experiences to develop more profound compassion. On some level, we each know what it is to suffer emotional or physical pain. Using that awareness can inspire us to do what we can to help and heal others. When our children cry, we respond swiftly to their suffering. Why should we feel any less for anyone else's child? Even wild animals have a mother and a home to return to at night.

Reflecting on the examples of compassionate men and women of all times, including today, can help us open our hearts and minds and increase our ability to practice loving-kindness in everything we do. Abraham Lincoln once said, 'I care not for a man's religion whose dog or cat are not the better for it.'

◆ ***The Practice of Warmth and Kindness*** The Dalai Lama recently said that the most important thing in life is human warmth and affection. How simple, how wise, how human. How do we practice warmth, kindness, and affection? Simply by making others feel loved. When you meet the Dalai Lama, he immediately makes you feel that he cares about you.

Warmth and affection is a way of conveying feelings of love, caring, and acceptance. We try to be warm and affectionate to our children, to our friends and family, to our neighbors, colleagues, acquaintances, and strangers. The question we need to ask ourselves is whether we can try harder.

Can we be a little kinder, gentler, more loving to those around us? This requires a certain amount of conscious determination. I find that it is important to think about speaking kindly and gently, and being more present with others, even when we feel burdened and busy. We have to think about using words that convey acceptance and support. We have to think about being more generous with what we have – with our time, with what we know, with our financial resources, and with our feelings and emotions. A little kindness, a little warmth, a little affection, a little empathy goes a long way in all our relationships. We know this is true with our children, our mates, and our friends. But it's also true with others – even in chance encounters with those we may never see again. We need to live in ways that express our belief that loving-kindness matters.

◆ *The Practice of Joy*

> *Joy is prayer; joy is strength; joy is love . . . A joyful heart is the inevitable result of a heart burning with love.*
>
> MOTHER TERESA

Spirit means joy! Awakening is joyful. Life is a miracle to be celebrated and loved.

It's important for all of us to find ourselves and follow our 'joy path.' When we are joyful, when we are happy, we spontaneously share love. So think about what makes your heart sing. What do you do to make yourself happy? What feeds your spirit and vivifies the love in your heart? Remember that the spiritual life is vibrant, not dull; ecstatic, not static. Finding ways to bring more joy into your life helps spread it around.

Not only does joy light up our faces, it heals our ills. Doesn't it make you feel happy when you see a child smile? Doesn't it make you feel happy when you see joy around you? We smile at joyous occasions – a baby's birth or any special celebration of love. These are broad smiles of love. Recently I met a young mother whose two-month-old daughter had just recovered from surgery to correct a serious birth defect. The child had been very ill, but after surgery the prognosis was that the baby would be fine, healthy, and normal. Now the mother was taking her healthy baby to visit her family, and her joy was so intense that it jumped from her face and swept up everyone who came near her. Sometimes another person's joy – or even our own – is so wonderful that it moves us to tears.

I always love being with Tibetans because they are so exuberantly cheerful and joyous. It must have something to do with the pure high mountain air combined with their indomitable faith. People love being around the Dalai Lama because he exudes joy, such in-the-moment presence, that it's contagious. I recently read a piece in *George* magazine that John F. Kennedy, Jr, wrote about meeting the Dalai Lama. In it he said that when the Dalai Lama left, it felt suddenly darker, as though the guy with the lantern had just exited the room. I've also experienced that feeling when with His Holiness. Perhaps you've experienced it too with someone, or something, special in your own sacred life.

The path of joy is the path of open-heartedness – the path of a heart filled with love. So smile. Make somebody happy. Make yourself happy. Learn to love. Spread love. Be love. You'll love it.

◆ ***The Practice of Peace*** The peaceable kingdom is a world filled with love and nonviolence. We become part of the peace effort by working for reconciliation in all areas of life and by reconciling all the various parts of our own lives. We try to make peace with those we love; we try to make peace with those with whom we've experienced conflict; we try to make peace with the earth itself. Here are some peace practices:

Plant a tree. The Buddha exhorted his monks to plant at least one tree every year to repay the earth for its abundance.

Make peace with yourself by grounding yourself and giving yourself permission to rest. Rest is sacred.

Make peace with the Divine by connecting to your inner goodness or by saying a prayer.

Work for peace in every possible way, every day. Gentle yourself and be peace.

Help a life; help a soul. The Talmud says that to save one life is to save the whole world.

In an essay titled 'Hope, Despair, and Memory,' Nobel Peace Prize-winner Elie Weisel wrote, 'Mankind must remember that peace is not God's gift to his creatures, it is our gift to each other.' Thich Nhat Hanh says: 'Be peace, don't just talk about it.'

Om Shanti, Shanti, Shanti. Peace, peace, peace.

* * *

Love is very complicated, and we show our love in ways we don't even realize. As parents the world over know, sometimes the most loving thing we can do is to say 'no'; sometimes the most loving thing we can do is to 'let go.' I have a friend who told me that when she gave birth to her first child, she was in labor for dozens of hours, struggling and crying, and it seemed as though the baby was never going to be born. Finally, the nurse midwife said, 'Push once more.' My friend angrily replied, 'I can't.' And the wise midwife shouted, 'Scream that you hate the baby!' And my friend screamed, 'I hate this baby!' and suddenly something in her let go, and the beautiful and healthy little girl was born.

Subtle and mysterious are the ways of love.

Last year my friend Kathy travelled to Indiana in order to attend the memorial service of a woman named Mary Davis. Mrs Davis, who was eighty-nine when she died, was the much beloved mother of four loving children. At the service, my friend Kathy was sitting in the row behind Mary's daughter, Margi, and one of Mary's grandsons, Jonathan, who was giving a eulogy.

When Jonathan, now a confident and successful man, stood up to speak, he told the congregants about some of his experiences growing up. He said that as a child he had learning disabilities that made him very discouraged. He said that he remembered days when he felt as though he couldn't get anything right, and he hated school. He said that one of the most inspiring, meaningful, and confidence-building things in his growing up was a family prayer taught by his grandmother, Mary, to his mother, Margi, who in turn taught it to him. Every morning before Jonathan went to school, his mother would take his hands, look him in the eye, and repeat this prayer. This was Mary's legacy to her family. I never knew Mary, but I often think of her and her prayer of love.

MARY'S PRAYER

I am the place that God shines through.
He and I are one not two.
He needs me where and as I am.
I need not doubt, not fear, nor plan.
If I but be relaxed and free,
He'll work his plan of love through me.

Part Two

◆

Approaches to Spiritual Practice

It is not a matter of faith.
It is a matter of practice.
THICH NHAT HANH

◆

Your innate goodness needs tending. When we build and maintain a spiritual practice, we are acknowledging that we take our spiritual lives seriously. Every time we meditate, pray, or engage in spiritual reading or any other spiritual practice, we are honoring our innate Buddha-nature – honoring the light within, honoring our best selves and our highest potential. We are attuning ourselves with the sacred.

There is so much that we have to do every day, so much work, so much personal maintenance. Wake up, wash, brush, comb, drink juice, get the kids to school, commute to work, have a meeting, go to lunch, visit the dermatologist, do the laundry, pick up the dry cleaning, spend time with significant other, attend PTA meetings, call friends, buy a birthday present for Mom, walk the dog, not to mention thinking about what's on TV and what's for dinner. We all could go on at length about all the things we have to do, and all the things we want to do. And they are all important. But that doesn't mean that your spiritual life should be neglected.

There are many good people, sincere seekers, who resist the idea of spiritual practice. They honestly believe that the sacred is found in miracles and chance encounters. Sometimes they simply haven't found a practice that suits them. Often they don't understand exactly what it is that meditation, for example, is supposed to do. Spiritual practices like meditation help us stay connected to the sacred in ourselves. If we get lost, practice helps us find ourselves. Practice is how we cultivate our spiritual gardens. Different people tend to prefer different practices, just as different gardens grow different plants. But I'm positive that there is some form of regular spiritual practice for everybody.

A friend recently attended a yoga class, and the instructor started the class by telling the students that she was a practising Roman Catholic who had never managed to feel completely connected to her faith until she began teaching yoga. I strongly identified with that. I assure you that even though I am a Tibetan Buddhist lama, I still feel very connected to my Jewish heritage. But starting from the time I was in my teens, I knew I was looking for something that the religions of the West weren't giving me. I simply never felt fully engaged – body and soul.

Maybe it was my failing that I couldn't get turned on by what was going on in my local synagogue when I was growing up. But when I discovered practices such as meditation and chanting, a world opened up for me. As a Westerner, religious training to me was about being righteous, faithful, and following the laws of God. It was a powerful message, but it was still very cerebral. I certainly never heard anyone talk about the body-mind-spirit connection.

One of the major contributions brought from East to West – and captured in Eastern spiritual practices – is the holistic awareness that the mind, body, and spirit are intrinsically connected. When the Sufis of the East whirl, for example, they are using the movement of the body to center and balance their spirits and souls. For thousands of years the mystic yogis have known that we can use physical postures to change a state of mind. Meditation and breathing exercises alter body chemistry, which in turn can affect physical and mental healing. All over the world, people of all faiths are beginning to further examine the healing power of prayer. Spiritual practice can work on many levels.

All forms of spiritual practice share a common essence and purpose. They help us distinguish reality from delusion; they help us experience the clear light of understanding and divine wisdom. A great Zen master once said that when enlightenment experiences happen, they are accidents. He then added, but spiritual practice makes us accident prone.

Maintain a spiritual practice; even if you don't get enlightened in this lifetime, you'll get lit up. As they say, practice makes perfect. Or even better, practice is perfect.

To Simplify Your Life, Simplify and Clarify Your Mind: Building and Deepening a Meditation Practice

◆

There is no greater magic than meditation. To transform the negative into the positive. To transform darkness into light – that is the miracle of meditation.

BHAGWAN RAJNEESH

Sitting meditation is the basis and foundation on which Buddhist practice is built. Meditation itself reflects the essence of simplicity. You close your eyes, breathe in and out through your nostrils, pay attention, and something amazing happens.

'What?' people ask me. 'Exactly what happens from meditation?'

'Clarity,' is my one-word response. 'Serenity,' I often add.

Here is a longer list of some of the other amazing benefits of meditation:

- Meditation helps our minds empty themselves of clutter and confusion.

- It makes us feel calm, peaceful, and more aware of our inner resources.
- It brings a sense of being centered, grounded, and balanced.
- It makes our senses and perceptions more vivid.
- It helps us see how everything in life fits together.
- Meditation helps us become more skillful at navigating life and, consequently, less likely to be buffeted about by the winds of fate.
- It helps us gain greater insight into our personal issues and hangups.
- It helps us become less egotistical and self-centered.
- It helps us increase our capacity and ability to love.
- It helps us gain greater insight into the nature of reality.
- It helps us become more mindful and able to lead our lives with greater awareness and understanding.
- It stops us from sleepwalking away our lives; it wakes us up and makes us more conscious.
- It provides numerous health benefits and has been credited with aiding in the healing process and improving ailments such as asthma, hypertension, migraine headaches, and stress, as well as some attention deficit disorders.

In retrospect, I can't exactly remember my initial reasons for meditating. I was a not-yet-twenty-year-old college student. I have a memory of being someone who was always trying to run over his feelings with a lot of restless activity. As my grandmother used to say, 'So long as you're busy, Jeffrey, you'll be happy.' Recently, going through the contents of an old cigar box stored in my parents' home in Long Island, I found a little poem I had written back then as a politically active college freshman. One line said, 'I am lost amidst the motions we all mistake for meaning.' It seems apparent that I began meditating because I was looking for something, even if I wasn't sure what that something was. And probably meditation seemed like a good thing to do. One more activity!

I remember my first ten-day Insight Meditation course in India in 1971. Of course I experienced some initial difficulties, physical discomfort, and awkwardness, but once they were worked through, I was amazed at how much inner peace, buoyancy, and love I felt. Everything seemed significantly more clear, spacious, and possible. For me, something amazing began to happen. My experience is not unique. Meditators tend to be so enthusiastic about the practice that we sometimes make people nervous. No one is more fanatical than a recent convert. But we've discovered something wonderful that we want to share. I remember wanting to write home to everyone I knew to tell them all about it and encourage them to try it.

To those who have yet to experience the benefits of meditation, enthusiastic meditators don't always make sense. The Buddha always told people that the only way they could find out whether meditation was going to do for them what it did for millions of others was to try it and see. It's like a scientific experiment, performed in our own personal, interior laboratory. If we replicate the steps of the Buddha's experiment, we will replicate his results – in ourselves.

When Westerners think about meditation, the image that almost inevitably comes to mind is the one we have of the man known as the Buddha, sitting eyes closed, cross-legged in the lotus position. In Asia, one sees this image everywhere – in store windows as well as temples. Even here in the United States, the image is so familiar that many people tend to think that meditation originated with the Buddha, who was born in 563 B.C. In fact, meditation is an even more timeless yogic practice, so ancient that we don't know who the original meditators were, who taught them, or when the practice began. We do know that the Buddha first learned to meditate after he left his father's palace. We also know that soon thereafter, the Buddha had the help of at least two teachers, famous Hindu yogis, and that, at the time, the Buddha was also known as a yogi.

During the Buddha's lifetime, yogis typically withdrew from society and its materialistic values and concerns in order to dedicate themselves to a profound purpose – the search for truth, the quest for the sacred. The Buddha and his contemporaries trained long and hard in order to discipline, purify, and transcend mind and body. The purpose of this was to achieve a higher, more unified, divine consciousness. In this way, individual practitioners would be better able to perceive truth, or reality. They would thus be able to see the connection between the personal and the absolute. This is spiritual realization.

The Buddha did not meditate in halls, temples, or rooms as we do today. In his quest for truth the Buddha wandered through the dense jungles and forests of northern India. There, he meditated night and day. The Buddha's reasons for meditating were exclusively spiritual. He meditated in order to see the difference between truth and illusion, the finite and the infinite, death and eternity. He meditated in order to be free, liberated, aware, and awake. He meditated in order to understand the convoluted workings of ignorance, attachment, and desire. He meditated in order to end suffering – personal and universal. In short, the Buddha meditated in order to become illumined and fully awake.

Today Westerners come to meditation for many different and multilayered reasons, spiritual as well as emotional and physical. Here are some of them:

- to cultivate ideals like wisdom, love, and compassion
- to slow down minds that are restless, 'speedy,' or detached
- to help handle physical problems that have a mental or emotional component
- to reconnect the soul, body, and spirit
- to control minds that are filled with uncontrollable fearful, angry, or obsessive thoughts
- to get more understanding into their own behavior
- to meet fellow seekers
- to open the heart and awaken the mind
- to realize God
- to become enlightened

Meditation is exquisitely simple. It's practical as well as healthy. It makes good sense. It's safe and non-invasive; it doesn't fill you with toxic chemicals; it's not un-American. Our tribal ancestors from Jesus and Gandhi to Thoreau, Emerson, and my Uncle Max from the old country meditated. It's natural, organic, and homegrown. It feels good, and it's good for us. 'A meditation a day keeps depression away.' Anyone can do it.

Meditation isn't exactly what people think it is. It's not always about just sitting still and closing your eyes. There are numerous other ways to meditate, including meditation as movement or dance and meditations on sound, music, and visual imagery. Some people do chanting meditation; some people do visualization meditation; and some people do guided meditation. There are also many different schools of meditation. By extension anything that helps you connect to your natural mind, your innate wakefulness and awareness, the divine within and all around us – that is meditation.

I think it's important to remember that there is a kind of meditation that is available to everyone. I know that some people who are in the middle of a clinical depression find that sitting meditation doesn't suit their state of mind. Sometimes when we're depressed what we really need to do is get the energy moving. Walking meditation or a natural meditation that includes movement may be what's called for.

The primary goal of meditation is the cultivation of mindfulness. Thus anything that helps us reach that goal can legitimately be defined as meditation. As Thich Nhat Hanh says, 'Every act done in the sunlight of awareness becomes sacred.' That means washing dishes, scrubbing a floor, or changing a diaper can be part of our spiritual practice. Manual labor, because it requires concentration and attention, is particularly conducive to the cultivation of meditative awareness.

Yes, learning a particular meditation technique is very helpful, but each of us can find in our own lives examples of activities that naturally encourage and cultivate meditative awareness. These are called Natural Meditations, because they help us reconnect to our natural Buddha-mind and inner clarity. Natural Meditations require little effort. Here are some examples.

For my friend Marie, gardening is a natural meditation. As she weeds, waters, and turns the soil, she is completely *there*, fully attentive to what she is doing. 'There is just nothing else to be or worry about, and nowhere else I'd rather be,' she says.

James finds meditative awareness while playing the piano. Each note requires perfect attention and total mindfulness. If thoughts intrude, the off-key notes provide instant feedback.

For Sada, it's walking her dog in the park. She and the dog become perfectly attuned. She walks slowly, noticing everything on the path, hearing every sound, every bird call, every rustling leaf. There is nowhere to go, nothing else to do. Nothing missing and nothing in excess. The best of all possible worlds.

For me, it's being near water or the sound of water. Sitting on a beach, I feel as though the waves are washing everything away. I don't have to watch my breath, the waves do it for me.

As we say, the techniques leading us to meditation are many, but meditative awareness is one. Meditative awareness is whole and flowing – ecstatic, not static.

The thing about meditation that is so remarkable is that the experience is replicable. Meditation is a time-tested inner science based on a technique that has been practiced for centuries. Those who meditate today derive the same sense of well-being from the practice as those who meditated twenty-five hundred years ago, providing verifiable proof that centuries come and go, but the nature of the heart-mind stays the same.

Basic instructions for sitting meditation are deceptively simple and not very different now than they were twenty-five hundred years ago. This is how my teachers were taught to meditate; this is how I was taught to meditate; this is how I, in turn, teach others.

1. Sit on a cushion or a mat with your legs crossed in as comfortable a position as possible. If you find it difficult to get comfortable in this position, don't give up on meditation. Remember that we meditate with our minds, not our knees. Sit in a chair or on a couch.
2. Keep your back as straight as possible. Relax and don't tense up. Don't tilt or lean; your head and neck should be centered. Let your shoulders fall naturally. Put your hands comfortably in your lap or on your knees.
3. You can keep your eyes open, closed, or half-closed; most people prefer to begin with eyes that are closed or half-closed.
4. Breathe in and out through your nostrils. As you do this, concentrate on the physical sensation of air

going in and out through the nostrils. Feel the physical sensation. Focus on your breathing and on nothing else. If you like, you can count your breaths in the following way: Breathe in through your nostrils, counting one. Breathe out through your nostrils, counting two. Breathe in through your nostrils, three. Breathe out through your nostrils, four. Continue doing this until you count to ten; then begin again.

5. Relax; stay open and loose. Keep your body quiet and your breathing calm, natural, and easy. Let everything settle naturally, in its own way, its own place, its own time.
6. Stay in the moment, in the holy now, in the present.
7. Whenever a thought, feeling, perception, or memory occurs while you are meditating, let it go, and don't follow it. Simply concentrate on the breathing. Do the same thing with all other forms of distraction. If you hear a noise, feel an itch, or see a movement, let it go and keep your mind focused on the breathing. When the mind wanders, as it will, simply bring it back to the object of attention, the breath sensation at the nostrils. Keep returning again and again to the breath, to the simple awareness of inhaling.

   This is mindfulness of breathing as a basic meditation.

THE THREE STAGES OF MEDITATION

A meditation session can generally be thought of as having three stages. For a few minutes, let's imagine that we are able to watch and feel what other meditators experience. Tony and Sophia, for example, are both experienced meditators who have just arrived at the side of a lovely country lake. They plan to sit here and meditate for approximately thirty minutes. Let's watch what these two friends do and see what we can learn.

Stage One – Arriving and Centering

Tony and Sophia are both settling down. Tony unbuckles his backpack. Sophia spreads out the mat and small cushion she plans to sit on. They both get comfortable. Sophia is able to get comfortable sitting in a half-lotus position, but Tony's knee is bothering him today, so he is sitting upright on a folding beach chair that he carries with him in the trunk of his car. Both of our meditators are carefully positioning themselves so that their spines are straight. Sophia wiggles her shoulders a little until she feels comfortable and relaxed, at home on her seat.

Once they have 'found' their seats, their balance, Tony and Sophia start settling their minds. They start cultivating mindfulness of the present moment; they start 'letting go' of the thoughts they have been carrying with them. Tony has been meditating longer than Sophia, and he has an easier time with this process. Sophia usually finds that it takes her a few minutes to relax and grip less tightly to her thoughts. Many of these thoughts revolve around work because several unfinished projects loom large in her head. Sophia also just put her little daughter on a bus to camp; she is concerned that she will feel lonely and her child will be homesick. Sophia has been meditating for six months – long enough to know that once she relaxes and centers herself, her thoughts will slow down. Still, it does take some time and some patience.

From the moment they sit down, Tony and Sophia start to be more attentive, conscious, and mindful of their breathing. Slowly and easily, they begin breathing in and out through the nostrils. Watching Tony and Sophia breathe, we can see that something is happening to their bodies. Their shoulders are relaxing, their backs are becoming straighter. Their faces begin to look calmer and more relaxed. Sophia particularly delights in the first stage of the meditation process; as her thoughts fall away, she begins to feel unburdened and liberated, like a huge weight is being lifted.

Although Tony and Sophia are both using the breath as a focus point to help them relax and meditate, they are using slightly different techniques: Tony simply focuses on the sensation of the breath coming in and out of his nostrils; Sophia finds it easier to count breaths. Either way, it is the awareness, the mindful attention, that matters, not whether the meditator is focusing on the breath or the number.

Sophia counts:

One . . . she slowly breathes in

Two . . . she exhales out

Three . . . watching the breath coming in

Four . . . watching the breath going out

Sophia continues counting up to ten, and then she starts all over again.

By the time Sophia has counted to ten, her meditation as well as Tony's has progressed to Stage Two.

Stage Two – Intensifying and Focusing

Both meditators are making a strong, determined, and conscious effort to pay attention to exactly what is happening: They are sitting and breathing. They focus on the inhalation; they focus on the exhalation.

With every breath, Sophie is feeling more and more comfortable, and more and more removed from the traffic jam of scattered thoughts that were bouncing around in her head only a short time before. For a fleeting second, she feels proud of her accomplishment. She lets that thought go by and continues to focus on breathing and breathing alone. She would like to congratulate herself on her ability to concentrate and focus, but she knows, as her teacher told her, that 'thinking about thinking is also just more thinking.' Sophia is having a good meditation, and starting to enjoy herself.

Tony, however, is having a harder time. Suddenly out of nowhere the spectre of the woman he was dating last summer has appeared in his mind. 'What is she doing right now?' he wonders. A follow-up thought pops into his head: 'Maybe I should call her.' He lets it go and watches it disappear. It takes some effort on Tony's part to let go of this train of thought, but he manages to do so. He breathes in and out several times. The woman is gone. Then he has another thought, 'Did I remember to bring a bathing suit so I can go swimming later?' This thought sticks in his head. Tony, however, brings his wandering mind back to his nostrils and continues to concentrate on the breathing, and eventually that thought too grows weaker and disappears. This is meditation: watching the show; knowing the knower; staying with the simplicity of just breathing; remaining free and untangled.

Stage Three – Releasing and Allowing

Tony and Sophia continue to meditate. They have both naturally and unself-consciously arrived at the place they wanted to be – namely, the present moment, the sacred now. They are both sensitized, receptive, and calm; they are both experiencing the peace and joy of meditation.

The lake itself is abuzz with activity. A bird sings in the trees; a soft wind rustles the leaves; a dragonfly whirls near the meditators' heads. A plane flies over head; a truck on the not-too-distant road screeches its brakes; across the lake a small child cries. Tony and Sophia hear each sound clearly at the moment it happens. They are both aware of this, aware of that – the sound, the smell, the thought, the ache in the knee. *Awareness of moment-to-moment happenings is the meditation*. This is it. This is meditation.

Meditation is being aware of what is, just as it is. Just *being*, without judgments or opinions. Tony and Sophia are aware of things arising and dissolving as they happen, as they come up and then pass away. In the meditative mind, there is room for everything. Nothing needs to be suppressed. If Tony and Sophia were to try to suppress their thoughts, for example, they would be going too far. Meditation is not a passive experience. It is simply dynamic, vibrant being.

Meditation cultivates an awareness of what is happening in the present moment. This is how we become more conscious. This is how we wake up. The sounds, thoughts, and feelings that arise during meditation are not distractions. They are grist for the mill of panoramic present-moment awareness.

When we first start meditating, we can't easily handle too many distractions, so we try to keep the surroundings and the stimulation very simple. Later, when we get more experienced, we can meditate anywhere. All thoughts, interruptions, and distractions become like wood in the bonfire of awareness. As awareness develops, everything that arises makes the bonfire blaze up more brightly. We become so able to handle distractions and thoughts that a great fearlessness and inner certainty arises within us.

In this third stage of meditation Tony and Sophia rely more on effortless being, a natural flow and natural mindfulness, rather than an effort to meditate and concentrate. In the final few minutes of their meditation, both meditators are feeling calm, centered, complete, and whole. They feel more alert and energized; they have also become ultra-aware of what is taking place around them on the lake. Everything seems brighter and lighter than it did when they first sat down. The sounds seem clearer and more distinct; the smells seem more pronounced; the breezes feel fresher. As they get closer to the natural state, they feel in closer harmony with everything in the natural world. When we look at them, we can see that they have both relaxed. Even their faces look less lined and younger than they did when the meditation began. They both feel more centered and clear, at peace with themselves and the entire world. It feels like the dawn of a new day.

Post Meditation – Transition and Integration

Tony and Sophia stand and stretch. Together, as planned, they do a little walking meditation. They walk carefully, focusing on the lakeside path beneath their feet. They begin slowly reintegrating their calm, focused minds into daily life activities. They move slowly and attentively at first; then they gradually pick up the pace. Finally they ease out of the meditation by having a nature walk together.

One of the primary reasons Sophia meditates is to get a sense that she is in control of her own destiny. Sophia often feels that she is too much of a reactor. In her life she has made many mistakes because she responds reflexively, often saying yes when it would be wiser to say no. Meditation is showing her that just as she is able to be aware of a car's horn without responding, she can be aware of what other people are doing and saying without becoming involved in activities or relationships that she should avoid. She hopes that this awareness will keep her from making quick and foolish decisions, as she has in the past.

Tony has come to meditation because he feels overworked and harried. For him, life seems to be nothing more than a series of appointments, chores, and tasks to be performed at high speed, one after another. He has found that meditative awareness helps him slow down and savor the precious individual moments of life. He is feeling less pressured because he is putting less pressure on himself. When he stops doing so much, things seem to fall into place.

Meditation helps us cultivate mindful awareness in every situation. The challenge Tony and Sophia face in the post-meditation period is to continue their lives with greater meditative awareness. The practice of meditation is showing them that awareness slows things down long enough so that they can see what is happening before they react. This is empowering. This is freedom.

The Great Zen master Dogen lived from 1200 to 1253. About meditation, he wrote:

'Meditation is not a way to enlightenment, nor is it a

method of achieving anything at all. It is peace and blessedness itself. It is the actualization of wisdom, the ultimate truth of the oneness of all things.

'In your meditation, you are the mirror reflecting the solution to your problems. The human mind has absolute freedom within its true nature. You can attain this freedom intuitively. Don't work toward freedom; but allow the work itself to be freedom . . .

'Practice . . . meditation in the morning or in the evening or at any leisure time during the day. You will soon realize that your mental burdens are dropping away one by one, and that you are gaining an intuitive power that you could not have previously dreamed possible.

'There have been thousands upon thousands of people who have practiced meditation and obtained its fruits. Don't doubt its possibilities because of the simplicity of its method. If you can't find the truth right where you are, where else do you think you will find it?'

DOES MEDITATION HAVE TO BE DONE IN A SPECIAL PLACE?

Sometimes I still see outdated cartoon-like representations of meditators and their surroundings. I think of the image of the young man or woman wearing bell bottoms, sitting cross-legged on the floor of a candlelit room that is filled with psychedelic posters, incense, or Eastern art. The home reflects middle-class comfort; the room can best be described as 'far out.'

A voice yells, 'I smell smoke. What's going on in there? What's that smell?'

The meditator replies, 'Nothing, Dad, I'm just meditating.'

The fact is that you can meditate anywhere. When we think of Zen Buddhists, we visualize gardens, shrine rooms, and zendos of starkly beautiful simplicity. Tibetans frequently meditate in halls filled with gilded icons, brass bells, and brocade tapestries, the brilliant colors – red, gold, and orange – splashed all over the ceiling, walls, and carpeted floors. Many Tibetan yogis and lamas, however, chose not to meditate in these vibrant surroundings. Milarepa, Tibet's great mountain yogi, meditated in Himalayan caves; Tilopa, the wandering tenth-century Indian yogi, meditated under bridges near the bank of a river in Bengal. There, free of material values or distractions, he sang, 'It is not objects that entangle us. It is inner clinging that entangles us.' He subsisted on what was discarded by the local fishermen.

If you were to wander far enough into the jungles and forests of Burma and Thailand, even today on the cusp of the twenty-first century, you might well come across mosquito netting hanging under a tree. And sitting happily under that protective netting, isolated from the zillions of insects of all sizes and descriptions, would be a meditating monk, a forest ascetic.

Today the very spot in India where the Buddha attained perfect enlightenment is in the middle of what appears to be almost a desert. During the Buddha's lifetime, it was a lush but treacherous forest filled with animals, snakes, and insects.

Here in the West, we can choose to meditate with groups at various Ys, churches, synagogues, and meditation and retreat centers. We can meditate with teachers; we can meditate with friends; or we can meditate alone. Some people meditate at the edge of oceans, lakes, and streams; some people meditate in their bedrooms, offices, or walk-in closets. Recently I was walking in Brooklyn's Prospect Park, and I saw a woman on a bench in a meditation pose. Her eyes were closed, her face relaxed as she sat facing the morning sun. The woman looked like she meditated on the same bench every morning. Others nearby in the park were practicing tai-chi.

New meditation students frequently ask me whether I think they should create a special place for meditation in their home. I think it's a good idea to have such a space simply because it will help remind you of your intention and commitment to meditation. In most matters, there is something to be said for finding a personal comfort zone. The same is true of spiritual practice. Some people, for example, always go to the same church or synagogue; often they sit in exactly the same seat. There is a comfortable sense of belonging and rightness to the familiar. Although it's not absolutely necessary, when you first start a spiritual practice, it will probably help if you meditate regularly in the same place. Most people discover, as I did, that your meditation space, no matter where it is, seems to become invested with its own spiritual energy and blessings. Later, you will be able to carry this atmosphere and energy with you wherever you go.

Some people prefer meditating in groups because it helps them maintain discipline. In Zen meditation halls, you sometimes see meditators facing each other in rows. In other zendos they sit facing blank walls so that they can limit the distractions if they so choose. At our retreat center in France, one of my Dzogchen teachers, Nyoshul Khenpo Rinpoche, used to wander off each day to find places to meditate away from everybody. One of his favorite spots was under a large tree, another was in a rickety old tool shed that he said reminded him of his Himalayan hermitage. The shed had no windows and a dirt floor; its solitude and simplicity felt familiar and sacred. All over the world, particularly in the East, where these traditions are still carried on, there are especially blessed caves and mountaintops, as well as churches and temples, which are considered sacred sites. These cathedrals of the spirit are believed to be imbued with a special energy. They are often located on top of conjunctions of underground rivers and streams. People go there even today to feel a sense of holy or divine presence.

When I first arrived in Nepal, I heard about one such site, a cave high up Mount Shivapuri where it was said that hardy ones would go alone to meditate. At the turn of the century it had been inhabited for decades by an old holy man, known as the Shivapuri Baba. Local legends said that the Shivapuri Baba had lived for 120 years. His cave was near a stream so it had a supply of water; it also had a splendid view of the snowcapped Himalayas. Very excited about the prospect of meditating in such a holy place, I went up there expecting to stay five days, but if truth be told I only lasted three and a half. The water dripping down from the rocks overhead made the cave incredibly damp. It didn't take long for my sleeping bag to turn soggy, and, to compound my discomfort, unseen creatures nibbled at my supplies throughout the night. Finally, common sense got the better of my youthful enthusiasm and determination. All in all it was a positive experience and served a definite purpose: It helped me realize that spiritual practice is not intended to be some form of penance. An excess of discomfort can make it difficult to meditate for long periods. At least this has proven to be true for this Westerner.

Some Tibetan lamas I knew in Darjeeling meditated almost around the clock, sitting up all night in a meditation seat or box. They lived, ate, and meditated in the same spot. Although it required enormous discipline, it was part of the culture and seemed natural in that environment. When I was on three-year retreat, we all spent the night in similar meditation boxes. Again, I confess there were times when I stretched out on the floor in something closer to my normal sleeping position.

I have a separate meditation room in my house. When I'm home, I love going in there to meditate. To me it feels consecrated with the blessings of my entire spiritual lineage and Buddhist teachings. I prefer this spot to anywhere else in the house. I live at the edge of a lake so I also like to meditate in the garden or down by the dock.

There is a form of Tibetan meditation called Dzogchen Sky-Gazing, which is often practiced outdoors. However, even that practice is adaptable to suit the individual practitioner. One renowned Tibetan lama of old, Dudjom Lingpa, had a hut in which he cut out very high windows like skylights; there, he meditated with open eyes and an upward gaze.

So to meditators who ask whether they need a special space, the answer is that often it's not so much a matter of creating your space as it is of *finding* your space. This is not about restriction or limitation – like only being able to eat in your own kitchen or only being able to meditate in one or two specific places. It's more about opening up and finding who you are, wherever you are.

In one way the spiritual life is about transformation. It's like the caterpillar shaking off its skin and becoming a butterfly. That image implies getting out of one's rut and personal comfort zone. On the other hand, the underlying spiritual principle is one of coming home and finding what we seek in our own heart-mind. That's the deepest comfort zone. Once you have begun to access the deeper comfort zones of your own being, you'll carry your own meditation space with you. Start finding that space. That's your natural mind, your natural comfort zone – your true spiritual nature, which accompanies you every second of your life.

Think about what kind of environment makes you feel most relaxed. When the world is too much with you, where can you go? Where *do* you go – in either outer or inner space? Do you feel most at home when you can hear the sound of the waves, or is your favorite place a corner of the living room couch when nobody else is home? Some people tell me that they reach a meditative state when they work around the kitchen, chopping vegetables; others recognize baking bread, scrubbing floors, or sewing as meditative practices. The place you reach inside your own mind when you meditate is the place you want to be. Learn to get there, memorize the signposts on the way, and recognize it for what it is when you arrive at your destination. Do this, and you'll be able to find your own natural contemplative space whenever you need it. In this way you'll always have an internal sanctuary that helps you come home to what counts.

IS IT NECESSARY TO HAVE A SPECIAL TIME FOR MEDITATION?

The answer is both yes and no. Most people feel that it helps them maintain a regular ongoing year-round practice if they commit themselves to a certain time each day. The Dalai Lama, for example, meditates in the early morning hours, and then again before going to bed. When we meditate at the same time every day, we develop self-discipline as well as continuity. After all, we're trying to build a spiritual life, not just experience an interesting interlude. But meditating every morning or evening shouldn't preclude meditating at other times as well. Meditation is like prayer; it's not limited to the Sabbath.

Even though they teach meditation and meditate in groups regularly, almost all the teachers I know still have a daily meditation practice, and they look forward to it. Meditation practice is about practice; 'practice' is the important word. You have to keep doing it, practicing it, regularly. This is like physical exercise. The muscle you are stretching is the muscle of your spirit. Once you get in the habit of meditating regularly it becomes a cherished routine. The meditation habit is an intentional groove created by skillful means. By struggling against the rut-like grooves that until now have kept you stuck in unsatisfying behavior, you are creating new grooves that will speed your path to transformation.

DO WE NEED SPECIAL CLOTHING FOR MEDITATION?

Of course you can meditate in a business suit, or even formal evening wear. However, there are some good reasons why you might prefer different clothing. Many of these reasons are practical: You will be more comfortable and get more pleasure from meditation if you are comfortable. That's why monks and holy people often wear flowing tunics and robes or wrap themselves in soft shawls, capes, and blankets. So when you choose clothing for meditation, look for something loose that doesn't pull or pinch around the waist, knees, neck, wrists, ankles, or buttocks. Try to wear something that stretches with your body and feels comfy. Before you start meditating, take weather and temperature into consideration. If it's a hot day, dress accordingly. If you are meditating outdoors, in cool pre-dawn hours, or in an unheated meditation hall, don't forget to wear something warm. Sometimes I wear my old maroon monastic lama robe as a shawl or put it across my lap. I also have several comfortable hooded sweatshirts that I wear when I'm meditating outdoors as well as a hooded parka for wild weather meditation in the mountains. If you're meditating outdoors, wear hats, sunglasses, and gloves as needed; you can even carry a small waterproof butt-pillow. Why not?

If you meditate with your eyes open, you might want to keep your glasses on. If you meditate with your eyes closed, take them off. It doesn't matter too much. I take off my watch when I meditate, and place it on the floor. You might also feel less encumbered if you remove your jewelry and put it someplace safe. This is, of course, a matter of personal preference. One ancient king in India who didn't remove his jewelry was instructed by his guru that instead of renouncing it, he could meditate on the crystal clear, luminous diamond on his ring finger. In this way, the king became enlightened.

If you are sitting in a chair or doing walking meditation, then you can keep your shoes on or off. If you are sitting in a cross-legged position, take them off. Shoe soles don't flex enough to make them practical choices, although I've known practitioners who wore soft moccasins. Shoe socks also work quite well in cold weather.

The other reasons for having special meditation clothing have to do with setting the mood and reminding yourself that what you are doing has a spiritual purpose. I have meditation clothing that I wear only when I meditate. Many meditators do. Is this necessary? No, of course not. You also don't need special clothes in order to exercise or ski, but it helps. When you open your closet and put your ski clothes on, the outfit helps remind you of your intention to spend the day on a snow-covered slope. It brings a vision, an ambiance, a mood. In your ski clothes you act differently than you do when you are wearing the clothes you normally wear to work. Similarly if you put on the same clothing whenever you meditate, those clothes begin to carry their own aura. Just seeing them in a drawer or a closet can make you want to meditate.

ARE ALTARS OR RELIGIOUS SYMBOLS NECESSARY COMPONENTS OF MEDITATION?

Of course not. But sometimes they help. Looking at spiritual symbols can be very supportive and facilitating.

Ideally everything we touch could feel spiritual and consecrated. But in our day-to-day world, that's not what happens. If you meditate in the kitchen with a view of your pots and pans, you're more likely to think about the dinner you're planning to cook than you are about your spiritual development. Your pots and pans symbolize food and cooking. If you were to replace them with symbols of your spiritual life, your thoughts would be more likely to veer in that direction.

In all religions and practices, there are certain kinds of symbols, clothing, behavior, ritual instruments, haircuts, and other 'props' that we associate with spiritual activities. In Orthodox Judaism, for example, for thousands of years, men have been entering temples, removing their business jackets, and putting on their tasselled prayer shawls for morning prayer. When they do this, it brings to mind the Lord's instructions to Moses, 'Speak to the people of Israel, and bid them to make tassels on the corners of their garments through their generations and to put upon the tassel of each corner a cord of blue, and it shall be to you a tassel to look upon and remember all the commandments of the Lord.' The blue tassels are a concrete and not-to-be-forgotten symbol reminding Jewish men of the commitment they feel to their God. Blue is the color of Zion. It reminds us of our spiritual identity.

Similarly in meditation practice, we try to create an atmosphere that *reminds* us of our inner work. Because of this I absolutely think it helps to create a special spot that will help you come home to who and what you are. So ask yourself, what resonates with your spirit? When you open your eyes, what do you want to see? What makes you feel grounded and more in touch with your own Buddha-nature? What lifts your heart and brings you spiritually home to where you want to be?

People surround themselves with all kinds of objects when they meditate: flowers, candles, statues. But not everybody has or is moved by the same things. You might say that you're allergic to flowers or the smell of incense, or that you're forgetful and don't want to run any risk of fire from a candle. You might say that you're so uncomfortable with statues and icons that you find them distracting. We each get to decide for ourselves.

Reality is the ultimate temple. Nature, therefore, is one of the best places in which to meditate. If you don't have a garden or a window with a view, you can always hang a picture that speaks to your spirit. I have a friend who loves Montana and the Rocky Mountains. She has a picture of mountain goats clambering up a craggy peak on a cloudless day. She's never been to this particular site, but she knows it's spring because there are little flowers poking out around the rocks. She says it makes her feel grounded. Perhaps you can't meditate in front of a waterfall, but you can meditate in front of a photo and imagine the sound. I have a Himalayan panorama on a wall in my living room.

Do I have religious symbols in my meditation room? Yes, I have many symbols, including a statue of a Buddha that I love as well as photographs of my primary teachers. These things resonate with my spiritual and karmic past. You don't need the same kinds of objects. Find something that you love, something that seems sacred to you.

WHAT DO YOU DO IF YOU FEEL UNCOMFORTABLE AROUND BUDDHIST STATUES AND IMAGES?

Many Westerners who start a Buddhist-based meditation practice say that they are initially uncomfortable with statues of the Buddha and other religious icons. The vast majority of us grew up in Judeo-Christian households. We were given very firm instructions about worshiping 'graven' images. This prohibition is embedded in our collective psyche. Some Westerners don't like icons or symbols because they remind them of their past religious conflicts and seem at odds with the deeper invisible truths they seek.

When I first arrived in Asia, I would often think, 'What's with the gilded Buddha statues and ornate altars?' If formless truth is everything, then why were these images necessary? Eventually these symbols grew to have meaning for me. In Asia where so much of the oral tradition was carried by symbols and images rather than by written precepts or commandments, the symbols took on a great deal of richness and meaning. Certain iconographic images – mandalas, for instance – are like mystical road maps encoding volumes of information and inspiration, when we know how to read them.

Symbols are simply reminders of what it is that we seek. Buddhahood means our own potential Buddhaness. Images of the Buddha remind us that the Buddha was not a God; he was a man – a man who was able to become enlightened. When we look at images of the Buddha, we are reminded of our own innate Buddhanature. A Buddha-rupa or statue is like a mirror reflecting our true selves and highest potential for enlightenment.

Yes, all spiritual symbols and objects have a great deal to do with form, and may not necessarily reflect the essence or depth of a spiritual practice. But right now we are all human beings, not yet enlightened beings. And there are few, if any, among us who don't occasionally need forms to help remind us of divine essence.

If you personally don't want to do anything that could be construed as worshipping images, the Buddha agrees with you. Remember that the Buddha was a social reformer twenty-five hundred years ago in a polytheistic land of countless god and goddess images. The Buddha discouraged his disciples from displaying images or statues of himself. He consistently told followers to focus on the teachings, not the teacher. He never stopped reminding people that although he was enlightened, he was a man, not a god, and that he should not be worshiped.

When the Buddha died, he was cremated according to Indian custom. Because his followers wanted to keep his ashes as a remembrance, the ashes were divided up and stupas, or holy places, were built to enshrine them. Human nature being what it is, people then began placing stone statues of the Buddha on top of these stupas. Legend has it that about fifty years after his death, a very elderly woman who had seen the Buddha in person described him in detail to an artist who then drew his portrait on cloth, and that became the first Buddha image.

Some people want to look on the face of God, and so they paint faces and create holy images as a way, by extension, to imagine the face of God. In the same way you can look for the face of God in everything – in nature, in the face of every animal and small child, in light shining on the water, and even in the face of your adversaries.

Often we find the face of God in blessed moments of awareness. We listen to a piece of music that we love, and are magically transported to a new level. Music is seen as sacred because of its ability to inspire us to go beyond ourselves to a sense of the divine. Think of the soaring heights reached by Beethoven's 'Ode to Joy.' The same thing can be true of any art form, particularly when it is able to shock us and show us other faces of reality.

In many ways I think art is really the religion of today – it wakes us into new *seeing*. The spiritual moment really is that time when we are briefly shocked into wakefulness. The sudden inhalation of breath, and the awe we feel at the marvelous beyond – beyond ourselves, beyond our habitual self-consciousness and preoccupations – that is the spiritual moment.

Re-Envision Yourself and Your World

◆

The soul never thinks without an image.
ARISTOTLE

Visualization is an important part of spiritual practice because it has to do with how we see both the world and ourselves. It has existed ever since mankind began thinking of gods and goddesses as the ultimate in form, and it may well be the oldest form of meditation. Today, it's an integral part of many guided relaxation meditations.

We all have the capacity for visualization. All we have to do is replace the image already in front of us with another image of our own making, or from our own memory. In visualization, we intentionally cause something to arise in the mind. If we use our mind to bring forth the same object often enough, it can even become part of our memory, making the next visualization of this object that much easier.

Take a moment right now and visualize your favorite place in nature. Close your eyes and let your mind take you to an ocean, a waterfall, a country setting. Visit there for a moment. Feel the gentle breeze, smell the ocean or freshly mowed hay.

Visualization is also beginning to be used with success in alternative healing therapies and techniques. When my friend Kathy's father, who lived in Kentucky, was first diagnosed with cancer, he started reading a book on imaging techniques. He was interested in the book for several reasons: He had been told that imaging techniques would help him reduce the stress he carried with him, which in turn would help his immune system fight cancer; and he was interested in finding greater inner peace.

From his reading he learned a visualization technique that instructed him to (a) think of a beautiful and peaceful place that he loved and (b) imagine himself enjoying that spot. The place he chose to travel to in his mind was by the side of a mountain stream, called Little Pigeon River, located in the Smoky Mountains. He had visited this idyllic spot many times with his family; they all vividly remembered picnics and outings by the stream. There were boulders in the river, and the children used to jump from rock to rock.

Three times a day for the next six years of his illness, Kathy's father would use his mind to envision himself by the stream he loved. At the end of each of these meditation sessions, he would finish by using his mind to send loving energy and thoughts to certain people he cared and worried about. He felt that this practice gave him strength and great peace of mind. His family felt the same way. His practice seemed to help center him and make him much more present and available. He had always been a man of great strength who was accustomed to taking charge. With his illness, he learned to soften and let go. Shortly before he died, he told his children, 'I'm so fortunate; I have almost no regrets.'

In Tibetan Buddhism, we regularly use visualization

techniques to help us connect with a more sacred reality. We might, for example, visualize ourselves in a Buddha-field of luminous light. Writing about images of the absolute or God, Buddhist scholar and psychiatrist Roger Walsh said, 'Perhaps the most dramatic example among religious traditions is the so-called deity yoga of Tibetan Buddhism. Here the yogi visualizes himself first creating and then merging with a god-like figure who embodies virtue upon virtue – unconditional love, boundless compassion, profound wisdom, and more. The yogi attempts to move, speak, and act as the deity. In other words, embodying, experiencing, and expressing those qualities.'

I once asked the great meditation master Kalu Rinpoche about visualization. Why, I wondered, wasn't visualization simply another form of delusion? It was quite different, he assured me. Visualization is not about superimposing unreality on reality. Quite the opposite. Visualization is a way of getting closer to the mind, the source of the projection of the unreality that we think of as being real. In our Tibetan tantric Vajrayana practice, there are two main stages. In the initial stage, known as the 'kye-rim,' we intentionally generate a spiritual experience by creative imaging techniques, including visualization of an archetypical meditation deity, and we enter into the experience of that world through the visualization combined with chanting, breathing, music, and the like. Then this is completed in the second stage, the 'dzog-rim,' which is the completion or dissolution phase. Here we release the visualization and let it dissolve back into the luminous open light of awareness, the light from which it arose. Then we rest in the ultimate completion of the two stages, the innate clarity of natural-mind, Dzogchen. In this way, we transform our ordinary perceptions into the pure visionary perceptions of the Buddha-field. We then let the visualization resolve back into the openness from which the light of pure awareness rose. That's the natural completion stage. The point is to experience and return to that natural state. This is a central practice of all forms of Himalayan Buddhism, and it is taught and practiced by all lamas.

Visualization can help us retool and rethink our self-concepts. We all have certain images and concepts of self that we cling to erroneously. Some people think of themselves as overweight even when they are not; others think of themselves as incompetent or lacking in some basic way. We can all revisualize ourselves in more satisfying and edifying ways. In this way, we begin to realize that we don't have to be stuck with the old labels about who we are. We can use these techniques to help us grow our spiritual selves by seeing ourselves as compassionate, warm, and loving. We can be anything we want to be; in fact, we already are.

VISUALIZATION MEDITATION

Sit down and relax.
Take rest.
Find your true seat,
balanced, centered, at home and at ease.

Breathe several times gently,
in and out.
In and out.
In and out.

Relax. Close your eyes.
Slow down.
Breathe naturally.
Let everything go.
Let go of all tension in your body,
and let go of all your thoughts and inner dialogues.
Just sit. Just breathe. Just be.
Relaxed, at home, and free.

Now, begin the visualization process
imagining yourself and your body
as a clear ball of light;
crystal clear, luminous,
sphere of white light/pure being.

Envision a golden sun
at the heart center,
warm, radiant, splendid.
Breathing in and out through the heart center,
imagine this inner spiritual sun
opening up like a golden sunflower,
petal by petal.
It opens a little more with each breath
radiating outward
warming up first your chest, then your entire body,
and then your whole being.

Light rays reaching out to all,
touching all, blessing all,
illumining all.
Warming up and illumining
all who wander like sleepwalkers
through the darkness of ignorance and delusion,

awakening the clear light of spiritual awareness and
joy
like a blessed, blissful dawn
throughout the world.

Then let go and just rest in the empty, open,
luminous afterglow
of this great awakening,
in your natural state of authentic presence,
pure Being. Just simply being,
enjoying the joy and peace
of meditation.

Mindfulness: Living Fully in the Present Moment

◆

Again and again, examine
Every aspect of your mental and physical activities.
In brief, that is the very way of observing mindfulness.
SHANTIDEVA

The other morning, Eric woke up, took a look around his apartment, and wondered, 'How the hell did this happen to me? And how can I make it stop happening?'

What Eric was looking at was an avalanche of small reminders that his life seemed out of his control: a desk piled high with papers that he had brought home from a job that he wished he didn't have; a stack of bills representing a lifestyle that Eric wasn't enjoying; a crammed appointment calendar; several interesting-looking books that he never seemed to have time to read; a wall filled with Post-its reminding him to call his mother, pay the parking tickets, and get an extension on his taxes. Right now there are times when Eric feels as though his life is completely cluttered with nothing more than a series of mistakes, unwelcome obligations, and almost meaningless details.

Many of us go through our days almost as though we are sleepwalking. Every now and then, we wake up for a brief instant of clarity, and cry out, 'What the hell is happening here?' And then we fall back into our semi-conscious state as we continue bumbling about, half asleep at the wheel of our lives. We don't pay sufficient attention to what we are doing as we are doing it, and then we wonder why we end up in the predicaments we do.

Have you ever had the experience of making a mistake, and even as you were doing it, you were saying to yourself, 'This is a mistake. Why am I doing this?' We've all had this experience, haven't we? Buddhism teaches that, to some extent, we are all aware of what we are doing. We all have innate awareness. It's always there. Where else would it go? Unfortunately this awareness is rarely operating at full efficiency. It's buried, covered over, obscured by temporary distractions, veiled by our illusions and confusions, submerged under layers of habit and learned behavior.

When we talk about mindfulness, we are describing conscious living and alert presence of mind. Mindfulness helps us bring our innate awareness into sharper focus; it helps us *pay attention* to what we are doing as we are doing it. Paying attention helps us live in, and appreciate, the present moment in all its richness and depth. It helps us see – truly see – what is actually going on. Simply put, paying attention pays off.

Mindlessness – heedlessness – is the opposite of mindfulness, and it seems to be a symptom of our age. We see it in our leaders, in our friends, in our partners, and in ourselves. Within the last decade we've had many examples of lack of mindfulness, not the least of which was an American president apologizing on national television for heedless and careless behavior.

Mindfulness practice is a way of training ourselves to notice the causal relations and interconnections between actions and their effects; it trains us to pay attention to the karmic implications and ramifications of personal behavior. Mindfulness practice helps us slow down and utilize more of our innate intelligence and sensitivity; it helps us savor and experience the full texture and feel of our experience. Mindfulness helps us smell the roses, but first it helps us *see* the roses.

Mindfulness helps us live in a more impeccable way: We can shed those layers and layers of habits and learned responses that lead to careless actions and thoughts. We can learn to look before we leap and think before we act; we can stop living like moths who are inevitably attracted to bright, dangerous flames. We can shake free of our knee-jerk behaviors and responses to life; we can let go of dissatisfying and unhealthy patterns. And, as we become more mindful, our innate wakefulness – our spiritual intelligence and inner wisdom – begins to blaze forth. This is the whole purpose of mindfulness practice.

Mindfulness is at the heart of Buddhist meditation practice. In fact, the most basic Buddhist sitting meditation is called Mindfulness of Breathing. When we do sitting meditation, we are training ourselves in the conscious practice of mindfulness.

Think about what happens when we practice sitting meditation: We sit, we relax, we collect ourselves, we center and stabilize our busy discursive minds by calming down with breathing and relaxation exercises. We focus our attention on the present moment by attending totally to the breathing process and nothing but the breathing process. We are aware of inhaling as we breathe in; then we are aware of exhaling as we breathe out. Breathing in, calming the mind . . . breathing out, relaxing, and smiling.

As we slow down, we become more aware of everything that is taking place. We become conscious of the small intermission between inhaling and exhaling. As we break it down even more, we notice more details; we see that even one single inhalation has different phases and parts – the breath enters through the nostrils, makes its way down through the throat into the chest and into the abdomen and so on. It may even have a little sound, a little whistle across the prairie of the body. Try this yourself. Breathe, and as you slowly and carefully inhale and exhale, notice how slow and precise each moment, each nanosecond becomes.

Of course we are not breath worshippers. Worship is not the purpose of meditation, nor is the breathing process at the top of my list of objects of veneration and reverence. What we are doing in meditation is training ourselves to bring the same attentive mindfulness, or precisely focused attention, to bear on anything and everything. We can concentrate on a candle flame, a flower, a star, washing dishes, eating a peach, or taking a walk. Mindfulness helps us stay in touch with our bodies, our emotions, and our minds. Mindfulness is the best and only antidote to heedlessness. When we are mindful, we have fewer accidents and we make fewer mistakes and fewer errors of judgment.

All mindfulness exercises, by definition, are repetitive. We are reminding ourselves time and time again to be mindful about life. A classic mindfulness exercise is called Mindfulness of Walking. In this meditation exercise, we breathe in as we slowly raise the right foot. Then as we slowly breathe out, we lower the right foot to the ground. Then we do the same thing with the left foot. We breathe in as we raise the foot; we breathe out as we place the foot on the ground.

We do everything slowly and carefully. We do it mindfully. We practice being totally aware of the physical sensation of raising the foot. We are mindful of the sensation of placing the foot slowly on the ground. We are fully conscious of the foot hitting the ground – first the heel, then the sole. As we are mindful of this activity, we are also aware of any feelings we have about how we are placing one foot directly in front of the other and how we are breathing. We place our full focused attention on this activity. If we don't do this, we get immediate feedback. If our mind wavers, we wobble. We do this again and again while walking slowly. Repetition is the essence of training.

This is traditional walking meditation. It is a way of cultivating mindfulness in action. In this way, we begin to integrate attentive mindfulness and present awareness into every aspect of our lives. We want to be able to bring the same kind of alertness and attentiveness into everything we do – mindful at any speed so to speak. In this way, we can know exactly what we are doing.

The Buddha, by the way, did not limit mindfulness to physical activity. Quite the contrary – he told his followers to observe their feelings as well as their actions. In fact, the Buddha may have been the first person to talk about what it means to 'be in touch with your feelings.' When asked how a monk should observe his feelings, the Buddha replied: 'A monk when experiencing a pleasant feeling knows, I experience a pleasant feeling; when experiencing a painful feeling, he knows, I experience a painful feeling.'

When we practice mindfulness meditations, it's easy to notice how much resistance we have to paying attention. We want to go speeding ahead, doing what we usually do. I like the following walking meditation because it forces the practitioner to really pay attention.

WALKING THE LINE WITH MINDFULNESS

Look around the area where you live or work and see if you can find a natural line that you can use to practice mindfulness. Perhaps there is a curb, a low seawall, a hallway, or an actual painted line in a tennis court, sports field, or empty parking lot. Maybe you can find a boardwalk by the ocean? Or even the water's edge by a lake or ocean. If all else fails, perhaps there is a line formed in your own home by the planks of a hardwood floor. One of my teachers in Thailand used to advise us to find two trees and do our walking meditation for hours back and forth between the two of them. If you do this long enough, the ground becomes worn, and you will have created your own path. This is a metaphor for how we create our own spiritual practice.

This walking meditation doesn't necessarily have to be done slowly, but it must be done carefully. Start toeing the line, one foot carefully placed after the other. As you are doing this, breathe through your nose. Coordinate your breathing with your walking. Inhale, and place your left foot down. Exhale, place your right foot down. Do this synchronized breathing and walking meditation long enough so that you feel as though you have created a new groove for yourself.

Take regular steps like a sewing machine needle going slowly up and down. I find that this walking meditation can have a refreshing, centering effect, and I do it often, especially when I travel. As you walk the line, you are also centering and collecting yourself. Use your breath as a touchstone or anchor, a reminder to keep bringing you back to the moment.

As in all mindfulness meditations, simply be aware of your thoughts. That's all you have to do. Just have a nice walk. Feel the ground beneath your feet. Keep your eyes relaxed, softly focused, gaze down, slightly in front of you. Don't let your eyes wander; wandering eyes are a symptom of an overactive mind. Instead use a gentle gaze to keep paying attention to the line in front of you. When the mind wanders, as it will, just bring it back to what you are doing. You are walking and breathing. That is all. That is it. That's enough!

Let this meditation help bring order to your chaotic world. Somebody once said to me, 'Surya, I don't understand, why is this behavior any different from that of a compulsive personality who feels compelled to step on every line?' This is a good question, but to me the answer is very clear. When we do walking meditation, we do it intentionally. We are not victims at the mercy of out-of-control behavior. Walking in this way helps us intentionally find order amid the confusions of the day. We are creating space and clarity in our busy lives.

Variations on this meditation can be done on nature trails or anyplace else where you have to be mindful of carefully placing your feet one in front of the other.

Three Breaths to Mindfulness: Ten Natural Exercises in the Mindful Pilgrim's Day

◆

In Buddhism, the most important precept is to live in awareness, to know what is going on.

THICH NHAT HANH

The men and women who enter monastic life quickly discover how much emphasis is placed on the discipline of careful moment-to-moment attention. This is true in all spiritual traditions, Eastern and Western. There are myriad ways to bring mindfulness into daily life. Tibetan monks, for example, frequently practice a moment of mindfulness each and every time they walk through a door. Sometimes they do this by remembering to recite a certain verse or mantra as they do so. Try this yourself for a day. Every time you walk through a door, pause, take a moment, breathe in and out. Bring yourself back to the moment. Then cross the threshold and walk on.

If you were to visit Thich Nhat Hanh's Plum Village Meditation Center in the beautiful Dordogne region of southern France, you would discover that throughout the day there are mindfulness bells to remind everyone to slow down and be aware of the present moment. Whenever the gong is rung, everyone – children as well as adults – take advantage of this time. They stop whatever they are doing and practice a moment of mindfulness in order to more fully experience their experience.

In our own lives, we can develop some simple rituals to help remind us to pay attention by creating moments of mindfulness. Choose ten things that you do every day, and as you do each of them, take a moment to be mindful. For example:

1. *Mindful Waking Up*

> *. . . of all human doings, nothing approaches in strangeness or wonder that most ordinary of daily events, the simple act of waking up. We come to ourselves each morning, and each morning it seems like a miracle. Shamanistic traditions from Siberia to New South Wales teach that the soul quits the body during sleep to wander in unmapped dimensions of space and time; who knows what contortions our travel-weary soul must go through to reenter its human abode? I have a friend who kisses his bedroom wall each morning upon opening his eyes, so astonished is he at his good luck in making it back to the right address.*
>
> From *Gifts of the Spirit*, by PHILIP ZALESKI and PAUL KAUFMAN

Each day presents itself as a new opportunity for awakening in a sacred manner. We can intentionally start our days in a more mindful fashion. After he had become enlightened, the Buddha was asked who he was. Was he a god, a spirit, an incarnation of God? The Buddha answered simply, 'I am awake.' Thus he became known as Buddha, which means 'The Awakened One.' Each morning, then, as we wipe the sleep from our eyes, we can remind ourselves of what it means to become genuinely awake and stay awake.

I like to think of each day presenting itself as the microcosm of an entire year. The morning represents spring; noon=summer; evening=fall; night=winter. When we settle in at night and pull the covers over our heads, we become semidormant, much like a garden in winter. Spring, like morning, always surprises us. Children almost always wake up fresh, happy, and fully energized; adults, more beaten down by life's travails and exigencies, are more likely to wake feeling as though they need coffee and more sleep. I think it's a good idea if we can remind ourselves each morning that the inner light of awareness – your essential Buddha-nature, well beyond the ups and downs of daily life – is never asleep. This Little Buddha within us – Tibetans call it the Clear Light Mind – is always bright-eyed, bushy-tailed, and ready to go. So wake up, get settled in the moment, and take three mindful breaths.

Inhale . . . Exhale . . . One.
Inhale . . . Exhale . . . Two.
Inhale . . . Exhale . . . Three.

Then.

Breathe out! Say Aaaah!

Clear yourself of the stale airs and humors. Breathe out the residue of last night's dreams. Expel any negativity you might be feeling. Greeting the morning with a giant outbreath is an ancient Tibetan practice.

Yeas ago when I was first living in a monastery in Darjeeling, I found it very difficult to wake up at 3:30 or 4 A.M., the hour at which monks and nuns normally begin their daily routines. When I told this to my meditation teacher, he said that I should wake up like a lion. Through a translator, I told him that this sounded very poetic, but what did it actually mean? And he showed me. He looked up and roared . . . *Aaahhh! . . . !*

THE LION'S ROAR

As you prepare to start your day, envision a large happy lion stretching and roaring.

Now get out of bed.

Stand up facing the morning and the day that awaits you. If you have a window, you might want to face in that direction.

Assume the Giant's Stance: Stand up straight, legs a little apart.

Raise your arms to shoulder level and spread them wide, like wings, with the palms *forward.*

Breathe out. *Aaah!!!!*

Stretch.

Take a deep breath.

Breathe out again. *Aaah!*

Feel the stretch; feel your breath expand in your lungs and chest.

Now, like the lion, leap forward into action, spring forward into the day; stride fearlessly forward like the king of the jungle.

Yes, I know at first this approach may seem absurd. Perhaps all you want to do is shamble off to the bathroom, with semiclosed eyes, hoping to stay awake. However, I ask you to just try this mindful lion's approach to the dawn of a new day and see if it doesn't make a difference.

2. ***Mindful Toothbrushing***

Stand in front of the mirror. Take three breaths in and out, relax for a moment, and look into the mirror with fresh eyes. See who is there. Look into your eyes. Can you get a fresh view every day? Now brush your teeth mindfully. Be gentle. Be mindful. Slow and careful. Pay careful attention. You're showing your teeth. So give yourself a little smile to start the day. It's a good day. Enjoy yourself.

3. ***Mindful Bathing***

As you approach your morning shower, reflect upon the many sacred rituals the world over in which water plays an intrinsic part. All traditions recognize sacred rivers, lakes, ponds, springs, and waterfalls. Water is used to both bless and anoint. We can all partake of these blessings through a transformative moment of calm, mindful reflection as we practice our daily ablutions.

Stop for a moment beneath the showerhead with the water running over your head and face. Become aware of your feelings. Drop your hands. Just stand there. Breathe in and out a few times and relax. Feel the hot water running over your head, your neck, your shoulders and back. Let the current blast on high for a solid minute. Listen to the water and feel it on the back of your neck and shoulders. Completely immerse yourself in this unusual sensual experience, which can be likened to a waterfall of blessings, a veritable baptismal font. Stay in the moment for a little longer if possible and let all ills, transgressions, and preoccupations be washed away. Experience the divine experience of water. Listen, merge, dissolve. Flow free and easy, at ease. In the flow.

4. *Mindful Walking Out the Door*

How many times in a day, a week, or even a year do we walk through the door on our way to work, shop, school, or anywhere else our karma calls us? How can we do this mindfully?

As you get ready to leave your home, consciously approach the door. Stop and stand up straight in front of it. Take three slow breaths; mindfully inhale and exhale three times. Use your breathing to help you be more present. You're at the door, ready to depart. Do you have what you need? Do you have your wallet, your umbrella, your pocketbook? There are entire industries devoted to helping people combat carelessness with keys. But we don't need any of that because we are mindfully alert. We have our wits about us, as well as all the different keys. *No problem!*

Walk out the door and enter the world with your eyes wide open and a smile on your face. Thich Nhat Hanh says that a smile helps us start being part-time Buddhas right now.

5. *Mindful Commuting*

When you first sit down in the car, train, or bus, take three easy breaths in and out through your nostrils.

Count the breaths to yourself. Collect yourself. Be mindful and aware of what you are feeling. Fully inhabit your experience. Know where you are. You are sitting down. Your commute is about to begin.

Look out the window. Is the sun shining? Is there a falling rain? Are you on a subway in a grimy station so far underground that you have no awareness of the weather? Look around. Pay attention to what you see. Feel the texture of the moment. Don't jump far ahead and outside of yourself, trying to get where you're going before you've barely begun the journey. Stay right where you are. Feel the atmosphere, space, and time around you. Experience the moment. Give it a chance to reveal itself before you jump on to your next stop. You are present and fully accounted for, right now. Make the most of it by 'being here now,' as Ram Dass likes to say.

6. *Mindful Arriving*

Whenever you arrive at your destination – whether it's the supermarket or the Supreme Court – let yourself fully arrive. Pay attention. Stop and take three breaths. Attend to the moment. Explore the moment. Let your three breaths bring you in touch with where you are. Be conscious, be awake, be aware. Notice the surroundings. Then take your place.

7. *Mindful Waiting*

We all do a lot of waiting, don't we? On movie lines, at water coolers, in waiting rooms of various kinds, at red lights and traffic jams while driving. The next time you're waiting anywhere, don't just kill time or try to distract yourself to keep from feeling bored or annoyed. Instead, use this opportunity to create a rich and sacred moment of mindfulness. Breathe three or seven times, and refresh yourself through the magic power of awareness.

The thing about mindfulness meditations is that they help us create a sense of more and better quality time. When we are totally aware, time opens up. With mindfulness, we can experience the eternal moment. Breathe in and out three times and watch time slow down. Isn't it wonderful to experience life, as opposed to watching it whiz by? Savor these precious moments of mindfulness. This is your life, your sacred life.

8. *Mindful Time Out*

Whether it's a coffee break, a visit to the bathroom or water-cooler, or simply a short walk up and down the hall to stretch our legs, we all need time during the day to reconnect to who we are. So whenever you feel that things seem to be spinning out of control, just stop, be mindful, and breathe in and out three times. Offer a prayer. Say a mantra. Maybe you could even play a chanting tape. Better yet, try a little chanting yourself. Whatever it takes, just do it.

If there is a window available, look out and practice your three breaths of mindfulness while you gaze at the view. Use this window of mindful time to regain your balance and sanity, collect yourself, and re-arrive in the present moment. Let the fresh air in and the stale atmosphere out. Pay attention and appreciate those surprising spring breezes of the spirit. Spirit is as spirit does. Regain your sense of humor, perhaps by making a funny face at yourself. Laughing, after all, is a way of loving.

9. *Mindful Eating*

Mindfulness of eating is an ancient spiritual practice. In Asia some Buddhists practice chewing each mouthful of brown rice a hundred times before taking the next chopstick full. Mindfulness of eating helps us experience the taste, texture, and temperature of what we put in our mouths; it helps us become aware of how, when, and why we nourish ourselves; it helps us handle food and dietary issues with greater consciousness.

When you sit down to eat, take three breaths to remind yourself to enjoy a moment of mindfulness. Smile, and appreciate a little post-denominational moment of grace. Put your hands in front of you and inhabit the moment. Then for the first bite or two, try chewing your food fifteen or twenty times. How does it feel? How does the food taste? Are you getting nourished? Be grateful for this moment of grace, for it is always there. By opening up to it, we experience the moment.

10. *Mindful Homecoming*

After his enlightenment, the Buddha said, 'Done is what had to be done.' That's a good feeling, isn't it?

Now that you are home, rejoice. Stand in front of your door and appreciate the moment of your arrival. Breathe in and out three times. Mark the passage and completeness of the circle. Feel the satisfaction. Feel your feelings. Just be there for a moment. Now open the door and step inside. Home is a temple; enter your sacred domain. Come home to yourself. Oh, and don't forget to be mindful of where you place your keys. You may want them for further journeying.

The Buddha was once asked, 'What do you and your disciples practice?' The Buddha answered, 'We sit, we walk, and we eat.'

The questioner was confused. 'But,' he continued, 'doesn't everyone sit, walk, and eat?'

'Yes,' said the Buddha, 'but when we sit, we know we are sitting. When we walk, we know we are walking. When we eat, we know we are eating.'

This is the essence of mindful living.

The Practice of Studying with a Spiritual Teacher

◆

Your own self is your ultimate teacher. The outer teacher is merely a milestone. It is only your inner teacher that will walk with you to the goal, for he is the goal.
NISARGADATTA MAHARAJ, author of *I Am That*

Recently I saw an article in the *New York Times* about how to find the best pizza in New York City. The *Times* listed several of its favorites and then went on to map the lineage of the pizza makers. It turned out that most of the great pizza makers of New York had all studied with the same Italian chef or with one of his students. This produced a lineage of excellence, at least as far as pizza is concerned. Historically, in all crafts and disciplines, people apprenticed to masters in order to learn. This is how mastery is handed down from teacher to student; this is how Socrates, for example, passed on what he knew to his student Plato, who in turn taught Aristotle. Spiritual traditions and lineages have long been passed on in the same way.

In our lifetimes we are exposed to many different kinds of teachers and teachings. In turn, we pass what we have learned on to others. Sometimes the lessons we give and receive are formal, but just as often they are seemingly accidental. The changing nature of the student-teacher relationship today is one of the hottest issues of Dharma transmission in the Western world.

Although the classic guru-disciple relationship has long been out of fashion in Western society, it continues to exist and function in Asia. Some of the more traditional teachers still feel that this is the best way for a student to grow spiritually. In these traditional relationships, the student would make a commitment and stay with one teacher, usually for an entire lifetime. But during the many years when this practice was standard operating procedure, it may have been as much a reflection of the times as anything else.

Today we are exposed to much that our forbears never dreamed possible, and there are so many more options for change and social mobility. A contemporary seeker can get on a plane and take a seminar with a teacher in California before returning to the East Coast for a meditation weekend or Sabbath ceremony with someone totally different. We can do this today in a way that our spiritual predecessors could not. My personal feeling is that for the most part this is a good thing; being committed to studying music doesn't mean that you can't appreciate or even study dance. The major downside to all this opportunity for choice, eclecticism, and cross-fertilization is the danger of dilettantism and weak, watered-down teachings.

Students who want to learn Dharma understandably would like to have some assurance that they are studying in traditions that produce verifiable results. Western students have numerous excellent choices. The great Asian masters taught their disciples, who in turn taught others, who in turn now teach others. Today's seekers can find Asian teachers who moved to the West after years of study with acknowledged Dharma masters; they can find Western teachers who spent time in Asia studying the great Eastern traditions; or they can find Western teachers who were trained by Westerners. They can, of course, also still make the journey to the East in person, if they wish.

People who know me know how important my lamas and teachers have been to me. Just being with some of them could be transformative. My first Dzogchen master, Kanjur Rinpoche, for example, was an elderly Tibetan refugee. Once in Darjeeling a visiting friend asked if she could meet him. I took my friend to his room, and froze when I opened his door and saw him meditating on his bed.

My eyes saw far more than an old man sitting cross-legged on a worn blanket. My teacher was literally blazing with light in the form of a magnificent blue Buddha. It was such a blast that I almost fell over backward. My friend just stood there, transfixed. It was more than twenty-five years ago, and I can still see it as though it were yesterday. That light is still streaming into me. Another friend of mine said that he had a transformative experience the first time he met Kanjur Rinpoche, when Rinpoche asked him to turn inward and see if his mind was round or square. This inward turning startled him into an epiphany.

If the karma is right, we can all receive enlightening transmissions from teachers. It has always been taught that the teacher or guru principle manifests as a mirror of our deeper, higher self – our own Buddha-nature. If we are fortunate enough to meet such a fully actualized being, we can see our own potential fulfilled. This is what we can become. In this way we are confronting our own highest truth. Sometimes these truths are mirrored to us in crescendo break-through experiences. More often they are gradual and happen over time. Martin Buber once wrote, 'Everyone has in him something precious that is in no one else.' A good teacher can help you find your true and precious self.

When I began living with my Tibetan teachers in Nepal, one of the most important things I came to understand was that sacred traditions are built around the experiences of individuals, men and women who have had direct knowledge of the spiritual path. In this country, if we plan a trip and belong to AAA, we can get free and reliable road maps that spell out the best way to reach our destination. Similarly in Asia I discovered that there were guides and teachers who were able to provide spiritual road maps, pointing out pitfalls as well as shortcuts. These road maps are there for all of us so we don't have to keep reinventing the wheel. Experienced teachers *can* help seekers understand these maps and develop and grow along the path. For those who don't have access to teachers, the teachings still exist in texts that lay out in great detail the stages that people go through as they take the tried and true spiritual journey.

The ideal teacher is someone who has exemplary talents and inspirational qualities that combine wisdom, character, generosity, and unselfishness. From such a teacher we learn more than we could ever have intended. There is an old Jewish story about a beloved rabbi who travelled for many days in order to visit and study with another even greater rabbi. When the first rabbi returned, one of his students ran up to him and said, 'Teacher, what did you learn from the rebbe, the holiest of holies?' The rabbi replied, 'I didn't learn anything. I just went there to see how he ties his shoes.' The meaning, of course, is that the greatest lessons are to be learned from watching how a master lives, day to day. There are lessons to be absorbed through body English, as it were – by living with and serving the masters. This kind of experiential learning can't be garnered from books.

The question the typical student asks, of course, is 'How can I find such a master teacher?' There is an old saying that most of us have heard: *When the student is ready, the teacher appears*. I often joke that it works both ways: When the teacher is ready, the students appear. This seems to be especially true today; there is such great spiritual hunger as well as a sense of a moral and ethical vacuum in the world.

Tibetan masters talk about what happens when a karmically ripe student meets a teacher who is karmically ready for such a student. Such a situation provides the groundwork for a cosmic boom of enlightenment. The right teacher acts like a master jeweler who knows precisely where to strike the uncut diamond. However, this doesn't happen every day, and it's not wise to bring your heirloom diamond to just anybody who happens to own a hammer. The results could be very disappointing.

It's important to note that there are many different kinds of teachers as well as many different levels of spiritual readiness. A student may need different kinds and styles of guidance at different stages along the way. We can learn on numerous levels, and we don't always need someone of the caliber of the Dalai Lama to help us move along on the spiritual path. I think the teacher's principal job is to facilitate the seeker's next step. It's a little like teaching children to walk. We don't really teach them; we help them find their feet and we remove as many objects from the path as possible. And we attend patiently, gently, and lovingly to their inevitable trials and tribulations, as if midwifing their spiritual rebirths.

In the Tibetan Buddhist tradition – and in Hinduism too – the guru-disciple relationship has always been crucial. Tibetan teachers say that just by watching someone bow, they can identify that person's teacher and tradition. Other Buddhist traditions, such as Vipassana or Zen, place less emphasis on the teacher and more on the teachings, the practice, and the techniques of practice. In the West, I think this pragmatic emphasis can be a healthy way to begin. Although many people consider me their teacher, I tend to think of myself as more of a spiritual coach or trainer – a player-coach, perhaps. The truth is that I feel as though I learn as much from my students as they do from me. Here in the West it seems appropriate that student and teacher should share Dharma in this way, finding their way together.

In the original Buddhist scriptures there was only one word used for teacher and it was not 'master,' but 'kalyana-mitra,' or good spiritual friend. I want to assure readers that this is not some kind of New Age theory that's being developed specifically for Western students. Last week I was on vacation, staying in the house of a Dharma friend, and I came upon an old book by the late great patriarch of Thai Buddhism, the Venerable Buddhadasa Bikkhu, in which he says, 'In truth, even in the old training systems they did not talk much about an "acharya" (teacher, master). Such a person was called a good friend (kalyana-mitra). It is correct to refer to this person as a friend. A friend is an advisor who can help us with certain matters. We should not forget, however, the basic principle that no one can directly help someone else . . . Although he or she is able to answer questions and explain some difficulties, it's not necessary for a friend to sit over us and supervise every breath. A good friend who will answer questions and help us work through certain obstacles is more than enough.'

Seekers are often searching for the 'perfect' and enlightened teacher. I think it's important, however, that we remember the original scriptures and focus, instead, on finding teachers who are first and foremost good and wise spiritual friends.

Those in positions of power and authority sometimes have feet of clay, and spiritual leaders are no exception. Consequently, I know a lot of men and women who became disillusioned by experiences with various gurus and teachers. Some of these disillusioned students devoted years of their lives to following one specific master or another, only to become embittered because things were not what they seemed to be. And yet many of these people now realize that much of the problem was that they overidealized their gurus and teachers. As in all things, the higher the pedestal, the further the fall. If we expect perfection in our teachers, we are setting ourselves up for disappointment except in the rarest of cases. There is no real need to expect so much. Our true journey does not require that.

In the spring of 1998, the Dalai Lama came to Branderis University in Massachusetts to give a public talk. It was a major event that Americans of all faiths, as well as Tibetans, had been preparing for for months. Banks of beautiful flowers were arranged around the podium, and when the Dalai Lama took the podium and looked over the sea of flowers and shining, eager, expectant faces, he said, 'I have nothing to give you.' This was a very profound teaching. The Dalai Lama went on to say that life is a matter of the heart, a matter of living in a way that reflects our best intentions. I have many times heard the Dalai Lama play down his role as teacher. 'Just listen to me as a person giving information,' he is fond of saying, 'before you start to take it up as your own.'

The true teacher can be likened to a midwife who helps the student find his or her internal guru or inner truth. That's the promise of enlightenment. It's always a mistake to assume that the only way to walk the path is by copying everything our teaches do. I myself have seen the downfall of people imitating the teacher in everything, bad and good. Thus the followers of one great teacher who drank too much also drank too much, and the followers of the teacher who preached celibacy while philandering had students who did likewise. Authentic teachers and teachings should enhance your life, not control it.

I love the story about the king in ancient India who had the most renowned stables in the entire land. For years the king's horses had been cared for by one highly skilled master trainer, and the horses flourished. When this particular trainer grew old, he retired. The king told his courtiers to hire another fine trainer, which they did. The horses continued to look as beautiful and healthy as they had before, and they continued to carry the king's soldiers. But one by one, the horses all developed limps on their left sides. When the king noticed the horses limping, he didn't understand what was going wrong.

Up until that time, the king had never met the new trainer face to face. He therefore asked to have the trainer brought to the palace to discuss the problem. When the trainer walked into the room, the king understood everything – for the trainer was also limping on his left side.

Some of the best teachers have had students who were able to equal and even go beyond their masters. This can sometimes be tricky, but in the spiritual realm, teachers who can't accept and mentor the best students run the risk of reproducing their own weaknesses. It may be hard for any student to go beyond the fully enlightened perfect Buddha, but we will worry about that when it happens.

I think it's wise for seekers to carefully check out prospective teachers before committing themselves. The Dalai Lama has said, 'Why not learn from everyone as much as you can, wherever you can? Go and listen to ordinary instructors, taking what you find useful and leaving the rest. But if you're considering taking on a certain teacher as a guru, check them out meticulously for many years before signing your life away. Spy on them!'

This is wise advice from one of the best spiritual teachers in the world. It can save us a lot of heartache.

GUIDELINES ON WHAT TO EXPECT FROM A TEACHER

A good teacher is a blessing as well as a source of inspiration. Here's a list of some of the practical things a student can expect to receive from a spiritual teacher or guide:

- specific instruction in various practices such as meditation, visualization techniques, chanting, yoga, prayer, ritual music and dance, and contemplative arts.
- information on spiritual history, philosophy, epistemology, and logic
- empowerments and initiations
- guidance on walking a spiritual path, including answers to help clarify your questions and your doubts (The best teachers understand that sincere students are full of beans.)
- an ethical, compassionate, patient, and generous attitude
- help in working through spiritual breakthroughs, energy eruptions, dreams, visions, epiphanies, and mystical and religious experiences.
- wisdom and inspiration in helping you persevere through the ups, downs, and plateaus of the spiritual journey.

In ancient Buddhism there were often two separate and distinct kinds of teachers. One of them was called the 'acharya,' a term that was applied to masters who themselves were usually enlightened. The acharya stressed the essence of the teachings and practice. The second kind of teacher, known as the 'upadhyaya,' emphasized the various rules and rites that were part of the religious life of the time. Although these two distinct categories have become blended together over time, often we find even today that different teachers emphasize different approaches.

Is it too clichéd to say that the best teachers practice what they preach and live by the values they espouse? These men and women are able to set an example of how to integrate wisdom teachings into life. The best teachers embody and exemplify the truth of Dharma. They have more wisdom than just an encyclopedic knowledge of religious rules and scripture. The humility, generosity, and compassion of a genuine teacher resonates at a level we can barely comprehend and compels us to go further than we could possibly go on our own.

We learn from everything we do. All creatures can be our teachers. We also learn from everything that happens, good and bad. In fact sometimes our adversaries provide us with our most precious teachings.

Confucius once said, 'If you meet a noble man, try to equal him. When you see an evil one, examine yourself thoroughly.'

Sangha and the Gift of Spiritual Friendship

◆

The Buddha's faithful attendant Ananda once asked the Buddha:

Is it true that the sangha, the community of spiritual friends, is half of the holy life?

The Buddha replied, 'No, Ananda, the sangha community is the whole of the holy life.'

Seekers need spiritual friends. Even the awakened Buddha reached out to others who shared his priorities and interests. In fact, one of the first things the Buddha did in the days following his enlightenment was to go and find his friends so that he could share with them what he had learned. This small group became the first Buddhist 'sangha.'

'Sangha,' a Sanskrit word, is literally translated as 'group, congregation, or gathering.' The traditional notion of sangha describes a group or holy order of monks, nuns, and lay seekers coming together around spiritual teachers or practice. Later, sanghas came to be seen as groups that gathered together around one specific teacher or master. But these are very limited definitions that don't always work in the modern age when we are connected on so many different levels and form communities in so many various ways.

When I'm watching a show on television, for example, there may be a million or more people viewing it at the same time. If the program has a spiritual component, a million people can be sharing an experience that makes them temporary members of the same sangha or spiritual community. Sometimes I've turned on the television to see fund-raising on a large scale for some worthwhile group. It's amazing what human energy combined with goodwill can accomplish! These events create other kinds of temporary sanghas or fellowships of people who are trying to do spiritual work by helping others.

Many spiritual groups sponsor regular retreats. My own group, the Dzogchen Foundation, for example, has week-long retreats four times a year. The people who attend these retreats are members of a sangha community, even though we may not get together for months at a time. Any collection of people working to relieve suffering on this planet can be thought of as a sangha. Ecological groups would certainly fit into this category. At Brandeis, at Passover, we have started to have yearly Tibetan Buddhist-Jewish seders for about three hundred people. This is a sangha. The members of the peace movement around the globe belong to the same sangha. Twelve-step programs such as AA provide good examples of modern Western sanghas formed not around a leader, but as a circle.

The idea of spiritual community is hardly original with Buddhism. America was founded by religious groups whose members helped and supported each other. Focused spiritual energy is a powerful force capable of doing great things on a material as well as spiritual level. I love seeing pictures of the Amish farmers collectively raising barns. The idea of an entire community joining together to help one another is very moving.

There was a time, in this country at least, when we could take a sense of community a little bit for granted. Growing up, we walked to neighborhood schools, shopped in mom-and-pop stores, and attended local churches and temples, which were as much social centers as they were places of worship. We knew our neighbors, and we pretty much knew where we belonged. All that has changed of course. Today our children need transportation to get to school, we shop in large malls where nobody knows our name, and the doors of the local churches and temples are locked for much of the week. Our neighbors are often shadowy figures hurrying back and forth to work, and we are in dire need of a sense of belonging.

It's natural for people to want to spend time with others who share similar interests, goals, and problems. That's when sangha, the community of fellow seekers, can become our refuge.

WHERE DO WE FIND SANGHA OR SPIRITUAL COMMUNITY?

People often ask me how they can find a fellowship of spiritual friends. I typically respond by asking them to think about the people they consider kindred spirits. Whom do they want to be with as they walk the spiritual path?

If you were in Asia and wanted to find a traditional

Buddhist sangha, you would visit the nearest monastery. Here, you might start your search by looking in Buddhist magazines such as *Tricycle*. In the back you will find numerous listings of groups and monasteries. If you have access to the Internet, search for terms such as Buddhist, Tibetan, Zen, Vipassana, or Theravadin, and you will find a great deal of information. You could also search on the Net using www.dharma.net or by using the many links to other Buddhist websites from my own Dzogchen Foundation site – www.dzogchen.org. Visit the local spiritual bookstore, and read the bulletin board. Also, Shambhala Publications publishes a book called *The Complete Guide to Buddhist America*, by Don Morreale, which is chock full of information about various Buddhist groups.

If you want a less formal spiritual experience, visit the local spiritual bookstore and look at magazines like *Yoga Journal*, *New Age*, *Utne Reader*, and *Common Boundary*. Check out the bulletin board. Ask questions; you may find that you almost immediately become a member of a helpful sangha. If you want to start with some meditation classes, try the nearest New Age center, yoga center, YMCA, or health club. Your own Christian or Jewish center may be sponsoring classes in meditation that will help you connect with others who have similar spiritual interests. Senior centers around the country offer meditation, yoga, and tai-chi.

Because meditation is prescribed for physical ailments, many medical doctors and health professionals can turn into your personal sangha mentors by giving advice on how and where to start a meditation practice. Look into weekend retreats sponsored by groups such as the Omega Institute or Esalen. These can provide ways to meet people who share your interests and a simple way of easing into a meditation-based spiritual practice.

Other fellowship experiences can be found by joining the 12-step programs that are frequently sponsored by churches and community centers. Any religious congregation can provide a sense of sangha or spiritual community. My Quaker friends consistently tell me what an important role Quaker meetings play in their lives.

We can also create temporary sanghas in our own life by introducing a spiritual component to gatherings, holidays, and special celebrations. My friend Wendy, for example, is expecting a baby. When her friends were invited to a baby shower, they were asked to bring some written spiritual advice for the new mother to be. Some of her friends wrote down quotations or poems that they thought would be meaningful to Wendy; others wrote down some of their own feelings about parenting. In this way, Wendy's baby shower became a deeper and more meaningful event.

WHAT CAN A SEEKER EXPECT TO GET FROM SANGHA?

In Tibet it is said that only intrepid snow lions can go into the icy wilderness forest alone. Everyone else needs community. Here's why:

- ***Spiritual friendships help us maintain spiritual priorities.*** Maintaining spiritual priorities, day in and out, is not so easy.

'I'm tired this morning; I don't want to meditate.'

'It's cold outside. I don't want to be a compassionate person and drive Claudia home because it's raining. She can take a bus. Why do we both have to suffer?'

'Sure I care about the planet, but nobody else recycles. Why do I have to waste my time rinsing those cans and bottles?'

'What's wrong with a little attachment, a little greed every now and then?'

Turning toward the spirit and living a more spiritual life requires diligence, mindfulness, and care in everything we do. With every moment, every breath, every word, and every act, we have choices to make; these choices determine our quality of life and our karmic destiny. Spiritual friends remind us of what's important. They help us increase in virtue and loving and keep us on track.

- ***A spiritual community provides elders and mentors.*** It's supportive to be with people who have worked through some of the same problems you may be facing in your practice and your life. The advice they can give is sometimes theoretical, but more often it is practical, such as useful tips and hints on meditation postures, diet, and books to read. Fellow seekers are likely to be aware of lectures and events that are worth attending, as well as pilgrimages or eco-tours with spirited teachers. It's encouraging and inspiring to spend time with men and women who are further along on the spiritual path. We learn by their example and are buoyed up and carried along by their living presence in our lives.

- ***Spiritual sangha gives us a safe space to share our good intentions and tender hearts.*** A woman recently told me that she was embarrassed because she had loaned money to a friend who hadn't returned it. It made her feel foolish. She didn't even want to tell anybody about the loan because she was afraid they would think she had been naïve and gullible. In the world today, generosity can sometimes seem foolish.

  Let's face it, it's sometimes difficult to expose our vulnerable, tender hearts and our kindness and sensitivity. Within the safe sacred space that is sangha, we don't have to feel embarrassed about letting our feelings show. We don't have to worry that someone will make fun of our spiritual inclinations and our desire to do good. We are more likely to be accepted as we are, with all our personal hopes, fears, faults, and foibles. Sangha means community, common embrace, communion; it's a sanctuary, a safe place to let down our guard.

  Often an individual seeker will find that his or her aspirations for enlightenment are not very supported by society as a whole. Many seekers of various persuasions have told me that their nearest and dearest don't understand what they are doing or why. A sangha of like-minded spirits will support and reinforce your aspirations and commitment when obstacles and distractions might get in your way.

  I come from New York, where many people know the fine old Yiddish word 'mishpoche'; it's a word we use when we are talking about family or our nearest and dearest. I like to think of sangha as a spiritual mishpoche. When we're with the sangha, we know we're with family so we feel safe.

- ***Sangha surrounds us with sacred energy and blessings.*** People who meditate or pray with a group have experienced firsthand the beautiful energy that can envelop the room. It's palpable and real. Engaging in any spiritual practice with a group can be incredibly uplifting and inspiring.

  Some people need a minyan of ten for daily prayer. Some need an exercise partner or golf buddy to help overcome inertia and motivate them to 'get out there.' Everyone feels the joy of connecting to others in a common pursuit. That's why Jesus said, 'For where two or three are gathered in my name, I am there among them.' My personal feeling is that whenever I connect and truly commune with others, I connect and commune with that which is greater than any of us. This is simply spiritual logic.

Service to the Universal Sangha

◆

All God's critters got a place in the choir. Some sing low, some sing higher, some sing out loud on the telephone wire.

BILL STAINES

For the ultimate benefit of all beings without exception, throughout this and all my lifetimes, I dedicate myself to the practice and realization of enlightenment.

From *The Bodhisattva Vow*

When I asked my generous teachers how I could ever repay them, they said to pass it on. When the Buddha told his faithful servant Ananda that the sangha represented the whole of spiritual life, he was reminding Ananda that as inhabitants of this planet, we are all members of the interwoven single sangha of beings, for which Thich Nhat Hanh coined the term 'interbeing.'

A unique and essential feature of Mahayana Buddhism is the belief in the definite possibility of universal enlightenment. The highest ideal I've ever encountered is known among Buddhists as the Bodhisattva Vow. In traditional Buddhist sanghas, throughout the world, the members chant this vow every day:

> Sentient beings are numberless: I vow to liberate them.
> Delusions are inexhaustible: I vow to transcend them.
> Dharma teachings are boundless: I vow to master them.
> The Buddha's enlightened way is unsurpassable: I vow to embody it.

When we repeat this vow, making this commitment, we dedicate ourselves to seeing the bigger picture. We are not alone; we live in a world inhabited by innumerable fellow beings, all of whom want happiness as much as we do. The great Tibetan teacher in America, Chogyam Trungpa Rinpoche, once said that the basic vision of Mahayana Buddhism is to help people think bigger.

Finding practical ways of helping others helps us learn to extend real love, not just an I'll-love-you-if-you-love-me kind of love. This is how we grow spiritually. When the American boxer Muhammad Ali started his career, he was known as the arrogant-appearing Cassius Clay, who loved to rhyme and create poems about himself. As a young man, his slogan was 'I'm the greatest.' A few years ago, as an older and wiser man, Muhammad Ali was asked to give an extemporaneous poem. He said, 'Me, We.' Look at how tight and vast this is. Look at what these two words say. This is a real one-two punch that harms no one and elevates everyone. I say this is the greatest.

The intention to help others is an essential part of a

spiritual practice. Before his enlightenment, the Buddha said that he had spent five hundred previous lifetimes as a Bodhisattva, dedicating himself to the welfare and alleviation of suffering of all creatures in all possible worlds and the myriad dimensions of being. The Bodhisattva Vow reminds us that our intention to become wiser, less selfish, and more loving exists not only for the benefit of ourselves but for the benefit of all beings. We take the vow realizing that everyone has difficulties and confusion, but that each of us actually has the power to address the problem. We realize that it is possible to work for the alleviation of universal suffering. We all pretty much want and need the same things. We are just struggling in different ways.

As spiritual seekers, it's incumbent upon us to try to help others in this, our universal sangha, which is an inclusive circle of all beings. This is a participatory mandala. Every part is the center of the whole web of existence. How much you do to help the whole is up to you.

When we look at the sun, the greatest visible energy source in our world, we can feel the light rays reaching out and touching whatever is there. In the same way, the loving heart is naturally warm; it reaches out to the community at large. In this way we share our gifts and the treasure we have inherited.

The list of ways we can help is as big as our imagination and spirit; there are countless opportunities to serve and contribute. People sometimes tell me that they want to volunteer, but they don't know where to begin. There are some suggestions for how to get started in the Resources section at the back of the book.

Inner Work: Therapy and Dharma

◆

If we really want to live a full life, both the ancient tradition of Buddhism and the modern one of psychotherapy tell us that we must recover the capacity to feel. Avoiding emotions will only wall us off from our true selves – in fact, there can be no wholeness without an integration of feelings.

DR MARK EPSTEIN

At the base of Buddhist teachings rests the premise that when we know who we are, then we will be able to understand the universe. But we all need some help in knowing who we are. Sometimes we have trouble knowing what we feel; sometimes we have difficulty in seeing what we do. If we are indeed committed to self-knowledge as well as knowledge and understanding in general, it makes sense that we avail ourselves of any and all possible techniques and tools, ancient and modern.

I believe that we all have within us a spiritual thirst – a 'divine gene' that compels us to look ever deeper and wider for wisdom, love, understanding, satisfaction, and happiness. I also believe that it's foolish to say that there is only one way, one method, one answer that will work for everyone or indeed for all the countless dilemmas, contradictions, and crises that are part and parcel of our era. We all need more holistic and integrative solutions to our common and specific problems. Many seekers have found that integrating a meditation practice with therapy allows them to enjoy the benefits of a more holistic approach than either system or practice provides on its own.

Buddha Dharma and psychotherapy have a great deal in common. The principle purpose of Dharma is to alleviate suffering through wise attention and awareness, which in turn loosens our entangling attachments and fixations, thus awakening us from the bondage of illusion and delusion. This is enlightenment. Therapy's avowed purpose is to free us from conflict and suffering, to loosen our neuroses, and to help bring about self-acceptance and love. This is mental health.

Etymological definitions of the ancient word 'Dharma' include truth, teaching, wise counsel, universal law, and spiritual doctrine. An often overlooked derivation of the original meaning of the word 'Dharma' is 'that which heals.' I think it's fair to say that both Dharma and psychotherapy are healings of a broad and deep kind. There is, therefore, a huge overlap between these two Dharmas or teachings. Dharma practice and therapy both require 'inner work'; they both require honest self-observation and self-inquiry. Ideally the two practices complement and augment each other in helping the seeker find balance, fulfillment, serenity, and meaning.

Because I am a lama and teacher, people come to me with their personal problems every day. Often I feel that these problems would be better addressed in depth over a period of time with a psychotherapist or counselor. I myself started seeing a therapist when I was in my forties. I did this in order to explore some inter-personal and emotional issues that had not been entirely resolved through my meditation training. I believe that I have gotten a lot of insight, self-acceptance, and freedom from therapy.

This is not to negate the benefits of a meditation practice. I see therapy and Dharma to be completely complementary and mutually supportive. Buddhism has always been seen as a deep psychology and an ethical philosophy as much as a religion. In fact, one-third of traditional Buddhism is the 'Abhidharma' (collection of special teachings on Buddhist psychology). The Abhidharma is one of the three original 'baskets,' or collections, of classical Buddhist canonical teaching, known as the 'Tripitika.' The Abhidharma includes elaborate detailed analyses of the multitude of states of mind, of the various emotions, the nature of mind and reality, and the dimensions and dynamics of consciousness.

Modern Buddhism today is more psychologically astute and insight-oriented than ever. We understand that meditation is far more than watching the navel or the breath, or repeating a mantra, or calming and quieting the mind. It also includes analytical exercises and introspective inquiries into the very nature of mind and identity. Buddhist practice can abound with rich symbols and detailed visualizations that help unlock the subconscious and open the unconscious to our investigating gaze. Even so, it sometimes takes the reflective, nonjudgmental wisdom of an experienced therapist to help a seeker work through the labyrinth of his or her questions and under-the-surface personal issues to 'see' what needs to be seen. This can help free us from the past and liberate us into the natural perfection of the here and now.

Some traditional authorities may disagree with this approach. I have known Asian Buddhist hierarchs, learned and spiritually accomplished, who in their compassionate wish to help their Western students told them, and I quote, 'Don't go into therapy. Better tell it to a stone or a tree!' or 'Therapy? That is "samsara," worldly business. Better to meditate and donate your money to monasteries and meditation centers so you accumulate merits for better rebirths in future lives.'

Somehow this approach reminds me of being told not to consult with medical doctors when we are ill, but instead to just rely on the power of prayer. I think it's important that we not be naïve about spiritual matters. The fact is that for most of us, the alleviation of suffering and removal of confusion is paramount. If something works, we can utilize it. The Buddha himself, when advising his followers about how to judge situations in their daily lives, said that the criteria to use was whether something was both good and wholesome. He said that when judging things, we should trust our own experience. Let none of us forget that Buddhism is at heart a practical teaching for here and now.

I believe that psychotherapy in the hands of an able therapist provides a new Dharma-like teaching that can help anyone to better understand his or her life and experience. Buddha Dharma has many teachings that address habitual self-destructive patterns, and yet often individuals can't unlock the psychological construction that holds these patterns in place without guidance and help. This is where good therapeutic treatment comes into play. A skilled therapist helps people explore the mind and psyche and in so doing helps the client or patient attain deeper knowledge and self-acceptance.

I should also say that I am acutely aware that in some quarters, spirituality and therapy are seen to be at odds. On the one hand, some inadequately informed spiritual teachers would have us believe that psychology and psychoanalysis are merely head games and fail to touch the deeper dimensions of the soul. Some psychologists and psychoanalysts, on the other hand, might tell us that seekers are merely using spiritual practice as a way of avoiding or denying their problems. Some among the devoutly religious tell me that psychology only concerns this world and this life, while spirituality goes far beyond. I think this is not clearly an either/or situation; ideally those of us who want to reach deeper and understand more about ourselves should be able to skillfully merge the two approaches, recognizing the strength and limitations of both, similar to a more evolved modern understanding of science and religion.

Much of the perceived conflict between spirituality and therapy revolves around a misunderstanding of the role of ego in our lives. It has erroneously been believed by Westerners new to Buddhist thought that the purpose of Dharma practice is the annihilation of ego or sense of self. The oft-stated goal of therapy, on the other hand, is to strengthen self-esteem and heal the ego. In fact, one needs a healthy sense of self in order to progress in spiritual practice. Meditation practice is not usually helpful for people who have not matured and grown up sufficiently to have an individual adult ego; meditation can sometimes even be counterproductive for people suffering from problems such as manic depression or extreme anxiety.

Psychologist and meditation teacher Jack Engler of

the Harvard Medical School perhaps states it best in his well-known essay 'Becoming Somebody and Nobody; Psychoanalysis and Buddhism.' In it, he says:

'One has to be somebody before one can be nobody . . . The attempt to bypass the developmental tasks of identity formation and object constancy through a misguided spiritual attempt to 'annihilate the ego' has fateful and pathological consequences . . . What is needed and what has been missing from both clinical and meditative perspectives is a developmental psychology that includes the full developmental spectrum . . . Both a sense of self and a sense of no-self – in that order – seem to be necessary to realize that state of optimal psychological well-being that Freud once described as an "ideal fiction" and the Buddha long before described as "the end of suffering" and the one thing he taught.'

In short, for all of us, some sense of mature identity (self) has to be established before spiritual practice can work its many benefits. Responsible spiritual teachers recognize that it is entirely possible for seekers to use spiritual practice as a way of avoiding emotional difficulties. In this way we sometimes see introverts use the time taken up by meditation as a rationale for introverted patterns. Recluses do sometimes become more reclusive in the name of practice; dropouts can avoid the world in the name of renunciation; control freaks can become more controlling in the name of mindfulness; the narrowminded and dogmatic can become more so in the name of tradition and purity; even the ambitious and competitive can play out their patterns in the hierarchy of the spiritual or religious group. The ego can claim anything as its own, including spiritual practice; thus materialists transfer their worldliness into the

Dharma and become spiritual materialists, yet still acquisitive, competitive, proud, and so forth.

Spiritual teachings consistently tell us not to lose our basic common sense or to kid ourselves about what we are doing. Balance is the name of the game in all things. Honesty is its method. Integrity is the result. A sound therapist can help us stay honest with ourselves about what we are doing. Spiritual practice should help us better understand reality, not avoid it; spiritual practice should help us lead balanced lives. Ethical education and values along with mind training and contemplative exercises help us develop character and cultivate our ultimate potential.

THERAPY AND A LOVING HEART

Therapy can also help each of us heal. After all, the primary purpose of spiritual practice is to be able to live and love with a more free and open heart. Well, the truth is that many of us have had life experiences that have made us close down. Life isn't always easy; we don't always get the love and nurturing we need. We don't always have the material, physical, and emotional security we would like. It's hard to feel love, if the primary emotions we experience are anger, sadness, or anxiety. When we are wrapped up in ourselves and our own difficulties, as a protective reaction, we inadvertently cut ourselves off from the sources of love and goodness. We may know that the love is there buried in our hearts, but being able to access it can be a challenge. Students often ask me, for example, about ways of handling the anger and negativity they feel. They want to know how to soften the armor that surrounds their hearts. They ask how to disarm the violence in themselves as well as around themselves.

Meditators often find that the meditation experience brings up a whole range of emotions from their past; some of these are disturbing; some are liberating. In these instances, a teacher can help; a sangha or even one spiritual friend with a sympathetic ear can also help. So can a therapist who will probably be able to devote more time to helping the seeker further face, explore, and understand these feelings.

A therapeutic situation can help us deal with all the chiaroscuros of varied emotions ranging from anger and jealousy to fear, guilt, and confusion. This sort of inner self-inquiry can help us become more authentic and true to who we are and what we want. The Buddha told his followers to feel their feelings. Therapy can help us do just that. People sometimes misunderstand Buddhist teachings and believe that we should all emerge or merge into one great homogenized passive zombie-like state. Buddhism talks about equanimity, but that doesn't mean complacency or indifference. Pacifism is not passive at all; it is dynamic spiritual activism, compassion in action.

A Zen master once said that we should practice with 'eyes of ice and hearts afire.' He meant that we should be both clear seeing and warmhearted. We aspire to emotional maturity, spiritual maturity, and psychological maturity. We need to develop all three.

I personally also like to suggest therapy for seekers who want a more well-rounded and grounded approach to life because it can become too easy for some to be so devoted to the spiritual path that they fail to function adequately in the world. Our goal of clear-seeing really is better served by being able to integrate the entire spectrum of experience instead of just living in one narrow corner of life. That's why I always say, man cannot live by Dharma alone. And take my word for it, I've tried!

CHOOSING A THERAPEUTIC SITUATION

Often the biggest question seekers face is how to find a style of therapy that complements spiritual practice. It goes without saying that it's counterproductive to try to do inner work with anyone who doesn't understand your personal or spiritual aspirations. In the past, I have personally known several people who were encouraged by therapists to give up on prayer or meditation. Yet today we are fortunate in having many therapists who are themselves interested in spiritual matters. There is a whole school, in fact, called transpersonal psychology, which specifically attempts to integrate the spiritual with the psychological. Jungians are another group that has always integrated the spiritual and the psychological.

Appropriately prescribed pharmaceutical psychotherapy and drug treatment is a new and interesting field of exploration along this frontier. People from all walks of life are using new treatments to find equilibrium, serenity, and balance under the care of skilled doctors, psychiatrists, and therapists. Personal experience and modern horse sense indicates that for each of us there may very well be unconscious and karmic forces that are limiting our development. In many instances, new scientific or ancient alternative treatments and therapies may very well contribute to the sense of wholeness and transformation that we all seek.

Therapists, counselors, and social workers are best found by asking for a referral from someone you trust. If you are a member of a sangha, church, or temple, they might have a list of people whom they recommend. Your doctor would certainly have some referrals; so might your university or college if you are a student. A local hospital might also have a list that you can use to get started on researching a therapeutic situation that will work for you. No one therapist or counselor is going to work for everyone. So don't be afraid to shop around until you find a therapeutic situation that fulfills your requirements.

Many have financial concerns that can make regular therapy difficult. There are a wide variety of less expensive alternatives. Don't be afraid to ask. Many therapists can refer you to someone less expensive; some may have a sliding scale or they might be willing to work out a suitable payment plan. Another less expensive way of getting the benefits of therapy is group therapy. Even a men's or women's support group can be very helpful. Again, you have to be the one to seek help and support. If you really can't afford therapy, another way of getting support is through one of the various 12-step programs, which are based on the twelve steps of recovery as formulated by the original 12-step program, Alcoholics Anonymous. Some of these include:

> Co-dependents Anonymous – for men and women who find themselves acting out unfulfilling, needy relationship patterns that have a basis in dysfunctional family backgrounds

Alcoholics Anonymous – for those who have substance abuse problems

Adult Children of Alcoholics – for those who grew up in alcoholic or otherwise dysfunctional households

Al-Anon – for friends and families of those with substance abuse problems

Gamblers Anonymous – for those who handle their money in such a way that they are always living on the edge

Programs such as these exist throughout the United States. They often take place in churches or synagogues. Make a few phone calls, look at the announcements in your local paper, and look at notice boards in churches and temples.

I consider the 12-step programs, which are spiritually based and nondenominational, an indispensable part of our homegrown, organic, made-in-America Dharma. They have worked wonders for countless people. Twelve-step meetings are everywhere today. So, as they might advise, 'Let go and let God' . . . or Buddha help you. The first step for all of us is always acknowledging that we have a problem.

No great inner event befalls those who summon it not.

MAURICE MAETERLINCK

Yoga

◆

Yoga is that which stills the mind.
PATANJALI

The word 'yoga' means union, or reunion with the ultimate sacred energy source. It's a way of reconnecting the material with the spiritual, the seen with the unseen. Therefore, yoga is really any training that helps us transcend ego attachment and connect to our innate pure spiritual energy.

Yoga, as both concept and training, is thousands of years old. During his lifetime, the Buddha was considered a yogi, as were the fellow seekers and ascetics he first met when he started on the spiritual path. In fact, in the larger sense, anyone who is trying to connect with the divine can legitimately be called a yogi. Yogi means spiritual practitioner; the emphasis is on practice, not theory or belief.

The classic ancient treatise on yoga, known as the Yoga Sutra, is attributed to a sage named Patanjali who lived in northern India more than two thousand years ago. Patanjali outlines eight specific principles, each of which is a yogic practice intended to help the seeker reunite with the divine. They are: (1) ethical behavior; (2) discipline; (3) bodily postures; (4) breath control; (5)

withdrawal of the senses; (6) concentration; (7) meditation (8) ecstatic absorption.

Here in the West, the word 'yoga' seems to have become synonymous with 'hatha yoga,' a physical training designed to cleanse, purify, and stabilize the body. But yoga, properly defined, encompasses many different paths and styles of practice all directed toward (re)union with the divine. When we, for example, practice (a path of) good works and compassion in action, it is said to be 'karma yoga,' or union through selfless action. When we focus on honesty, truth, investigation of reality, intellect, and self-realization, we are following the path of wisdom known as 'jnana yoga.' A path devoted to devotional love is known as 'bhakti yoga.' And when we recite, chant, or silently say a mantra, we are following the path of sacred sound known as 'japa practice,' or 'mantra yoga.'

Yoga has always emphasized the mind-body-spirit connection. Now that Westerners are beginning to understand the wisdom in this kind of integrated, holistic thinking, hatha yoga is enjoying a well-deserved surge in popularity. I recently spoke to a couple who are both in their mid-fifties. About a year ago, on a whim, they started taking yoga classes together. Neither of them had ever done anything like this before. They now say they are completely hooked and take from two to four classes a week, saying they feel so much better as a result of the yoga that they would not be without it. Around the world, almost everyone – young and old – gives hatha yoga the same kind of endorsement. It's fun, it's relaxing, and it's good for us. And yes, it's spiritual. You can learn yoga at an ashram, health club, weekend yoga retreat, or at the local Y. There are magazines, books, videos, and websites dedicated to teaching Westerners more about yoga.

In hatha yoga, breath control and various physical postures ('asanas') are used to balance the seven energy or power centers of the body known as chakras. This is done in order to awaken the body's central energy source, known as 'kundalini' or the 'coiled serpent.' Unawakened kundalini energy is said to remain dormant at the body's first chakra like a coiled-up spring or snake. The practice of yoga awakens and channels this energy up through the various chakras until it reaches its highest center, in the crown chakra found above the very top of the head.

The first chakra in the body, where kundalini resides at rest, is located at the very base of the spinal column. This chakra is drawn as a four-petaled lotus. This energy vortex forms the basis of our survival instinct – our fight-or-flight response – as well as fear and aggression.

The second chakra, found at the genitals, is depicted as a lotus with six petals. It is the seat of sexual energy, reproductive forces, and other forms of sensual gratification and nurturance.

The third chakra, which is situated below and behind the navel, is frequently imaged as a whirling lotus with ten petals. This is the power and ego center from which mastery can be derived.

The fourth chakra is the heart chakra, sometimes called the heart lotus; this is the center of compassion and love. It is usually seen as a blue lotus with twelve petals.

The fifth chakra, which is found at the throat, has sixteen petals. Our longing for higher ideals, vision, and magical creativity stem from this transcendental center.

The sixth chakra, sometimes called the 'third eye,' is located behind the forehead between the eyebrows and up about an inch. Pictures of this energy center show only two petals. This is the wisdom center. The third eye represents unitary vision, bringing together and resolving the dualistic, divisive vision of our two normal eyes.

The seventh chakra, and topmost energy center, is found at the very top or crown of the head. It is frequently depicted as a thousand flowerlike petals resting flat above the top of the head. This is the center of cosmic union or enlightenment. When one reaches full awakening, this chakra blossoms and is activated, like a starburst. To me it looks like a fountain pouring downward over the head.

The yogic image is of the serpentlike power of kundalini raising up and pulsating through the energy channels of the body until it finally results in energy blossoming out of the seventh chakra and raining down all over the practitioner, filling him or her with a sense of life, light, completeness, and pure goodness. The energy then is recycled back into the body to be used again and again, an inexhaustible, pure source. When you tap into this cosmic source, blessings, energy, bliss, and joyous wisdom course through you.

I attended my first yoga class in Buffalo when I was still a college student. I approached this yoga class with some reservations. For someone into team sports, the idea of yoga seemed almost un-American. I quickly figured out that while yoga wasn't baseball, it also wasn't quite ballet. Finally I decided that is wasn't any less macho than the dance classes that all the boys had to attend back in the sixth grade. In fact, it was challenging, relaxing, and interesting in an incomprehensible sort of way.

Within a couple of classes, however, I discovered that yoga made me feel better than calisthenics or weight lifting. The only other exercise that I have ever found comparable is swimming, which is also well-rounded and relaxing as well as physically beneficial. As I began to do the postures and breath work associated with yoga, I found that, without any conceptual theology, I was becoming more centered and spiritual, more in touch with the sacred dimensions of both life and myself. It was extraordinarily experiential.

These feelings encouraged me to begin experimenting with and understanding more about the various yogic dietary suggestions as well. I began to see the value of eating light foods – fruit, vegetables, nuts, tofu, and yogurt. I became more sensitive to caffeine and sugar, all of which seemed to artificially buzz me up and then blindingly weigh me down. There is no question that yoga practice was helping me enter more fully into the present moment. I began to love it and even started doing it on my own, practicing in the sunny yard and on beaches, with girlfriends, and so on until yoga became part of my life. It would only take a few minutes, long enough for a couple of breaths and centering exercises, for me to connect with and directly contact that sacred dimension I had begun to visit more freely.

When I got to India in 1971 after graduating from college, yogis, of course, were everywhere. I stayed at an ashram in Rishikish on the Ganges River, and learned the system taught today by Swami Satchidananda through his Integral Yoga Institute. Then I went on a yoga retreat to an ashram near Benares. When I think about these halcyon days of my youth, the memory that comes up is one of learning yoga from my teacher in the sun early every morning along the banks of the Ganges.

From the outside looking in at a yoga class, it appears to be just a bunch of people stretching their bodies in an attempt to stay fit. And yoga can certainly serve such a purpose. In its essence, however, it is a much richer and sophisticated practice. Postures, breathing, and visualization all work together to balance and harmonize your energy and bring it into the central energy channel. Yoga helps align the skeleton and musculature, as well as stimulate internal organs in a way that can improve health and a sense of well-being. It smoothes our rough edges, extends and opens our breathing; it releases the energy knots in the psychic channel and energy pathways within our subtle body-mind complex. It helps iron us out.

Anyone interested in meditation would be well served by taking yoga classes, which can provide an excellent prelude to meditation. Most yoga classes end with a posture known as the corpse pose. In this posture you lie on your back and first tense and then totally relax your muscles until you are so relaxed that you feel as though you are one with the earth. After this pose, it's a great time for meditation. In fact, yoga is meditation from beginning to end. And meditation is a principal form of yoga.

In India, practitioners spend years practicing various forms of yoga in order to purify and free the mind, body, and soul. They do this through the use of visualization, diet, fasting, body movement and postures, chanting, prayer, meditation, and other purification practices. And many claims have been made for yoga. Yoga is said to increase longevity, vitality, sexual prowess, memory, mental activity, and health. Some of this is verifiable. In fact, studies have been done at respected medical institutions that show that some yogic practitioners are able to slow down their metabolism and heartbeat as well as alter their body temperature. This can significantly affect states of consciousness and encourage healing as well.

Many other supernormal claims have been made about the extraordinarily well trained yogis of Asia, who are known as 'fakirs.' Some have been said to be able to levitate, or to appear in two or more different places at the same time; others walk on hot coals without burning their feet or step on beds of thorns or nails. Some can certainly meditate for weeks at a time, going without food or water. I have witnessed it. One of the legends of Tibet revolves around Tibetan yogis of old, who were said to be capable of fast-walking dozens of miles each day while moving with such speed that their legs were literally so far above the ground that they appeared to be flying. Alexandra David-Neel, a French explorer who travelled in Tibet extensively at the turn of the twentieth century, said that she personally witnessed such fast-walking yogis perform their energy practice. In Tibet this is called 'Lung Gom' (Breath-Energy Meditation) or 'Fast Feet.'

There are, of course, also many examples of yogis who have been less than pure-hearted in their attempts to impress the impressionable, causing doubt to arise in many, sometimes when it's not deserved. Even today we have Sai Baba who has appeared on film pulling things out of the air and pouring holy ash out of empty clay pots. Many believe in him; others say he is a more accomplished sleight-of-hand artist than he is a yogi. Who knows?

Seekers are frequently warned about the extremes of yogic excess, for which some Indian fakirs have been famous. I once heard a story about a yogi who was able to slow his metabolism and his heartbeat down so much that people wondered if he was still alive. But a lama who passed by was less than impressed. 'Continue that way,' he said, 'and your metabolism will be so slow that you will be reborn as a great sluggish subterranean serpent.' The moral of this story is to remind us not to confuse the forms of practice with their transcendental purpose and essence.

The appropriate way to practice yoga, on any level, is to keep in mind your higher spiritual purpose. I know for a fact that it is possible for someone to use yogic practices in such a way that he or she is capable of performing amazing feats. But without a spiritual grounding, this is a fairly meaningless exercise. We are striving to cultivate spiritual depth, not perform carnival sideshow stunts. It's about the true miracle of enlightenment – psychic powers are merely special effects. Let's attend the real show.

The great state of yoga
is experienced
in that mind which has ceased
to identify itself
with its fluctuating waves of perception.
When this happens, the seer is revealed
resting in its own essential nature
and one realizes the true self.

From *The Yoga Sutra* by PATANJALI

The Yoga of Bowing

◆

The Buddha realized his great awakening while sitting in meditation under the Bodhi Tree at Bodh Gaya, India. At that moment, as the morning star rose in the heavens, the entire natural world bowed to the Buddha. According to the sutras, the earth trembled; trees, flowers, and even the tall blades of elephant grass bent down in respect.

A soft rain fell lightly from a cloudless sky, while fragrant breezes blew gently upon the Buddha's radiant countenance. Flowers and fresh fruit fell from the nearby trees, and lotus blossoms fell from the sky itself, dropped from the devas and angels like a cloud of blessings. The Buddha's fingers formed a 'mudra' (gesture) and with his right hand, he touched the earth, taking it as his witness. Morning came. The Buddha arose, fully awakened, as the Enlightened One.

Bowing reflects the essence of simplicity. We can all do it. In fact, many of us do it all over the world. In the 'old countries' of the East, bowing is the traditional way of greeting and parting. Instead of shaking hands, curtsying, hugging, or kissing cheeks, people bow and reach out to each other in this simple and beautiful gesture of mutual respect and reverence.

In India, they bow to each other and say, 'Namaste,' meaning 'I revere the light within you.' In Tibet, we bow and say, 'Tashi-delay,' which means excellent luck and auspicious fortune. In China and Japan too, there is a lot of bowing. When I lived in Kyoto, Japan, in the early Seventies, I was amazed at the lengths to which people go in terms of bowing. Even today at modern steel-and-glass airports, you see people bowing. Dressed in business suits, rushing to and fro with laptops, suitcases, carry-on bags, and cameras, they still take the time to bow, often whispering words of farewell – thank you, good-bye, be well. It's a wonderful sight. People going through the metal detectors at the security checkpoint bow to the checker, who bows back. Sometimes they continue this for minutes, each bow a little deeper than the one before.

Whenever we Buddhists enter or leave a sacred space such as a meditation room, temple, shrine, or Zen garden, we bow. This is very similar to Roman Catholics who kneel whenever they approach the altar, or Jews, who cover their heads before entering a synagogue, lowering oneself before God and acknowledging that there is something above them.

In some countries, like Burma, Thailand, and Tibet, bowing has become an intense spiritual practice. Practitioners don't just bow, they get down on their knees and then lower themselves face down and flat on the floor, in a full bow, called a prostration. We put our palms gently together and press them to the forehead, throat, and heart chakras. This gesture represents going for refuge to the three jewels of Buddha, Dharma, and Sangha – with body, speech, and mind. Bowing, we then lower ourselves to our knees; and with our hands placed near our ears almost as if we are doing a push-up, we prostrate ourselves until the entire body, forehead, and heart touch the ground. The hands and arms by now are outstretched directly in front of the body and also pressing into the ground. Sometimes the hands are placed palms up in a receiving gesture, ready to receive blessings. This position symbolizes yielding as well as taking refuge and offering respect. The practitioner is symbolically showing trust and surrender by putting him- or herself into such a powerless, vulnerable position. The hands, knees, and head touch the ground – five physical points symbolizing the five elements. It is another example of the mandala principle of wholeness – the microcosm (your body) returning to the macrocosm, as represented by the earth; the finite rejoining the infinite, from which it has never really been apart.

Prostrations such as these are an important part of the most common foundational practices of Tibetan Buddhism. Over the course of a few months, the new practitioner is expected to complete 111,000 of these full-body prostrations along with refuge prayers as part of these preliminary practices. This practice of bowing and taking refuge continues throughout the practitioner's life.

In Tibet we make many small bows as well, palms clasped together, bending gently at the waist. We do this three times when we enter a shrine or come into a master's presence. These little bows are also offered daily to parents, friends, and the environment whenever it feels appropriate. In Zen temples, one bows when entering or leaving; I follow a similar custom by bowing whenever I enter sacred space, including my meditation room. When I go to our Buddhist center in Cambridge for our weekly meditation group, I walk in and offer bows. If I go into my meditation garden near the stone Buddha statue, the first thing I do is bow.

I'm sure we've all seen photographs of the Dalai Lama putting his hands to his chest and bowing, often to the people who have come to hear him speak. Such a bow is not an empty gesture, but a yoga-like practice with many levels of meaning. It's a way of being, and a way of giving, of offering up oneself. In Buddhism we are taught to clasp our palms together and bow to all beings, seen and unseen. In this way, we show our intention to cherish and respect all forms of life. This is a vital spiritual principle.

I have a Tibetan lama friend who had polio as a child in India. Because he can't kneel down, he simply puts his hands to his chest, palms together, and bows in his mind. He assures me that one can even do Tibetan yoga in one's mind, through visualization as well as the use of breath and energy practices, since the mind is where it really must take place anyway. Such sincere purity of heart reflects the ultimate principle, any way you look at it.

I didn't always enjoy bowing as much as I do now. For the first few years that I lived in India and the Himalayas, bowing instead of shaking hands wasn't a problem for me, but the idea of prostrating myself before a shrine, temple, or even a master was anathema. It was so foreign to how I was brought up! 'I won't lower myself to anyone,' I thought, full of youthful arrogance. Eventually I got over this initial hesitation, and began to see bowing as the profound and beautiful practice it is.

Now I often think of bowing as an elegant traffic

signal of the body and mind. It says, 'Slow down, yield, meditation zone ahead. Quiet. Stop. Drop your ego.' Bowing is a mindfulness practice. When we walk into a meditation center or sacred space, bowing is a way of removing our mental and emotional armor, and any other ego baggage we may be carrying.

Even Westerners can become comfortable with bowing. For me, it's a little like taking off your hard boots or shoes when you enter the house and putting on a pair of soft, comfortable slippers. It's a centering practice that reminds us to divest ourselves of the more worldly personas that we carry with us as we walk around playing out our roles in the world. When we bow, we lower our guard and surrender to our spiritual nature.

Placing ourselves closer to the earth, as we do when we bow, reminds us to get closer to our own ground of being. We lower ourselves before the infinite mystery, the unknowable infinite universe. As the grass and trees of the forest did upon the Buddha's enlightenment, we too bow to the radiant Buddha-nature – the natural luminosity – within all beings. All creatures are our teachers. The earth is like an altar, and we are the gods and goddesses on it.

I bow to that. To that in you.

Fasting and Simplicity

◆

There's hidden sweetness in the stomach's emptiness.
We are lutes, no more, no less. If the soundbox
is stuffed full of anything, no music.
If the brain and the belly are burning clean
with fasting, every moment a new song comes out of the fire.

RUMI, Sufi teacher and poet, 1207–1273

Question: In your house, which door gets opened and closed with the greatest frequency?

Answer: The refrigerator door.

Fasting is not just about giving up food. Done properly in moderation, spiritual fasting will:

- help us understand more about our habits, desires, appetites, and attachments – how they work as well as how to loosen them.
- put us more closely in touch with the inner fullness and contentment that is our radiant spiritual core.
- increase awareness, mindfulness, and restraint.

The ancient practice of fasting, which is tied to the concept of renunciation and letting go, helps us introduce greater simplicity into our lives. Holy men and women have always intuitively understood that sometimes the best way to fill oneself with spiritual purpose is to empty oneself of everything else. The Buddha fasted, as did other spiritual seekers of his time. Even today, many Christians fast during the season of Lent.

My Muslim friends fast yearly during Ramadan, which is the ninth month of the Islamic calendar. For thirty days, nothing – no water or food – passes through a religious Muslim's lips from sunrise until sunset. During the daylight hours of Ramadan, Muslims also refrain from smoking and sex. Each night, the fast is broken with prayer and a meal. According to the Koran, Muslims can eat or drink while it is dark – 'until you can plainly distinguish a white thread from a black thread by the daylight; then keep the fast until night.' This definition of night and day, by the way, is very similar to one found in the ancient Buddhist tradition where we are told that night begins when we can no longer see the lines on the palms of our hands.

Fasting has always played an essential role in Judaism. Moses fasted forty days and forty nights before he came down from Mt Sinai with the Ten Commandments. And although the once-a-year Yom Kippur fast was the first fast commanded to Israel, there are other important fasting days in the religious calendar. Jewish traditions call for fasting at other times as well – by the bride and bridegroom immediately preceding the wedding, or after bad dreams as a way of clearing out the psyche. In Judaism, there are also days of celebration on which fasting is forbidden, and there are several ancient works that carefully delineate times when one should and shouldn't fast.

When I was growing up, my whole family would give up food for one day a year on Yom Kippur, the Holy Day of Atonement. I remember being told that all those who fast and atone for their sins on Yom Kippur would have their names inscribed into the divine Book of Life. It amuses me now, after all the disciplines I've practiced over the years, to remember how difficult it was to fast for just that one day. Once sundown came, my teenage friends and I would rush out of the synagogue and into a reception room in order to guzzle down fruit juice to break our fast. We would then go home with our parents for a late dinner.

The classic New Testament story of Jesus' fasting is told in the book of Matthew:

'Then Jesus was led up by the Spirit into the wilderness to be tempted by the devil. He fasted forty days and forty nights, and afterwards he was hungry. And the tempter came and said to him, "If you are the Son of God, command these stones to become loaves of bread." But He answered, "It is written, Man does not live by bread alone."'

That's sort of the point of fasting, isn't it? Fasting is another way of reminding ourselves that there is more to life than creature comforts and satisfying our appetites. When we fast, we are better able to focus on our spiritual values and priorities. We are often so full of ourselves that there is little room for anything else. As we empty our bodies of food, we become more sensitive and attuned to the bigger picture. Spiritual fasting helps us:

- practice a dietary discipline that will bring more consciousness into what goes in and out of our lives, as well as our mouths.
- detox and cleanse ourselves spiritually and emotionally as well as physically.
- center and rebalance.
- slow down and simplify.
- access our natural state, unadulterated by addiction.
- loosen some of our attachments and dependencies.
- empty ourselves of extraneous worldly values and become more open and sensitive to healing.
- become more sensitive to the spiritual dimension and more open to enlightenment experience.
- become more conscious of our innate luminosity.
- develop compassion and empathy for hungry ghosts, spirits, and addicts.

As we lead our lives, we will all inevitably go through soul-numbing moments, big and small. Too many of life's experiences are hurtful, frustrating, and annoying. These experiences can make us feel empty – emotionally hungry and needy. It's easy to get into the habit of responding to negative feelings by reaching for something that tastes good. I know I've done this. Haven't you?

Some experts say that women are most likely to reach for sweets – chocolate, ice cream, or cookies – and that men just concentrate on the fat – hot dogs, well-marbled steaks, potato chips. Recreational eating and drinking are favored activities here in the West. Small wonder so many of us treat chocolate or liquor as the preferred antidotes for every little mood swing. We use food and drink as a way of insulating ourselves from our feelings. We use food as a way of satisfying a variety of subtle underlying hungers.

Each time I fast I am also reminded of how much time and energy is taken up buying, preparing, and eating food, not to mention the time we spend thinking about food. We spend hours obsessing about what to eat and how to resolve our weight issues; then we spend even more time regretting our overindulgence.

Fasting, even for a few days, can make everything suddenly seem more vivid. Our senses seem to come alive; we can better taste and savor all of life, not just what we eat. Men and women who fast often say that they feel as though the doors to perception have been cleansed.

While on retreat in the vineyard regions of southern France. I once went on a grape fast. The red grapes were sweet, wonderful, and plentiful. When the fast was over, I remember noticing how the sky itself seemed so much brighter; even the air seemed sweeter and filled with energy. Another time I spent several days fasting and chanting on Mount Koya in a small temple in one of Japan's most ancient Tantric graveyards, close to where the great Zen master Kobo Daishi is interred in a cave. After completing the fast, as I was walking down the hill I saw a field of flowers. Looking into their little pink and yellow faces, it seemed as though every one of them was like a divine little universe. It looked like a glorious Buddha-field filled with mandalas of cosmic holographic design, each individually painted and embroidered on this holy mountain, near this ancient temple. Even today I only have to close my eyes to see them in my mind's eye, and almost smell them.

Fasting is a spiritual practice. It is meant to help seekers gain discipline and stay focused on the bigger picture. It's a way of learning how to refrain from excess. Completing a fast gives us a sense of mastery over the senses. We see that we don't have to be led around by our obsessions and worldly concerns.

A well-known Buddhist symbol is that of the Hungry Ghost. Hungry Ghosts are imaged as beings with enormous bellies, thin pipe cleaner-like necks, and insatiable appetites. Their physiology makes it impossible for them to be satisfied; they can never get enough down their skinny necks to satisfy their swollen stomachs. Hungry Ghosts symbolize greed as well as the hellish existence of anyone with cravings and desires that are out of control. The Hungry Ghost personifies addiction in all its forms.

There is, of course, a little bit of a Hungry Ghost buried in each of us; when this dissatisfied ghost emerges, it can take over. And it isn't just about food. Think of all the obsessions and activities that threaten to consume your life. If you can't get off the 'web' or stop playing computer solitaire, that's your Hungry Ghost. If you regularly shop for clothing you don't need, go through romantic partners like cannon fodder, can't stop working, need constant stimulation, or crave constant attention, these are all more examples of ghostly hunger. You get the picture.

Fasting is a regular practice in Tibetan monasteries. There are frequent day-and-a-half fasts on the full and new moon starting in the evening – from Friday night to Sunday morning, for example. Often these fasts are accompanied by a practice intended to purify the karma of Hungry Ghosts and all other beings who suffer from an overweening need for nourishment. In this practice, the fasting monks and nuns visualize radiating light rays that are powerful enough to satisfy the true desires of those who hunger and thirst, and thus offer their prayers to help their misery.

These monthly fasts reach back to antiquity and are among the most common purification practices in Himalayan Buddhism. The tradition originated with a great enlightened Indian Buddhist nun, known as Abbess Palmo, who is said to have cured herself of leprosy through long fasting and other purification practices related to Avalokitesvara, the Buddha of Love and Compassion. During her lifetime, Abbess Palmo had a vision of the Buddha of Love and Compassion feeding Hungry Ghosts and, in this way, fulfilling their needs and liberating them from addictive karma. Following this vision, she started doing this visualization practice on the full and new moon of each month; these lunar times are believed to be powerful and energetic turning points in both the macrocosm (universe) and the microcosm (individual person). Abbess Palmo thus established a lineage of compassion that continues today.

RELINQUISHING AND RENOUNCING CRAVINGS

When I was growing up, I remember hearing my Christian friends talking about what they would be giving up for Lent. One friend gave up gum; another, ice cream. A girl in my junior high school homeroom gave up dating her boyfriend for the entire period of Lent. With these renunciations, these innocent young people joined the procession of wise men and women throughout history who have relinquished attachments because they were interested in a different kind of sustenance.

In order to experience some of the spiritual gifts of fasting, we don't have to stop eating. We can just stop eating to excess. We don't have to give up shopping for food, but maybe we could stop filling our stuffed cabinets and overflowing refrigerator shelves with every conceivable flavor and variety of taste treat known to mankind. We can certainly simplify, as well as heal, our lives by renouncing some of the food and drink that isn't good for us. I know people who have chosen macrobiotic diets – eating mostly grains, vegetables (including sea vegetables), tofu, as well as small amounts of fish. They say it makes life less complicated. If done with the proper spirit and good medical advice, renouncing certain types of food gives us physical as well as spiritual benefits. We might even be able to heal ourselves through various dietary regimes, as did Abbess Palmo seventeen hundred years ago.

There is a story that is told about how a woman once came to Mahatma Gandhi to seek his help with a problem she was having with her son. It seems that the boy was completely addicted to Indian milk sugar sweets. He couldn't stop eating these candy-like treats. The woman asked Gandhi if he could help. Could he please, she implored, ask her son to give them up, and tell him how much better he would feel if he did so?

Gandhi looked at the distressed mother and replied, 'I

can't tell you that this week, but come back next week.'

The following week the mother arrived with her son, and Gandhi delivered an impassioned little lecture as the mother had requested.

'But Baba,' the mother asked, 'why did you make us wait a week?'

'Because,' Gandhi replied, 'last week I was also still eating too many milk sweets. I gave them up, and now I too feel better.'

HOW TO BRING THE BENEFITS OF FASTING INTO YOUR SPIRITUAL LIFE

Periodic fasting is a way of training ourselves to examine and reflect on our worldly attachments. During those days that we rearrange our eating habits, we can rearrange our priorities as well. In this way we can detox and cleanse the mind and spirit as well as the body.

Remember, a fast is a serious undertaking. *Don't just give up food.* That's not healthy, and it's not wise. *And don't ever, ever give up drinking water for very long!* One can too easily get dehydrated.

Here are some suggestions for getting started on a spiritual fast:

1. This is essential: Consult with your doctor, nutritionist, or health-care professional to make certain that he or she feels that it's okay for *you* to fast.

2. Go to the library, bookstore, World Wide Web, or health-food store and get some information on different kinds of fasts. Because fasts are meant to

help you detox physically as well as mentally, pick a fast for its health benefits. There are many books available about different kinds of fasts. There are juice fasts, grape fasts, and brown rice fasts, to name just a few. All of these fasts have different protocols that should be followed. Find the fast that best suits your personality and lifestyle.

3. *Don't fast if you have a medical problem without medical supervision.*
4. Don't fast for more than three days without medical supervision or advice, even if you're healthy.
5. Keep your fast healthy by choosing a fast that puts an emphasis on healthy diet choices.

KEEP YOUR FASTING DAYS SPIRITUAL

Use the days that you fast to slow down and maintain your spiritual priorities. Whenever possible, stay mindful and dedicate these precious days to prayer, meditation, spiritual readings, yoga, and solitude. Find joy in nature and your environment. Write in your journal and reflect on your life and your priorities. Done properly, your fasting days can help you learn restraint, mindfulness, discipline, and self-control.

SOME WARNINGS

When we stop eating, we become light-headed, and hallucinations as well as visions come more readily.

Your judgment can be easily thrown. Treat your fasting days as though they are private retreats with an emphasis on simplicity, prayer, and meditation. These are not days in which you should go places or do things. In this state, by the way, it's also easy to become more dependent on others. For these reasons, be aware that fasting has often been used as a means of mind control.

WHEN FASTING, FOLLOW THE BUDDHA'S LESSONS ON BALANCE AND RESTRAINT

Sensible fasting is a spiritual practice only so long as it is done with a sense of balance. When we go overboard with fasting, it ceases to be spiritual and becomes instead a way of fulfilling ego needs or feeding an inflated or inverted sense of self. This is true of everything, of course. Spiritual fasting is not meant to be used as a means of penance, self-mortification, or extreme deprivation. It should always be done in moderation. It should always be done in a way that is balanced and sane.

When the Buddha first began his spiritual journey, he went too far and practiced extreme asceticism. There were days when Gautama ate only one single grain of rice. He became so weak that, at one point, he staggered into the river and was almost swept away. The Buddha finally decided that such extreme austerity, though common among yogis in his day, wasn't achieving healthy results. Exhausted and near death, Gautama entered a village where a young woman gave him sweet milk and rice. Eating and regaining his strength, the thirty-five-year old Buddha realized that extreme austerity practices were a form of violence perpetrated upon the self. They push the limits of sanity. He renounced extreme asceticism, realizing that balance is an essential ingredient in a spiritual life. The Buddha's own experiences led to the development of his unique teachings on naturalness, nonviolence, balance, and harmony, known as the Middle Way.

Prayer – A Do-It-Yourself Experience of the Divine

◆

You say a prayer in your religion, and I will say a prayer as I know it. Together we will say this prayer, and it will be something beautiful to God.

MOTHER TERESA

Simone Weil says that prayer is undivided attention. St Paul's advice to his followers was that they should make every breath a prayer. Jesus told his followers: 'Whatever you ask for in prayer, believe that you have received it, and it will be yours.'

Throughout the ages, prayer has been a universal human practice – an essential connecting element – common to every person in every religious and ethnic group. Who among us hasn't uttered a little prayer, or petition, for help in times of need? Sometimes these prayers are entirely about one's own needs: 'Help! Is there anyone out there who hears me? Is there anyone out there who cares about me?' Sometimes these prayers are focused on others: 'Please help my friend Paulette, who is sick and is having a terrible time in her marriage.' These pleas or prayers, spoken and unspoken, take place the world over. The petitioner is praying for wisdom and divine intercession.

I think we can all agree that prayer is how we touch, or connect with, that which is beyond ourselves. Some people say prayer is how we talk to God; others say it is how we set things into motion. An old saying admonishes us to be careful what you pray for, you may get it. Oscar Wilde said that 'when the gods wish to punish us they answer our prayers.' Others say that if we pray for what we already have, our prayers are always answered.

Prayer, like meditation, is a complex concept with multilevel meanings from age to age, religion to religion, and culture to culture. The common theme in all traditions, however, revolves around the natural human wish to open our hearts and communicate with the sacred principle, a higher power or divine source. Whatever language we may use, prayer is the common language of the soul. Needless to say, prayer doesn't depend just on words. Some people pray by singing, and some people pray by keeping silent. Thomas Merton once said that 'God prays by dancing.'

Growing up in a Jewish household, God was the only divinity to whom I was taught to pray. My Protestant friends prayed to Jesus; my Catholic friends had a whole constellation of divine beings to whom they could direct their prayers. I remember friends who often asked for divine intercession in the daily activities of life from God, Jesus, and Mary, as well as dozens of really cool, interesting saints – St Jude, the patron saint of impossible cases; St Francis, who looks over animals as well as people; St Anthony of Padua, as the patron saint of lost things, to whom many pray.

When I was in France, a friend who was a Dominican

brother taught me a little prayer to St Theresa of Lisieux, who is also said to help find things. 'Little Flower at this hour, show your power.' I use it whenever I can't find my car keys or any one of a dozen objects that seem to disappear so mysteriously. The idea of an agnostic Buddhist Jew from New York praying to a Roman Catholic French saint may seem odd, but it does seem to help. I swear it by all that is sacred! Focusing on this prayer reminds me to stop, put a halt to frenetic searching for my lost possession, relax and become more present. To get centered, I meditate for a few seconds and pray. Sometimes just doing this helps me remember where I left the item I can't find.

I've personally never prayed for Muhammad's intercession, but I have friends who do. And I have certainly used many Sufi prayer songs, and chants from the Islamic tradition.

Carrie, a friend of mine with a bad back, recently visited a spiritual healer who, as Carrie said, began the session by asking for assistance and guidance from just about anybody who could give it. When the healer asked for help from the Divine Source, Carrie told me she felt very comfortable. The healer then went on to invoke the help of Eastern saints as well as Tibetan dakinis and Dharma Guardians. Carrie said that absolutely nobody was left out. At first Carrie felt silly, but then as the session turned into a prolonged meditation, it began to make sense. Carrie began to feel bathed in marvelously positive energy, and her back pain became a little less intense. She said she felt much better for days afterward, with or without back spasms.

Many studies have shown that every living thing responds positively to prayer. This is as true of plants sitting on a greenhouse shelf as it is for people lying in hospital beds. From the spiritually tended gardens of the New Age Findhorn community in Scotland to prestigious medical institutions like Harvard, the Menninger Clinic, and the Mayo Clinic, there is ample evidence of the power of prayer. Larry Dossey, M.D., author of the bestselling book *Healing Words: The Power of Prayer and the Practice of Medicine*, says that 'prayer is a bridge to the Absolute, a way of connecting with something higher, wiser, and more powerful than the individual self.'

Simply put: Prayer works. Why? Could it be that prayer has power because we are all interconnected and interdependent? Mother Teresa said, 'Everything starts from prayer.' When asked if she had any special wisdom to impart to others, she would often reply, 'My secret is very simple. I pray.'

Meditation practice is so central to Buddhism that many people forget that prayer is also a part of traditional Buddhist practice. Some Buddhist scholars go so far as to tell me that there are no prayers in Buddhism, but I think they are using a very limited definition of prayer as being solely theistic, or simply looking at only one school of the Buddhist tradition. The fact is that the Buddha prayed. The Dalai Lama prays – for hours every day. In fact all Himalayan lamas, monks, and nuns pray and so do laymen and women, as well as children. I very clearly remember a time when I was uncertain about what direction my spiritual life should take; one of my beloved old lama teachers in Nepal said that if I made 108 prayers at a certain holy power place I would certainly receive the guidance and direction I wanted, and it worked for me. Prayer is a vital part of the spiritual path. Prayer is a beautiful thing in our lives.

In Buddhism as in other religious traditions, there are many different levels of prayers for many different purposes. One of the questions people ask me all the time is how Buddhists direct their prayers. Traditional Buddhists do not believe in God. There is nobody to pray to. So what is the purpose of prayer?

Buddhism believes in karma – cause and effect. Everything we do, everything we say, everything we think causes some change in our environment, and has implications. When we pray, we cause a shift. Intentionality rises, mind moves, energy flows. Something definitely happens, even if it's only observable at first within ourselves. Say a prayer, put a thought into motion, and by definition there will be some effect. Thoughts, wishes, and ideas create worlds. Everyone knows the power of technology; few remember the radical changes that have taken place on this planet through love and truth and through the power of prayer. As many people have said many times, all prayers are answered, but sometimes not in the way we expect.

Here's a list of some of the different types of prayers and ways of bringing them into our lives:

- morning prayers, daily prayers, evening prayers, bedtime prayers, seasonal and holiday prayers
- prayers for healing and longevity
- prayers for reconciliation
- peace prayers
- bardo prayers for guidance at the time of death

- prayers of loving-kindness and compassion
- petitioning prayers and obstacle-removing prayers
- prayers for guidance and divine wisdom
- prayers of surrender and allowing
- prayers for a better rebirth
- benedictions, and prayers for blessings
- prayers of thanksgiving
- centering prayers
- silent prayers.

In *Autobiography of a Yogi*, the famed Hindu master Swami Yogananda says, 'Whether *He* replies or not, keep calling him.' Similarly, the mystic Rabbi Nachman said, 'Prayer is the Jew's main weapon . . . pray with all your might and with intense concentration to the point where your prayer will be like thunder.'

Spiritual practice implies repetition. Nowhere is this more true than with prayers. On the top of Mt Athos is a Greek Orthodox monastery that overlooks the Aegean Sea. The cloistered monks who live there strive to pray without ceasing, constantly repeating the prayer, 'Lord Jesus Christ, Son of God, have mercy on me, a sinner.' Many people who use this centering prayer do it as a practice, inhaling as they pray, and saying silently or out loud, 'Lord Jesus Christ, Son of God,' and then exhaling as they complete the prayer, 'Have mercy on me, a sinner.' Some shorten this prayer further by praying, 'Lord Jesus Christ, have mercy.'

There are beautiful legends that say that the Orthodox

monks repeat the prayer so frequently and with such faith and devotion that the prayer itself sometimes becomes inscribed on their hearts. In Tibet a similar statement is made about lamas, nuns, and monks who have chanted the same mantras every day of their lives. When these holy ones die, it is said that you can see the syllables inscribed on their hearts. Just recently I was in Nepal at the monastery of my late Dzogchen master, Urgyen Rinpoche. His son, the abbot of the monastery, showed me and the few other close disciples the skull of our master, which was wrapped with orange silk cloth and enshrined in a little stupa. The skull had emerged from the lama's funeral pyre intact, a symbolic representation of his adamantine, or diamond-like, vajra mind. On the jawbone was inscribed the Dzogchen mantra symbol 'Aah.' It didn't seem to me to be entirely coincidental that the fire had marked the jawbone in that way. My faith makes me feel free and easy about many of these things; I suppose others could harbor doubts. Prayer is powerful and profound.

ADAPTING AND PERSONALIZING YOUR PRAYERS

There are many Tibetan Buddhists who pray regularly to a whole assortment of Buddhas, Bodhisattvas, enlightened gurus, dakinis, Dharma Guardians, and minor deities. This practice is not that dissimilar to Westerners praying to individual saints, or the Confucians and Taoists praying to the Immortals and ancestors. Personally, I don't do this very often. On the Western side of my brain, this kind of prayer seems removed from where I'm coming from. However, many people I know use these prayers and get a great deal out of them.

Some of the prayers that I use include the concept of God or Divine Source or spirit. This is true of prayers from the Western mystical traditions as well as prayers from Hindu and Muslim traditions. As a buddhist *and* a Westerner, I am completely comfortable doing this. Others may feel differently.

One of the amazing well-documented characteristics of Buddhism has been its ability to adapt, absorb, and integrate into other cultures and religions. Tibetan Buddhism, for example, has clearly integrated the Tibetan indigenous religion of Bon, and incorporated its practices relating to the energies of the land and all five natural elements as well as energies of the body, mind, and spirit. It seems entirely reasonable that as Buddhism enters the West, it is able once again to stretch accordingly.

In prayer as in other spiritual practices, open-minded spiritual leaders realize that different forms can evolve and change without altering the essence. In the last twenty years, I've noticed the emergence of a new attitude toward God and prayer. I've been in Western Christian churches that have retained the essence of the Lord's Prayer, for example, while changing one line. Thus instead of praying 'Our Father who art in Heaven,' they loosen gender bias and pray, 'Our Mother and Father who art in Heaven.' Sometimes people abandon the anthropomorphic notion of a long-haired white-bearded God even further by praying, 'Our Divine Source (or Creator) who art in heaven.'

As spiritual seekers, I think it's important that we

stay open to understanding and accepting the many ways men and women use different words to describe essentially the same concepts. In Buddhism we usually think of our spiritual translations as being from Sanskrit or Pali to English, but in reality all words referring to spiritual practices are weak translations from the universal language of the spirit. So let's not get hung up on words. The great-souled Gandhi once said, 'It is better in prayer to have a heart without words than words without a heart.' Some words simply don't translate, but we know what is meant. The important thing is that we continue to open our hearts in prayer.

Create Your Own Personal Prayer Book

◆

When I started out in spiritual practice, I began to write down prayers that felt powerful or beautiful or simply spoke to my state of mind. At first I collected them on little scraps of paper. Soon I bought a little notebook, and I wrote them all down. A few years later, I bought a special new notebook, and a spiritual friend who was a calligrapher copied them down for me. I covered the notebook in a rich red and gold fabric. I carry this book with me wherever I go. It's been around the world several times. My personal prayer book functions as a talisman and is always with me.

Recently I was at a museum exhibit in New York called the Jewels of the Romanovs. The exhibit featured the Russian royal family's incredible jewelry as well as some clothing and personal possessions. In one of the glass-enclosed tables in the middle of the exhibit, I spotted two faded satin-covered books with gold lettering. These were individualized prayer books that had belonged to two members of that royal family who had lived a hundred years ago. I was sorry that the books were closed and there were no examples of the prayers enclosed within.

The idea of having a personal prayer collection is a

very beautiful one to me. You can collect your prayers any way you like. You can even do it on your computer. Personally I prefer doing it the old-fashioned way, by hand. I find it a more reflective and centering experience. Copying prayers is also an old and accepted way to gain spiritual merit. Remember that the word 'yoga' means connecting or reuniting. Copying spiritual writings is thus a form of yoga that connects you to the source. For me this is a practice of love as well as a way of practicing mindful attention. I also like carrying my prayer book with me wherever I go. I know the prayers in my book by heart, but for me that little book reverberates with spiritual energy.

So start collecting your prayers. They don't all have to be formal prayers. Sometimes we hear words, phrases, bits of hymns, chants, or even pop songs that speak to us in a very personal and spiritual way. Sometimes we can pray silently, and listen to whatever heartfelt words, affirmations, and aspirations may spontaneously come to us. These are our true prayers.

What follows are some of my favorite prayers. Maybe they can help you start on your way.

Peace Prayers

◆

Dona nobis pacem, pacem
– give us peace, peace –

Peace is of primary importance in all spiritual traditions. We all want peace; we all pray for peace – among all peoples, among all beings. Peace evolves from love; love evolves from peace. In many traditions, the two words are used almost synonymously. When Buddhists are asked to define nirvana, we often describe it as the peace that surpasses understanding, or the experience of divine and unconditional love that brings with it a sense of belonging or wholeness. We must become and be peace if we want to see a more peaceful world.

Many remember peace marches, with all the demonstrators chanting the Lennon-McCartney song 'Give Peace a Chance.' The Sanskrit word for profound peace is 'shanti.' As you walk through the streets of India, you can hear holy men and women chanting 'Om shanti, shanti, shanti.' Hindus believe that mankind's most ancient sacred scriptures, known as the Vedas, have a divine origin. Sanskrit is such an ancient language that it is often called the 'Language of the Gods.' 'Om Shanti' is one of the oldest mantras known to man.

A VEDIC PRAYER FOR PEACE

May there be peace in the higher regions;
may there be peace in the firmament;
may there be peace on earth.
May the waters flow peacefully; may the herbs and
plants grow peacefully; may all the divine powers
bring unto us peace.
The supreme Lord is peace.
May we all know peace, peace, and peace; and may
that peace come unto each of us.
Om Shanti, Shanti, Shanti.
Peace to all.

ST FRANCIS PRAYER

The following prayer, attributed to St Francis of Assisi, the Roman Catholic saint who was born in the late twelfth century, is deservedly very well known. The wish to become an instrument of peace is as profound as it is beautiful.

Lord, make me an instrument of your peace.
Where there is hatred, let me sow love,
Where there is injury, pardon;
Where there is doubt, faith;
Where there is despair, hope;
Where there is darkness, light;
And where there is sadness, joy.
Oh Divine Master, grant that I may not so much
seek to be consoled as to console,
to be understood as to understand,

to be loved, as to love.
For it is in giving
that we receive;
it is in pardoning
that we are pardoned;
and it is in dying
that we are born to eternal life.

BLESSINGS OF PEACE

For people the world over, words of peace are associated with blessings. Here are some familiar wishes of peace. Each of these wishes is a small prayer.

Go in Peace.

Pax.

Peace be with you.

May your feet be guided in the path of peace.

Shalom.

Healing Prayer

◆

The main reason for healing is love.
PARACELSUS (1493–1541)

'Heal her, God, I beseech thee.'

This simple heartfelt prayer was uttered by Moses, asking God to come to the aid of his sister Miriam, who had leprosy.

Like Moses, the rest of us often respond to illness, whether it be a loved one's or our own, with prayer. When we are scared, confused, or worried, praying seems the right thing to do. Back in the early 1970s when I was in India, one of my friends on the path suddenly came down with a serious illness that no one seemed to be able to diagnose. We didn't know what he had – malaria, meningitis, smallpox? Various Indian doctors gave us conflicting advice. Worried and unsure of the steps we should take, several of us finally left the monastery we were staying in, phoned our friend's parents, and put him on a plane to Switzerland to get medical treatment.

As soon as we returned from the airport, I remember going into our temple hall and praying. This was my first real experience of spontaneous prayer; I recall even now the urgency to my petition. There was nothing else I could do. I don't remember the words I used as I prayed, probably just, 'Please help my friend. Please help my fear.' I simply folded my hands, bowed my head before the immensity of it all, and prayed.

In Buddhism, healing prayers take on special significance, because when we pray for healing, we pray for healing in the very largest sense. We ask not only that the being for whom we are praying will be cured of a specific disease or frame of mind. We are also praying that this being will be cured in the deepest ways that karma itself be expiated, purified, and exhausted. A Buddhist prayer for healing implies a petition that the entire life (or lifetimes) be healed, not just the temporary affliction. The deepest healing brings a return to spiritual as well as physical well-being.

A HEALING PRAYER

We, who need help, pray for the healing of our
physical, emotional, and spiritual pains and difficulties.
Source of all blessings and power, heal us, empower
us, and bless us.
We realize that we can't do it alone, and we ask for
blessings from all those who have the power to
help, elevate, and heal.
We ask for the help from the sacred that is above
us.
We ask for the support of those around us, our
friends, families, and communities.
We pray for the wisdom to find ways to help
ourselves.

We ask for guidance to help us ease our way and heal our hearts.
May we open ourselves to the mystery that is beyond us, the source from which we are never apart.
May we be happy and whole.
May energy pour through us for the benefit of one and all.
May we dance and lift up our hands and our hearts in praise and rejoicing.

An Agnostic's Prayer

◆

Don't misunderstand me. I don't believe *in prayer. I only* do *it. Or perhaps it does* me.

SAM KEEN

My friend Sam Keen is an American philosopher, author, and thinker. In one of his many books, *Hymns to an Unknown God*, he speaks about what it means to be an American male. In one section, he says, 'As a modern American, my mentors in manhood have taught me by word and deed that I am expected to be self-sufficient. From Emerson I learned self-reliance. Erich Fromm taught me the virtue of autonomy. Gary Cooper, Clint Eastwood, and all the heroes of those great morality plays – the Western movies – showed me that a Marlboro man stands tall and goes it alone. Most recently a gaggle of pop psychologists have warned me against the terrible danger of codependency. No crutches, no leaning. I am a freestanding, self-supporting individual.

'It is with some embarrassment that I admit that on certain occasions I have been unable to keep myself from praying. Like a shipwrecked sailor, I have hurled my petition into the void:

Almighty Father, strong to save,
Whose arm hath bound the restless wave,
Who biddest the mighty ocean deep
Its own appointed limits keep:
O hear us when we cry to Thee
For those in peril on the sea.'

Before I started reading Sam's book, I looked at the title for a long time wondering what kind of 'unknown God' he was referring to. When I started reading the book and got to this section about prayer, I found that it really spoke to our times and generation. When the moments of crisis arise, Sam, like most of us, prays.

An All-Purpose Prayer for Divine Guidance

◆

In September 1972, I was driving the elderly sari-clad, American-born, India-trained, Hindu spiritual teacher Hilda Charleton to her weekly evening class in Greenwich Village. Her satsang group gathered one night a week to chant, sing, meditate, pray, and learn to love together. We were late for the gathering, and I was having trouble finding a parking spot.

Hilda said, 'Let's pray to God for a good spot near the hall. He will help us.'

'How can we ask God for such a small favor?' I asked her, with self-righteous indignation. 'There are many greater, more important things in the world to pray for.'

'Don't worry, Surya,' dear Hilda said, 'prayers get better by use. Let's just pray and find the space He has in mind for us.'

We found someone leaving a spot right near the front door. It felt almost magical that we got where we were going just on time.

I've thought about that evening and Hilda's words many times. Often what we are really praying for is that we will become so attuned to our universe that we will find the place we were meant to be.

In life there are endless times when we wish for divine guidance, or at least some sort of direction. The law of karma, or cause and effect, teaches us that everything that happens to us is the result of something that we did, said, or thought. Our destiny is in our own hands. Wouldn't it be wonderful if all of our decisions, words, and thoughts expressed divine compassion and wisdom? How much happier and more satisfying our future would be.

This prayer is adapted from an old English hymn. In just a few simple lines it eloquently asks that the sacred be part of all that we do and think.

Divine Presence, be in my head
And in my understanding.
Divine Presence, be in my eyes
And in my looking.
Divine Presence, be in my mouth
And in my speaking.
Divine Presence, be in my heart
And in my thinking.
Divine Presence, be at my end
And my departing.

Ancient Tibetan Prayers

◆

In Tibet, Padma Sambhava, 'The Lotus-Born,' is venerated as the second Buddha as well as the founder of Tibetan Buddhism. He is commonly referred to as 'Guru Rinpoche' (precious teacher).

Padma Sambhava, who lived in the eighth century, is said to have had twenty-five principal disciples – both men and women. Because he foresaw difficulties in the future continuance of his teachings, Padma Sambhava hid many of his religious writings and revelations in some 108 various hiding places, including the many mountain caves scattered throughout Tibet. Centuries later, the reincarnations of Padma Sambhava's original twenty-five disciples had visions and dreams telling them where they could find these hidden Dharma treasures, or 'termas,' as they are called. The most famous of these termas is the Dzogchen text known in English as *The Tibetan Book of the Dead.*

The following wish-fulfilling healing prayer was given by Padma Sambhava to the prince of Tibet in the eighth century. It was hidden and rediscovered in the nineteenth century by the visionary terma finder and master Choling Rinpoche. In this prayer, Padma Sambhava is personified as the reincarnation of the Medicine Buddha, the divine physician who can cure all ills. By praying to this archetypal form we enter into the healing current of transendental energy and blessings.

PADMA SAMBHAVA'S HEALING PRAYER (FROM THE CHOLING TREASURE)

The illusory bodies of all sentient beings suffer from fear, harm, and illness.
Through an indescribable ocean of misery, we pray to the power of the healing Buddha, the physician Buddha, the spiritual doctor who heals all ills and afflictions through his form as the Lotus-Born Buddha.
May our longevity and vitality be unhindered by illness, accidents, and suffering.
To the Lotus-Born Guru master we pray:
Please bestow the blessing to fulfill all our sterling wishes and aspirations.

I invite you to pray with us and all the lineage masters for this prayer to be fulfilled. By praying with these ancient power words spoken by Padma Sambhava himself, we enter into the ceaseless stream of blessings and inspiration, aligning ourselves with that cosmic principle of immutable wholeness, harmony, and perfection.

OBSTACLE-REMOVING PRAYER

The following prayer for removing obstacles on the spiritual path is another ancient terma from the same Tibetan tradition of Choling Treasures.

Precious Guru, Lotus-Born Buddha, Guru Rinpoche
One with all Awakened Ones throughout time and space,
Blissful presence and source of all spiritual accomplishments,
Fierce destroyer of illusion who dispels every obstruction—
We pray to you for blessings and inspiration:
Please remove all outer, inner, hidden, and unknown obstacles, and spontaneously fulfill our aspirations.
To you, and you alone, We pray.

Longevity Prayers

◆

Who can explain why some people lead longer, healthier lives than others, as well as have more life force, energy, or Chi, as it is sometimes called? It's a mystery. In Tibet there are specific prayers as well as empowerments that are used to increase energy and promote longevity. This is a significant practice in Vajrayana Buddhism, and all lamas rely on these practices to one extent or another. When Dudjom Rinpoche was in his sixties, for example, he became quite ill with emphysema after leaving the high Tibetan plateau and taking up residence as a refugee in the lower, more tropical climates of India. Yet despite this, he lived a long productive life. Everyone strongly believed that his vitality and ability to continue as an active and energetic teacher until well into his eighties was directly attributable to longevity practices as well as prayers, his wife's healing energy, and related techniques.

Usually these longevity prayers are directed to Amitayus, known as the Buddha of Infinite Life. This radiant ruby red Buddha manifestation is a common image in the East; he is usually depicted with the palms of his hands upturned, in his lap, and his fingers lightly joined in the meditation mudra. Often he is seated in a lotus blossom, which reinforces the purity of his nature. In his upturned palms is the overflowing vase of spiritual immortality. In Tibetan wall hangings, known as 'tangkas,' as well as throughout the Far East, where Amitayus Buddha is much venerated, he is frequently painted a bright sunset red, blazing with life, as it were.

When I was on retreat in France, two brothers were part of our group. Both of these men, trained as pilots, came from a French Catholic family. They were both engineers. While we were in retreat, their father was diagnosed with cancer. Their mother loved and respected the grand lamas who were our teachers; she and her children asked if the lamas could do anything even though Monsieur Father was disbelieving. Our teachers said they would bless Monsieur, pray for his longevity, and empower him. The entire monastery then became involved in making hand-rolled prayer 'pills' according to ancient medicinal recipes and visualization instructions. My friend's father lived another ten years, and his grateful family always believed that these practices and prayers were responsible. Even the cynical Monsieur became a believer and was grateful and very supportive of all of us.

Most Tibetan lamas have a special long-life prayer, called a 'shabten,' written personally for them, often by their own master. Here is an example of one, which was written for me by my teacher, Nyoshul Khenpo Rinpoche, at the request of my own students. I offer it up for your own prayers and protection. You can personalize it by substituting any name you wish instead of 'Sun.'

By the power and blessings of oceans of holy beings
of boundless life:
Lord and protector Buddha Amitayus, guardian of
boundless life, our guide the Lotus Buddha
Padma Sambhava and all others,
May he who bears the name 'Sun'
live long in this world, that his spiritual activity
may continue and vastly flourish.

If you want to write your own longevity prayers, it's worth noting that Tibetan longevity prayers typically ask not just that the person being prayed for live a long life. There is always a greater purpose implied – that the person's life be a vehicle for beneficial spiritual activity and to further the spread of wisdom, truth, and love, known as the Dharma.

A Sakyapa Prayer for Swift Progress on the Spiritual Path

◆

There are four primary schools of Tibetan Buddhism. The oldest original sect is the Nyingma, which was established by Padma Sambhava in the eighth century A.D. The others are the Kagyu, Gelug, and Sakya schools. This is the kind of information that might come in handy if you found yourself a contestant on a rather uniquely designed game of 'Jeopardy.' Although they have much in common, each school is renowned for different reasons. Sakyapas, for example, are known for tantric scholarship and monastic discipline.

The following prayer was given to me by my beloved late Sakyapa teacher, Deshung Rinpoche, who died in Nepal in the 1980s. His current incarnation was reborn in Seattle; *Little Buddha*, the delightful Bertolucci movie about a Tibetan lama's rebirth in America, is partially inspired by this story.

This prayer will speed one's spiritual progress.

By the blessing of the Triple Gem,
May the minds and hearts of all beings
Be attuned to the sublime Dharma.

Bless us to move forward on the path of true
understanding;
May the way be cleared of all impediments.

Bless us that the illusive vision may appear in the
clear light of the transcendent wisdom of Buddha;
May unwholesome thoughts and unskillful actions
cease to arise.

Bless us with the awakening of true love and
compassion.
May all beings together realize perfect enlightenment.

Prayer to Tara

◆

Depictions of the wondrous female Buddha, Tara, are found everywhere in Asia, especially in Tibetan Buddhism. Tara, whose name means star, embodies the sacred feminine energy found in all of us. Viewed like a brilliant light shining in the darkness, Holy Tara is the female complement of Chenresig, the Buddha of Love and Compassion. Tara is Tibet's all-encompassing, nurturing mother figure. Chenresig and Tara are both beloved protective deities who guard and take care of Tibet and its people.

Tara appears in twenty-one different forms and colors. The most common are White Tara and Green Tara. When seated in a lotus position, white Tara is usually seen with a white lotus in her right hand. She is peaceful, contemplative, and divinely aware. White Tara has five additional eyes, one in each palm, one in each foot, and, of course, the third eye in the middle of her forehead; this represents her watching over us at all times with the fully opened eye of wisdom and love.

Green Tara is often depicted with one leg out of the lotus position, extended down for a quick and decisive response when needed. Green Tara acts swiftly in answering prayers – like a lioness protecting her cubs.

In Tibet everyone seems to know, by heart, the

beautiful, lengthy prayer called Twenty-one Praises to Tara,' and so do I. Each four-line stanza of this prayer is dedicated to a different one of Tara's manifestations. In both monasteries and homes, this prayer is chanted twelve times each morning, which takes about an hour. Tibetan practitioners also condense this lengthy Tara prayer down to two evenly metered short lines.

When I first arrived in Darjeeling in 1973, and hadn't yet learned Tibetan, my Nyingma teacher, Bairo Rinpoche, told me that Tara always responds speedily to our prayers, and that if I could learn nothing else in Tibetan, I should learn how to get her attention quickly by calling out '*Tara Kye Kyenno.*' This is the shortest way to summon her.

Here is the condensed version of the Tara prayer, the first Tibetan prayer I memorized.

> Oh Tara, holy liberator, swift-acting mother, we
> pray and invoke your blessings;
> Please watch over us, protect us, and hold us in your
> loving embrace.

Albert Schweitzer's Prayer for the Animals

◆

Musician, theologian, doctor, writer, and medical missionary Albert Schweitzer, who died in 1965 at the age of ninety, was perhaps best known for the missionary hospital he established in Central Africa at Lamarene, Gabon. His ethical philosophy was based on a deep reverence for life.

The following Prayer for the Animals has always had meaning to me.

> Hear our humble prayer, O God, for our friends the animals, especially for animals who are suffering; for any that are hunted or lost, or deserted or frightened or hungry; for all that must be put to death. We entreat for them all thy mercy and pity and for those who deal with them we ask a heart of compassion and gentle hands and kindly words. Make us, ourselves, to be true friends to animals and so to share the blessings of the merciful.

Prayer of Thanksgiving and Praise

◆

How good to sing God's praise
How lovely the sound.
From Psalm 147

Americans tend to remember to be thankful on at least one day a year, Thanksgiving. A good way to get more in touch with the sacred year round is to maintain a grateful heart for everything that comes our way. St Theresa of Avila went even further, saying, 'I thank God for all the things I don't have.'

I think the following poem by E. E. Cummings is a wonderful expression of a grateful and joyous heart.

> i thank You God for most this amazing
> day: for the leaping greenly spirits of trees
> and a blue true dream of sky; and for everything
> which is natural which is infinite which is yes

E. E. CUMMINGS

Prayers of Blessing

◆

We all need blessings; we all need benedictions. We don't normally think of ourselves as giving blessings, although we do. We say 'God bless you' when someone sneezes. We say 'Be well, take care' to our friends. We say 'From your mouth to God's ear' to affirm another's spoken wishes.

Anyone who visits Israel feels warmed by hearing 'Shalom,' may you go in peace. When Tibetans say good-bye to one who is leaving, they say 'Go easily.' And the Tibetan who is departing says to the one who is staying 'Rest easily.'

Most of us have seen the following old Irish blessing. We see it inscribed on placemats, hanging on kitchen refrigerators, and posted over the bar in neighborhood saloons.

> May the road rise up to meet you
> May the wind be always at your back
> May the sun shine warm upon your face
> May the rain fall soft upon your field
> And, until we meet again, May God hold
> you in the palm of his hand.

The following profoundly beautiful Celtic blessing invokes peace in the form of the four elements – water, air, earth, and fire.

> Deep peace of the running wave to you.
> Deep peace of the flowing air to you.
> Deep peace of the quiet earth to you.
> Deep peace of the shining stars to you.

How to Pray

◆

Divine Spirit of Love,
Hear Our Prayers.

Yom Kippur is a day of fasting, atonement, and cosmic realignment. Once on this highest holy fast day of the Jewish year, an illiterate young shepherd entered the synagogue of Baal Shem Tov, the founder of the devotional Hasidic movement. Unable to follow the prayer book of the solemnly 'davenning' (praying) congregation and the soulful cantor's chanting, the young shepherd began to whistle aloud – for that was the one thing he knew he could do beautifully. He whistled as a gift, offering praiseful worship in the sight of God.

The horrified congregants looked up from their devotions as the templekeeper rushed to keep the shepherd boy from entering further into the temple. Whistling Prohibited!

The great sage Baal Shem observed this and quickly interceded. He announced, 'Until now, our prayers have been blocked from entering heaven. However, this innocent faithful youth's whistling prayer was so pure it opened the gates and brought all of our prayers directly to God.'

The point is that the Divine hears all prayers, in all languages. When I first lived with the lamas in the Himalayas, I didn't know how to speak or read Tibetan. Whole days were often spent in prayer, and I wondered how I would be able to be part of the group. 'How can I pray? How can I meditate?' I asked Kalu Rinpoche. He said, 'Just pray, however you can. As your practice develops, more ways will be readily available.'

Prayer is an essential, simple practice. It requires no special skills or, for that matter, instruction. We do it spontaneously and from our hearts. In short, the language of the sacred is expressed in purity of heart, no matter what the circumstances. Through this portal we see and are seen: we listen, we hear, and we are heard.

A friend of mine told me that some years back when her little boy was just a toddler, he became violently ill and was rushed straight to the isolation ward of a large metropolitan hospital. The child, who had a high fever, was vomiting violently and uncontrollably and doubling over in pain; the doctors suspected some form of serious viral or bacterial infection. The terrified child was hooked up to an IV drip; every time the doctors and nurses came in the room, they were covered with masks and disposable gloves and gowns. Although the boy wasn't allowed any other visitors, because he was still so young, his mother was permitted to stay with him around the clock. After the first day, my friend began to feel as ill as her son. She had chills and a fever, and she too began to vomit violently. She says that as she kneeled down on the hospital bathroom floor with her head over the toilet bowl, she began to pray. She was frightened not for herself, but for her child. If she was also ill, she was sure she would no longer be allowed to stay with him. He was just a little boy, and he was so scared. She prayed – with as much energy as she could muster. Then she says, literally and very graphically – in mid-vomit as it were – all her symptoms vanished. Suddenly she was well. Still sitting on the tiled floor, she was fine. Her prayers had been answered.

FINDING AUTHENTIC PRESENCE IN PRAYER

Many people have said that prayer, like meditation, begins with silence. True silence is a far different experience from just being quiet or not talking. In the inner silence of just being, it is easier to find Authentic Presence. In order to reach this kind of profound silence, we clear out the extraneous, the clutter, from our heads and our hearts as we attempt to connect with our innate Buddha-nature, our natural goodness – the center of our being.

C. S. Lewis once wrote, 'The prayer preceding all prayers is "May it be the real I who speaks. May it be the real Thou that I speak to."' When someone is ill and you're afraid, the real you – Authentic Presence – emerges. This is the true you speaking from the source within to the source of all blessings – Authentic Presence meets Divine Presence. Reunion.

So before we begin praying, we stop; we get silent. We become still. We get in touch with the divine within. Then with or without words, we unself-consciously speak what's in our hearts. The authentic longing of the heart-spirit expresses itself. We listen. This is where real being comes in. Sometimes we pray silently. These can be our truest prayers. Benedictine monk Brother David Steindl-Rast once said to me, 'Real prayer begins when one is no longer conscious of praying.'

DIRECTIVE AND NONDIRECTIVE PRAYER

Although many forms of prayers are directive in that they make specific requests, often the most powerful prayers are those that relinquish control. Most of us are familiar with the Christian Lord's Prayer, which asks that 'Thy will be done.' People who have attended 12-step programs are familiar with the phrase 'Let go and let God.' In Buddhism we think of this as emptying oneself of ego, learning to allow and let go. This is another example on the path of nonattachment. By doing this, we step aside and get out of our own way.

When seekers pray, they often try to find a balance between directive and nondirective prayer. As in 'I want what I want, but I also want to be in tune with the sacred.' Buddhist teachings encourage us to accept karma even while knowing that it can be changed for the better. We pray, therefore, for the wisdom to accept what is happening even as we try to find solutions to our human dilemmas. In this way we balance 'being' with 'doing.'

GROUP PRAYER

Across the world, there are groups of people who dedicate themselves to praying with others. Sometimes these groups assemble in the same space; often they simply agree upon a time when they will all offer up a prayer together. Frequently these groups are praying for a specific reason. At the end of a church service that I attended recently, the pastor asked if there were any announcements. Someone stood up and talked about an ill friend who had been a member of the church before moving away. During the following week, the speaker wanted to know, could everybody please set their clocks for 9 A.M., and offer a prayer for the friend's recovery?

To pray with a group is a lovely practice that generates great sacred energy, creating blessings and healing for all.

THE ROLE OF FAITH AND DEVOTION IN PRAYER

I am often asked about the role of faith in practices such as prayer. Yes, prayer implies faith, but it isn't just unidirectional faith. We can have faith in many things. We can have faith in the power of the conscious mind. We can believe, or have faith, that as we think, so we become.

Some people might say that it takes 'chutzpa' to pray. Others might think the belief that there is magic and mystery beyond what we can see is foolishness – which some perceive as divine foolishness. The fact is that it takes a certain amount of self-esteem to pray because self-esteem implies a belief in personal power. One of the sole requirements for prayer is the faith, or conviction, that we can alter circumstances. We have a part in our fate. We have a part in our karma; we have a part in our future. Believing this is faith enough.

It also take a certain amount of faith and trust to stop doing what we are doing long enough to pray. Jesus told his followers that even if their faith was as small as a mustard seed, it would be enough to move mountains. So even if you are, like me, someone who questions everything, you have enough faith to engage in prayer. If you believe that your questions are valid enough to be asked, then you have enough faith. Follow that faith, and sooner or later your questions and prayers *will* be answered. Listen. Receive. Empty your mind and open your heart and see what can fill it from beyond yourself. This is how we pray.

The Practice of Spiritual Reading

◆

How many a man has dated a new era in his life from the reading of a book! The book exists for us, perchance, that will explain our miracles and reveal new ones. The at present unutterable things we may find somewhere uttered.

HENRY DAVID THOREAU

Before our ancestors learned the techniques and skills of papermaking, writing, and printing, spiritual wisdom wasn't so easy to find. In fact, until Gutenberg and the spread of literacy, learning was for the privileged few. When the Buddha was alive, all spiritual teaching was done via oral transmission. There was no other way; consequently a seeker needed a living, breathing teacher. Today much of our spiritual heritage is handed down in book form. Just about all libraries and bookstores, actual or on the Net, have sections devoted to matters of the spirit. And this modern wisdom transmission is no longer confined to books. We have magazines devoted to spiritual matters, books on tape, videocassettes, CD-ROMs, Buddhist websites, and a host of emerging communication tools and learning technologies. How fortunate we Westerners are!

Buddhist spiritual practice puts so much emphasis on

meditation and emptying oneself of thoughts that it's easy to neglect the use of thoughts and analysis in spiritual practice. And yet it's fairly obvious that generations of seekers have found their way onto the path guided by the words of those who have analyzed and written down their thoughts, struggles, and experiences.

When I first arrived in Nepal as a young student, one of my aged Tibetan lamas told me that I shouldn't waste my mind reading newspapers, magazines, novels, or poetry. In fact, he said, the only book I ever needed to read was Gampopa's twelfth-century classic, *The Jewel Ornament of Liberation*, which is an extremely dry and detailed Buddhist text. For years I tried to follow this kind of anti-intellectual advice. I know some seekers today who still do so. But I came to see that it was not something particularly good for me. I mean, man cannot live by meditation alone! Take my word for it, I've tried.

Some ten years later, when I was in the traditional lama training, a cloistered meditation retreat, we didn't just practice meditation. Our teachers Dilgo Khyentse Rinpoche and Dudjom Rinpoche gave us two hours a day of teachings and study, and as we went along we occasionally had written and oral exams on some of the Buddhist texts, scriptures, and commentaries.

Dharma wisdom and truth *can* be found by contemplating and reflecting upon the written word. Reading *can* be transformative. In Tibet, it is taught that the process of learning or garnering wisdom has three steps: **1**) hearing wisdom; **2**) reflecting on what we have heard; **3**) meditating on what we have heard and making it part of who we are. Reading spiritual texts fulfills the first step. The other two are up to the individual seeker and involve introspection, self-exploration, and contemplation.

Oliver Wendell Holmes once wrote, 'Man's mind stretched to a new idea never goes back to its original dimensions.' Today, we have access to centuries of timeless wisdom. Most of the beautiful and illuminating ancient scriptures of the East exist in translated form. The newer generations of Dharma teachers – both Eastern and Western – have created shelves of books, which in turn are inspirational to seekers around the globe. This is true not only in Buddhism. Consider the generations of seekers and students of every faith and ethnicity who have poured over the Torah, the Bible, the Koran, the Tao Te Ching, the Bhagavad Gita, as well as countless Hindu and Buddhist scriptures.

Think about all the exhausted travelling salespeople who pick up the Gideon Bible in their lonely hotel rooms as well as the scholars who spend lifetimes studying arcane religious scriptures. How many times have you read something and been genuinely inspired – perhaps even enlightened – by the experience? If we could take all the energy generated by the accumulated hours people have spent in spiritual reading, it would completely light up the sky.

In Buddhism, reading wisdom scriptures has always been considered an honored enlightenment activity. One of my most beloved late Tibetan masters was the venerable abbot Deshung Rinpoche, generally considered to be one of the most learned lamas of his time. After escaping from Tibet in 1959, he and some of his followers, including other high lamas, were brought by the Rockefeller Foundation to Seattle, Washington, as part of an extraordinary university program in Asian Studies. Deshung Rinpoche told me that in Tibet he had spent three years in the great Tibetan-Sanskrit library in Derge, studying and memorizing Buddhist sutras until he knew thousands of them by heart. In the Tibetan tradition, this is considered to have great spiritual merit and to be the equivalent of a three-year retreat. Later in his life, when he lived in New York City, he showed me some of the many handwritten notebooks he had filled with his comments and observations since being in America.

Many Tibetan monks devoted their energy to making rice paper and carving Buddhist scriptures on old wooden printing blocks so that the wisdom scriptures could be preserved. This was always thought of as selfless and essential spiritual work. When the Chinese Communists invaded Tibet, one of the first things they did was burn down and destroy the written scriptures as well as the treasured wooden blocks, many of which were centuries old.

Book burning is nothing new. The history of human oppression – man's inhumanity to man – is tragically filled with examples of brutal armies destroying books as a way of destroying the spirit and culture of a people. In ways such as this, invading armies control the countries they invade. In 1975, the Khmer Rouge began their wholesale slaughter in Cambodia, killing millions in their attempt to eradicate the traditional culture. Among the first to be targeted were all the intellectuals and property owners – teachers, journalists, professionals, those who spoke foreign languages, and even anybody who wore glasses. The Khmer Rouge especially wages war on Buddhist teachings and singled out for persecution the gentle monks and nuns.

Peaceful men and women were killed for something as benign as talking about the Buddha or reciting scriptures. Almost all of Cambodia's more than three thousand Buddhist temples and scriptures were demolished. When the Khmer Rouge started its destruction, there were more than fifty thousand Buddhist monks; by the time they were finished, there were only three thousand.

One of those three thousand monks was the revered Maha Goshananda, who has dedicated his life to working for peace. In 1978, as Cambodian survivors began to arrive at refugee camps, they were met by Maha Goshananda wearing the forbidden saffron robe of a Buddhist monk. He began to pass out well-worn copies of the Metta Sutra, the Buddha's teachings on love, forgiveness, and compassion for all. The editors' introduction to Maha Goshananda's book *Step by Step* says: 'In that moment, great suffering and great love merged. Centuries of Buddhist devotion rushed into the consciousness of the refugees. Waves of survivors fell to their knees and prostrated, wailing loudly, their cries reverberating throughout the camp. Many say that the Dharma which had slept gently in their hearts as the Bodhi Tree burned was reawakened that day.'

How fortunate we are here in the West to be able to read the books, papers, and magazines we want to read, pray the prayers we want to pray, chant the chants we want to chant. Freedom of religion, one of the cornerstones upon which our great country was founded, is not something to take for granted.

Spiritual reading teaches us how to *listen* in order to hear the sacred in the timeless teachings of the wise men of the ages. Obviously men and women living today were never able to meet face to face with Gautama, the sage man known as the Buddha. But we have his words. We can read them whenever we want to, in just about any language we want.

Few people today plan to travel toward Kathmandu or Lhasa in the hope of meeting their guru on the path. Most wouldn't want to go that far even if they could. The good news is that they don't have to. They can walk to the nearest bookstore and learn meditation from Buddha, Milarepa, or Dogen; they can learn devotion and prayer from Rumi, haiku from Basso, and the principles of enlightened living from Lao Tsu. If you feel like it, you can spend an afternoon or evening hanging out with mystical writers like Rumi, Kabir, St John of the Cross, Han Shan (*Cold Mountain*), Weil, Whitman, and Ginsberg. If you're interested in more contemporary teachers, they abound: Sharon Salzberg, Pema Chodron, Stephen Mitchell, Sylvia Boorstein, Jack Kornfield, Joseph Goldstein, Thich Nhat Hanh, Jon Kabat-Zinn, to name just a few.

I think it's important for seekers to be very open-minded about finding spiritual inspiration in their reading. When we think about spiritual reading, our minds typically jump to the familiar volumes. Everybody knows about the Torah, the Bible, the Koran, and the Dhammapada (the words of the Buddha). But many of us began walking the spiritual path after reading books that seemed primarily popular, commercial, or introductory. One of their greatest virtues is that they are accessible.

In my own case, books were important stepping stones on my spiritual path. Over the years, I've discovered that the books I found inspirational weren't always so obvious. In my own case, when I was about twelve or thirteen I borrowed a book from a friend. It was *Franny and Zooey* by J. D. Salinger. If I remember correctly I thought it was going to be a love story. Those of you who have read the book will remember that the central character, Franny, clutches a copy of *The Way of a Pilgrim*, an old book that tells the story of an anonymous nineteenth-century spiritual wayfarer travelling through Russia on foot.

Reading *Franny and Zooey* pointed me in the direction of *The Way of a Pilgrim*. These days *The Way of the Pilgrim* is in most bookstores, but when I was in college in the Sixties, it was a hard book to find. Eventually I tracked down a copy; one of my friend's college-age brothers had it. It was a fascinating book. The anonymous pilgrim wants greater understanding about what St Paul said when he told his followers that they should turn their lives into prayers. Trying to lead a life of unceasing prayer, the pilgrim learns what is known as the Jesus Heart Prayer – 'Lord Jesus Christ Have Mercy on Me . . .'

Although I came from a Jewish family, it was meaningful to me to read about the power of all forms of prayer and faith in directing one's spiritual path. It was also very important to me to discover that I was not alone in my interests. I was gratified to find that intelligent people could be into prayer and spirituality. It wasn't just for the naïve and the gullible, as many in the suburbs around me would have had me believe. When I discovered Alan Watts and books about Zen, a world began to open up for me. The summer I was eighteen I worked in a large law firm on Fifth Avenue in New York City. One morning when I came in, the head partner, with his monogrammed shirt, Italian shoes, and custom-made everything else, called me into his office. He was often in his office so early that I used to imagine that he slept there.

'Jeffrey, come here,' he said to me that morning. He had picked up my copy of *The Tibetan Book of the Dead* from the top of my desk. 'What is this?' he asked. 'I want you to read this and tell me what the hell this is all about.' Even then, people were interested in learning more about Tibet – and also about the inner life, of course.

In those days, needless to say, I didn't know a Tibetan from anything else. But I remember finishing the book sitting in the firm's law library and becoming fascinated with what I learned about the passages after death known as the bardo, awakening in dreams, reincarnation, and the possibility of enlightenment in this lifetime. Did this book open the door to my Tibetan karma? Possibly.

My experience is certainly not unique. 'Yes,' we say when we read something that touches our hearts and our minds, 'that is so true.' Being a seeker implies that we are open and alert to hearing wisdom. Books contain so much of what we want to know. Kafka said, 'A book must be the axe for the frozen sea inside us.'

Create your own spiritual library. In that way, the books and words that have meaning to you will always have a place in your life. I think it helps if you make a special place or shelf for these inspirational volumes so that you can always find them when you want them. Place books that you love on your bedside table and read a little every night. Reading and rereading the books that help you awaken to the sacred will help you acknowledge to yourself, as well as others, that you have a commitment to the spiritual path. And if you don't like to read, many of these books are now available on audio tape.

> ***Outside of a dog, a book is man's best friend. Inside of a dog, it's too dark to read.***
>
> GROUCHO MARX

Create a Spiritual Notebook: Copying Words That Speak to Your Spirit

◆

Make your own Bible, select and collect all the words and sentences that in all your reading have been to you like the blast of triumph out of Shakespeare, Seneca, Moses, John and Paul.

RALPH WALDO EMERSON

When I am reading or listening to words that resonate with my life and experience I often write them down in my special little notebook. I have found this to be a very satisfying and enriching spiritual practice. I remember buying my first spiritual notebook in May 1991, soon after I first left the United States. (Is this beginning to sound like the J. Peterman catalogue?) It was in Istanbul and I had just had a meal at the Pudding Shop, which was one of the few places in Turkey where Americans could get food they could understand – even if items like milkshakes, pancakes, and burgers were rarely spelled correctly on the menu.

What I was thinking was that I needed a dedicated notebook in which I could write down my lists of places to go and things to do on my spiritual trek. I already had a black, bound poetry journal and a dream journal, but I felt as though I needed a journal specifically dedicated to matters of the spirit. Like my prayer book, the first 'spiritual notebook' I bought was red, and I liked it so much that every one since then has also been red. By now I have dozens, and I've kept them all. And I look at them regularly.

Sometimes we all lose track of our reasons for travelling the spiritual path, and our priorities can so easily be thrown out of balance. A spiritual notebook filled with ideas and quotations from the holy men and women who have walked before us – or who walk alongside of us – can help remind us of what's important and what we are doing and why.

Then and now, I prefer small notebooks that can fit into a jacket pocket so I can have them with me at the crucial moments when I read or hear something worth saving no matter where I am, not just when I'm sitting at my desk. That's how I managed to collect the many teachings, quotations, and stories I've heard over the years. Now, I use these notebooks in many of my own teachings and writings. A day rarely goes by without something being written in them.

I would like to suggest that you begin your own spiritual notebook by copying down the Buddha's words on kindness and love known as the Metta Sutra. This sutra is so inspirational that I believe it belongs in everyone's spiritual library. I keep a copy next to my meditation seat, along with my Tibetan prayer books.

Metta is loving-kindness. When we chant the words of the Metta Sutra, we remind ourselves to extend our love, compassion, forgiveness, empathy, and good will to *all* living beings, without exception. Read the Metta Sutra and think about what the Buddha meant when he said, 'Even as a mother protects with her life her child, her only child, so with a boundless heart should one cherish all living beings.'

It is said that chanting the Metta Sutra brings manifold blessings to the practitioner as well as to the entire environment. Among many Buddhists, 'metta' has become the code word for love and blessings. Along with other Vispassana meditation teachers, Sharon Salzberg, the author of *Lovingkindness*, has helped bring the concept of the metta into the spiritual mainstream. Sharon will often send e-mail to friends making requests that we send metta to specific beings who are ill or in need. When she does this, she is asking us to send our most powerful loving thoughts and radiate prayers of loving-kindness. Metta is a way of waking up to the true love in our heart; in this way we help heal and care for each other.

We increase our capacity for love by sending metta to all beings, but especially to those who are in need or suffering. Whenever I, for example, look up in the early autumn sky and see a V-formation of geese heading south for the winter, I send metta. I think *May they be safe, may they reach their destination, may they find food, may they be protected from harm.* I do the same thing for the occupants of those airplanes that cross my vision, or butterflies that cross my path.

I particularly send metta and spiritual blessings to all those who are helpless, of diminished capacity, and crying out for help. The more I have been doing this soulful practice over the years, the more it naturally comes up for me. When my dog chases deer and rabbits into the woods, I call her back. I can protect the creatures she's chasing from my dog, but I can't protect them from everything else, so I send metta, wishing *In gladness and safety, may all beings be at ease.*

As you copy down this sutra, be mindful of what the words mean.

THE METTA SUTRA

This is what should be done
By one who is skilled in goodness,
And who knows the paths of peace:
Let them be able and upright,
Straightforward and gentle in speech.
Humble and not conceited,
Contented and easily satisfied.
Unburdened with duties and frugal in their ways.
Peaceful and calm, and wise and skillful,
Not proud and demanding in nature.
Let them not do the slightest thing
that the wise would later reprove.
Wishing: In gladness and safety,
May all beings be at ease.
Whatever living beings there may be,
Whether they are weak or strong, omitting none,
The great or the mighty, medium, short or small,
The seen and the unseen,
Those living near and far away,
Those born and to-be born,
May all beings be at ease.

Let none deceive another,
Or despise any being in any state.

Let none through anger or ill will
Wish harm upon another.
Even as a mother protects with her life
Her child, her only child,
So with a boundless heart
Should one cherish all living beings;
Radiating kindness over the entire world
Spreading upwards to the skies,
And downwards to the depths;
Outwards and unbounded,
Freed from hatred and ill will.
Whether standing or walking, seated or lying
down
Free from drowsiness,
One should sustain this recollection.
This is said to be the sublime abiding.
By not holding to fixed views,
The purehearted one, having clarity of vision,
Being freed from all sense desires,
Is not born again into this world.

Chanting Practice

◆

That's the wise thrush; he sings each song twice over,
Lest you should think he never could recapture
The first fine careless rapture!

ROBERT BROWNING

Sound has power.

The Old Testament book of Joshua gives the following stunning example of what can be accomplished by sound:

'And the Lord said to Joshua . . . "You shall march around the city, all the warriors circling the city at once. Thus you shall do for six days, with seven priests bearing seven trumpets of rams' horns before the ark. On the seventh day you shall march around the city seven times, the priests blowing the trumpets. When they make a long blast with the ram's horn, as soon as you hear the sound of the trumpet, then all the people shall shout with a great shout; and the wall of the city will fall down flat."'

And from the energy and power of that great shout, those fabled walls of Jericho came tumbling down. It's actually a scientific fact: Sound vibrations can affect physical matter. The great Italian tenor Enrico Caruso was said to be able to hit certain notes with such intensity that glass would shatter. Although you and I may not have the vocal cords of Caruso, when we speak we each have our own unique not-to-be-duplicated sound or vibration.

As most of us can happily attest, sound has spiritual as well as physical impact. My spirits are often lifted by the power of music. Most of us have been blessed enough to have known times when concerts, choirs, and even parades have lifted us up and carried us along with the musical tones.

From drumming to melodic singing, sound has always been an integral part of the spiritual experience. Like most Jews, I grew up listening to the beautiful voice of the cantor leading our congregation by chanting prayers. Chanting is an ancient as well as universal practice intended to yoke the material and nonmaterial world. Spiritual seekers all over the world chant as a way of making contact with divine presence. Think of shamanistic practices, Native American chants, Gregorian chants, Hari Krishna chants, as well as Buddhist chants.

Chanting implies continuum. Chant one 'Om.' Repeat it again and again. Listen at the sound. Put your fingers at your throat and feel the vibration not just at your throat but also at your heart and your stomach. Chanting is a way of capturing spiritual vibration – the union of the one and the many. 'Om' is eternal. 'Om' ceases to be many and becomes one – the eternal now. The sound 'Om,' or Aum, is known as a 'bija,' or seed syllable. It is believed to have the power to connect the visible and the invisible world. 'Om,' for example, is actually more of a vibration or primal sound than it is a word as we know it. I like to think of 'Om' as the vibration that emanates from the sacred engine that drives all things. In India I often heard this seed sound compared to the seashell sound that emerges from deep within the conch.

The New Testament gospel of John says, 'In the beginning was the Word, and the Word was with God, and the Word was God.' Out of stillness comes sound. Out of emptiness comes vibration. A Tibetan tantra says, 'From within the infinite womb of emptiness arises like a shooting star, the seed syllable.'

As someone once said, the Divine isn't always listening so sometimes you have to repeat yourself. When we chant, the power of sound is united with the power of repetition. There is so much within the universe that is repetitive – seasons, monthly lunar cycles, tides, sunrise, sunset, and of course life itself. Much of Buddhist practice depends on repetition. In meditation we watch our breath, counting, in and out, until we have done it ten times. Then we start again. This simple repetition establishes a rhythm that takes on a life of its own. Doing this helps us get closer to our own natural vibration, our own nature – our innate Buddha-nature.

Chanting mantras is also a skillful way to break our identification with our own thoughts – and thus helps us free our minds. As we chant, we throw ourselves into the ocean of sound that is beyond ourselves; in this way we tune out the usual random thoughts that scatter across our consciousness and tune into the larger world of pure and simple being. I recently read somewhere that we have about two hundred thoughts a minute, or more than one a second. Ram Dass says that to break your identification with your own thoughts is to achieve freedom.

Start chanting and you surround yourself with a rhythm born of sacred sound and energy; in this way you begin to bridge the subtle gap that exists between the body and pure spirit. Try this: The next time you are out walking in the woods or on a beach, open your heart, throat, and chest and begin to chant. In this way, you can uninhibitedly create your own resonance; it's like creating a little cathedral, or magic circle, around yourself. In Tantric Buddhism, there is even a practice in which we use energy, breath, and sound to create and encapsulate blessings, as well as keep obstacles out.

Some people think that meditation and silence is the ultimate spiritual practice; others feel the same way about prayer. In fact, chanting combines elements of both meditation and prayer. I first became aware of devotional chanting when I was in India studying with Neem Karoli Baba. There, the continuous devotional chanting was accompanied by droning Indian instruments filled with undertones and overtones that help engage and awake the spirit.

There is a great deal of chanting in Tibetan Vajrayana Buddhism. Even the late head lama, Dudjom Rinpoche, who was master of the most subtle kinds of meditation, told me that when he was distracted, he would chant the one-hundred-syllable mantra to clear his energy and help him return to pure presence and awareness. In Tibetan monasteries, the lamas and monks always had a chant on their lips. Another high lama, Kalu Rinpoche, was known for the immense number of chants he had completed. Whenever I would see him, his beads would be in his hand. It is said that he has chanted the compassion mantra 'Om Mani Padmé Hung' a hundred million times.

In Tibetan Buddhism, we begin and end long retreats with extended chanting. When a group of us went into three-year retreat, for example, we began by chanting the Heart Sutra for one week. It helped clear the ground – as well as the air. The chanting fostered good spirits and helped create good energy and vibrations for all the beings seen and unseen.

Many Tibetan chanting practices are done outside. Monks, nuns, and lamas frequently go to chant in places that are by definition a little bit scary, like graveyards and cremation sites. They do this so that practitioners can use the energy of the chant to help confront and clear away their personal fears and demons. Chanting also plays an integral role in what is known as inner heat practice or 'tumo,' which is a mystic practice meant to intensify inner incandescence. The physical manifestation is heat; the spiritual effect is the blazing light of awareness.

Dudjom Rinpoche said that when he was a teenager he chanted outside with a group of monks in the Himalayan winter, and they created so much heat that the heavy snow melted around the circle; Rinpoche vividly remembered feeling warm and blissful. Chanting is a wonderful thing to do in a natural environment. Imagine for a moment what it feels like to be sitting in the falling snow with other practitioners in a circle, facing each other, chanting and breathing. When Dudjom Rinpoche lay on his death bed in his house next to our retreat monastery in Dordogne, France, we chanted in shifts twenty-four hours a day for more than a week.

The sixteenth Gyalwa Karmapa, one of the most important Tibetan lamas of our time, was known as the

Black Hat Lama because of a ceremonial crown that he wore during a specific empowerment ceremony. When Karmapa came to this country to teach in the 1970s, he was invited to visit the Hopi Indians, who welcomed him with great celebration. It seemed the Hopis had a prophecy that a great chief with a black headdress would someday come from the East.

The Karmapa happened to arrive at the time of a great drought in the four-corner region of the American Southwest. The Native Americans asked Karmapa and his entourage if they would join them in their prayers and chants for rain. The Karmapa led a ceremony of several hours' duration during which the Tibetans and Native Americans together played drums and chanted. And lo and behold, the clouds gathered, and not long after that ceremony, there *was* rain. Was it because of the chanting?

CHANTING 'OM' WITH THE IN CROWD

Westerners are now finding out what Easterners have always known: Chanting helps clear your head; it improves and purifies energy. Someone recently sent me a magazine article about various personalities like Jeff Goldblum and Meg Ryan who have discovered the benefits of chanting. Tina Turner has often been quoted as saying she chants daily. On her successful *Ray of Light* CD, Madonna sends out peaceful vibrations by chanting 'Om Shanti, Om Shanti, Shanti, Shanti, Shanti, Om.' Even the 'Material Girl' can reach the spiritual zone by chanting.

These people, and many others, are enjoying the emotional as well as physical benefits of chanting. I often recommend that people who are feeling anxious or depressed try a little chanting. I find that it seems to clear out negative energy while giving me a boost of good energy. It feels like spiritual caffeine with none of the negative side effects.

LEARNING TO CHANT

If you know how to hum, then you know how to chant. Start by breathing deeply, in and out through your nose until you have established a rhythm. Then on the out breath, find a musical tone that feels comfortable. Hum or chant 'Ahhh' with the out breath. Do this three times to experience a sense of chanting. Now let's learn a simple chant.

Just as you mastered chanting the simple seed syllable 'Ahhh,' take up Om (pronounced as in 'home'). Breathe in and then chant Om with the out breath. Hold the final sound with your mouth closed as long as you can. Notice how it turns into a hum.

Now breathe in and hum the syllable 'Ahh' on the out breath.

Finally, breathe in and chant Hum on your out breath, again holding the sound with your lips together as long as you can.

Now, let's put the mantra Om Ahh Hum together.

Breath in and then on the out breath chant the three syllables OM AHH HUM.

Again . . . OM AHH HUM

The syllable 'Om' represents the white chakra in the middle of the forehead; 'Ahh' represents the red throat chakra; 'Hum' represents the blue heart chakra. 'Om Ahh Hum' thus represents Buddha body, Buddha speech, and Buddha mind.

OM AHH HUM

Of course it is difficult to teach chanting in a book. I believe it helps if you start by listening to chanting. There are many different kinds of chants available on tapes and CDs. And there are teachers and groups that you can learn to chant with.

WHAT LANGUAGE DO YOU WANT TO CHANT IN?

I have a friend, Alexandra, who went to the Methodist church in the small town in which she grew up. But her grandparents had been Russian Orthodox. Now, as an adult, Alexandra makes a point of attending holiday services in an Orthodox cathedral because she loves the sound of the Russian chants. Even though she doesn't speak a word of Russian, the chants speak to her intuitively. When I arrived in Asia, I felt the same way about the Indian and Tibetan chants. I responded on a very deep level. But many people do not enjoy chanting in a language they don't understand. They want to know exactly what they are saying. If this is the way you feel, you may be happier chanting in your own language.

USE THE POWER OF CHANTING TO CHANGE THE ATMOSPHERE AROUND YOU

Chanting can have an extraordinary effect on your environment even if you yourself aren't doing it. One of my students told me that on a particularly stressful day in her life, she felt as though she was at her wit's end. Her phone was ringing nonstop, and her computer was sending her error messages. Everything was gong wrong, and she had a major deadline. She was exhausted, and to make matters worse, she had to drive two hours to an out-of-town meeting. She remembered my advice about chanting, and before she got into the car, she found a chanting tape. She said that she felt as though the chanting tape saved her life – and her spirit. Listening to it, she experienced the tension and stress roll away. She was able to settle into the moment, and enjoy the drive.

I play chanting tapes at home all the time. They light up the energy in the room. I play all kinds of chanting: Benedictine, Tibetan, Native American, Hindu, and anything else I can find. Chanting is enchanted.

Chenresig Practice: Cultivating the Heart of Love

◆

Earlier this year I was at an ecumenical meeting in Boston with ministers, rabbis, and priests from around the country. One of the people I spoke to was a Protestant woman minister from Texas. During the break she told me about something that had happened to her years earlier: One night after Bible class, a masked man came up to her in the parking lot, stuck a big revolver in her face, and demanded the money in her purse. She opened the purse, gave him the money and said, 'I wish I had more to give you. I love you.'

I was struck by the unself-conscious way she told this story; she just made it seem so normal. The attitude she conveyed was *Of course – I just came out of Bible class, what else would I do? How else would it happen?* It was no big deal to her because her mind had been so well trained to give and forgive. And I don't just mean from Bible class, but probably from years of learning to think and act in a loving way.

Afterward I asked her how she actually managed to do that. And she said, 'I just saw the fearful, lovable child in the eyes beneath the mask.' Ten years later a man in a suit approached her after church one day. He asked if she remembered him. She said no. He said he had held her up at night in a parking lot, and her words had shocked him into a reformed life.

The genuine spiritual path, no matter what practices you choose, helps us to love and cherish life, in all its forms. First you have to love, then you can see. This woman minister, through her own path – her Christian life – had learned how to love and let go. And that's the direction in which we all want to walk. In Tibet we call it mind training, or attitude transformation. This Texas minister's mind was so well trained that no matter what happened she instinctively responded with love. Her heart was so open that it spontaneously treated a midnight mugger as an errant, wayward son.

When we meet people who embody love, we are automatically moved. People often ask me why I became a Tibetan Buddhist and a lama. In response I always think first of the loving teachers I met in Nepal and India. Lamas like Kalu Rinpoche and Karmapa radiated so much love and wisdom that I wanted to be around them. I wanted to be like them. I once asked Kalu Rinpoche how I could ever possibly be as loving and accepting as he was. He said, 'Practice Chenresig meditation and radiate light rays of love to all.'

Chenresig is the Buddha of limitless Love and Compassion, often known as Avalokitesvara. The name 'Avalokita' means 'the Lord who sees and hears the cries of the world.' Avalokitesvara is sometimes depicted with eleven heads and a thousand arms. There is a legend that explains this form: One day as Avalokitesvara looked down at the world's suffering, his head burst from the pain he observed. When the pieces were put back together, it was in the form of extra heads, symbolically representing the divine quality of all-knowing and all-seeing. The many hands and arms are needed to help all the beings of the world; in the palm of each of the many palms is an open eye of awareness.

The Dalai Lama is considered to be Chenresig/Avalokitesvara's completely human embodiment here on earth. The Karmapa Lama is another embodiment. (Avalokitesvara has other names. In China, Avalokitesvara is called Kuan Yin; the name used in Japan is Kannon). Although I am using the pronoun 'he' to refer to Avalokitesvara or Chenresig, this is often regarded as an androgynous Buddha. In some parts of the Far East, for example, Kuan Yin is depicted as female, and is one of the most beautiful of all religious images in Asia.

In Tibet, followers of the Mahayana Bodhisattva path are devotedly attached to Chenresig. Chenresig's mantra, known as the mantra of love and compassion, is the very familiar six-syllable Om Mani Padmé Hung.

In Tibet this mantra is often called the 'Mani,' or jewel, mantra. Probably the oldest and most essential mantra in Tibetan Buddhism, the Mani is chanted everywhere, all the time. It can be translated simply as 'the jewel is in the lotus' – referring to the luminous spirit of Buddha-nature at the heart of one and all. The jewel of the enlightened mind is held within the lotus of individual consciousness. In a larger sense it also represents the priceless jewel of enlightenment springing up like a lotus flower from the very mud of this gritty world.

When Tibetan practitioners chant Om Mani Padmé Hung, it brings to mind the whole Bodhisattva path. Chanting this mantra, we visualize and cultivate ourselves as Bodhisattvas, radiant with loving-kindness, selflessly praying and striving for the liberation of all beings.

Kalu Rinpoche told me that chanting this mantra was his main practice. When people asked what he did during all those years he spent in retreat in a Tibetan cave, or on what he meditated every day, he replied, 'the Mani.' By this he meant the jewel or the luminous heart of Dharma. Kalu Rinpoche told me that Chenresig practice is the wish-fulfilling jewel, and he showed me a lovely silk scroll that depicted the four-handed Buddha of Compassion. The Buddha's two central hands hold the radiating wish-fulfilling jewel, representing the heart-essence of love and wisdom that is given freely in service to all. In the other two hands are the white lotus flower of Dharma and the 'mala' (rosary) beads that are used while chanting mantra.

I vividly remember Kalu Rinpoche pointing to the tangka scroll hanging on the wall over his altar and telling me that Chenresig was his tutelary deity. Rinpoche said that he had vowed a lifetime of practice in which he would complete an infinite number of these mantras. In Tibet, when one completes one hundred million recitations of Om Mani Padmé Hung, it is called a 'tungjor.' By the time Kalu Rinpoche died, he had completed three such tungjors. The mantra was always on his lips. I remember writing to a friend and saying that the venerable master Kalu Rinpoche had practiced the mantra of compassion so many times that his weathered face had started to look like a face-shaped heart.

When I was in Darjeeling, Kalu Rinpoche gave tantric empowerments and blessing, initiating us into the practice of the mantra of love and compassion. We were instructed to do the practice over a long enough period of time so that we could chant the mantra seven hundred thousand times.

Chenresig practice contains elements of meditation, chanting, and prayer. We begin this practice by visualizing or imagining an image of unconditional love and compassion. For Kalu Rinpoche this image was the Buddha of Love and Compassion, Chenresig. Many Westerners love the image of Chenresig, but others are more comfortable with a different image, perhaps one that seems more home-grown. The image could be Buddha, Padma Sambhava, Tara, Jesus, Mary, or a personal saint or spiritual teacher. Hold this image and cultivate thoughts of love, trust, and devotion.

As you do so, begin chanting.

Om Mani Padmé Hung . . . Om Mani Padmé Hung . . . Om Mani Padmé Hung. Repeat the lovely mantra of loving-kindness and get into it. *Om Mani Padmé Hung. Om Mani Padmé Hung.* Get it going; turn those prayer wheels in your heart!

As you chant, bring someone you care about into the light of your love. This could be a child, a parent, a spouse, a friend, or even a pet. Now let's send these beings our love along with the chant. Imagine or visualize them in front of you – bathed in the warmth of your love light. Pray for their healthy happiness, well-being, protection, and enlightenment.

Continue chanting and think of others you care for. Open your heart and offer each of them your love. Like the sun's spreading rays, when your love has grown along with the energy of the chant, begin to extend your compassionate love to others – to mere acquaintances, to strangers, to people who get on your nerves. Let your love reach as far as you can.

As you chant, keep reaching out, by extending the radiant visualized light rays of your love and compassion. Imagine that there is a warm glowing sun whose rays are streaming out of your heart chakra. Can you continue doing this, extending your love even to those people whom you dislike or who make you feel threatened? Reach out with your love. Give it out freely.

Om Mani Padmé Hung.

Om Mani Padmé Hung.

Think: May all beings have happiness and the cause of happiness, which is virtue.

Om Mani Padmé Hung.

Pray: May all beings remain free from suffering and the causes of suffering, which are nonvirtue and delusion.

Om Mani Padmé Hung.

Wish: May all beings remain unseparated from the sacred joy and happiness that is totally free from sorrow.

Om Mani Padmé Hung.

Pray: May all beings come to rest in the boundless, all-inclusive equanimity beyond attachment and aversion.

Om Mani Padmé Hung.

Affirm: May all beings be happy, content, and fulfilled.

Om Mani Padmé Hung.

May all be peaceful in harmony and at ease.

Om Mani Padmé Hung.
May all be protected from harm, fear, and danger.

Om Mani Padmé Hung.
May all have whatever they want, need, and aspire to.

Om Mani Padmé Hung.
May all be healed and whole again.

Om Mani Padmé Hung.
May this planet be healed and whole again.

Om Mani Padmé Hung.
May all beings awaken from their sleep of illusions and be liberated, enlightened, and free.

Om Mani Padmé Hung.
May all realize their true spiritual nature and thus awaken the Buddha within.

Om Mani Padmé Hung.
May all equally enjoy, actualize, and embody the innate great perfection.

Om Mani Padmé Hung.
Om Mani Padmé Hung.
Om Mani Padmé Hung.

Part Three

◆

Coming Home to Your True Nature

Spirituality is completely ordinary. Though we may speak of it as extraordinary, it is the most ordinary thing of all. Spirituality is simply a means of arousing one's spirit, of developing a kind of spiritedness. Through that we begin to have greater contact with reality.

If we open our eyes, if we open our minds, if we open our hearts, we will find that this world is a magical place. It is magical not because it tricks us or changes unexpectedly into something else, but because it can be *so vividly and brilliantly.*

CHOGYAM TRUNGPA RINPOCHE

◆

Dzogchen and Natural Meditations

◆

Sometimes people get the mistaken notion that spirituality is a separate department of life, the penthouse of our existence. But rightly understood, it is a vital awareness that pervades all realms of our being. Someone will say, 'I come alive when I listen to music,' or 'I come to life when I garden,' or 'I come alive when I play golf.' Wherever we may come alive, that is the area in which we are spiritual. To be vital, awake, aware, in all areas of our lives, is the task that is never accomplished, but it remains the goal.

BROTHER DAVID STEINDL-RAST, in *The Music of Silence*

Walking the spiritual path brings us in touch with pure being and the truth of who we are. What a relief! Spirituality is authentic and real. Spirituality is sane, natural, meaningful living.

Yes, philosophers and theologians agree: What we seek is naturally within us all. But exactly what is it that we seek? Some call it the True Self or Higher Self. Others call it clear inner light or innate luminosity. Hindus call it the Supreme Self to distinguish this true self from the ego. Many call it Authentic Presence or Pure Being.

Think about what the terms 'Pure Being' or 'Authentic Presence' mean. Think about aliveness, that indefinable yet vivid sense of being the right person in the right place at the right time. Then think about your day-to-day life and whether your activities help you feel more or less connected to your *true self*. Doesn't it seem as though we all spend too much time pretending to be something we're not, telling ourselves stories about how it could be otherwise, if only . . . ? Pretense is habit-forming as well as unnatural; every time we put on a pretense we are inauthentic and we stray further and further away from our true nature, our true self. We become completely accustomed to gluing on personas that prove to the world that we are 'fine,' 'cool,' 'confident,' 'cheerful,' 'desirable,' and 'something special.' It can be deadening. Let's admit it, to some degree, we all guard ourselves against being known. It can feel easier to hide out behind the masks we wear to protect us from the world. It's how we go through life: We create this kind of dream, and then we forget that we're dreaming.

What would it feel like if you could stop pretending to yourself or anyone else? Wouldn't it be great if you were able to give yourself unconditional acceptance and permission to be the person you really are? Think about the bliss of being at one with things just as they are. Think about the bliss of just being.

To understand what 'essential' or 'pure' being is doesn't require years in monasteries or any advanced degrees. It simply involves getting in touch with your inner sacred core. Everyone has experienced at least one brief moment of feeling totally alive, grounded, connected, confident, and real. These moments give us a glimpse of the natural state – the Garden of Eden that exists within all of us. That's Authentic Presence.

The highest teaching of Tibet is called Dzogchen, which is translated as 'Innate Great Perfection.' Dzogchen practitioners are said to be able to attain enlightenment – Buddhahood, or total self-actualization – within one lifetime of assiduous practice. When one first hears about Dzogchen one assumes that the teachings must be very difficult and knotty – intricate, involved, mysterious, and complicated. At least that's what I thought when I first heard Dzogchen, which I was also told were the 'secret' teachings of Tibet. In fact I was warned off Dzogchen by people who told me that it was only for students of superior faculties – those who had already mastered the advanced Buddhist teachings on renunciation, emptiness (sunyata), and Bodhicitta (selfless love and compassion).

In truth, the teachings of Dzogchen reflect bare essence. The difficulty in accessing them comes about because they are simple, naked, and pure. The principle teaching of Dzogchen is so open, vast, and clear that it is sometimes said that only the most evolved spirits can understand it.

To see the world with the eyes of a Dzogchen master, we must ourselves begin to strip away all our unnecessary baggage and enter the path of primordial purity and innate wakefulness. Then we will genuinely be able to see the world with pure perception and nondual awareness. This is the eye of oneness – the wisdom eye that sees things as they are. (Think again about the meaning of the much-quoted saying – 'The secret remains for those with eyes unclouded by longing.') The practice of Dzogchen helps us cultivate such clear awareness and true seeing. It is a visionary practice grounded in the most practical details of daily life, a Dharma to be integrated in the street.

> *Since religion is dead, religion is everywhere. Religion was once an affair of the church; it is now in the streets, in each man's heart. Once there were priests; now every man's a priest.*
>
> RICHARD WRIGHT in *The Outsider*

Direct Access to Our Original Nature

◆

Dzogchen is based on seeing things as they are. We call this 'resting in the View.' The View is like the vast sky without limits, corners, distortions, or bias. It's clear, radiant, and complete. It's simple, profound, peaceful, and naturally at rest. This is the nature of the sky; it is also the nature of mind. These are all qualities of nirvana itself. When we are able to rest in the View, seeing things as they are, boundaries drop away; we see into luminous infinity.

Dzogchen is the Natural Buddha Meditation. What this means is that you, me, and everyone else are all Buddhas by nature. We have only to realize it. *The practice of Dzogchen is about recognizing and realizing who we are.* Dzogchen provides direct access to what is already there, right here. Right now. Other levels of Buddhist teaching talk about the many lifetimes that are necessary before one can become fully awakened, enlightened, and free. According to the consummate teachings of Dzogchen, the entire journey of enlightenment can take place in one lifetime. All we have to do is be open to the truth about who we are. The three vital points of Dzogchen, the Natural Great Perfection, say that what we need to do is recognize it, gain certainty and experience in it, and then stabilize that inner conviction.

Dzogchen meditation is grounded in the following principles, which will help you gain direct access to Authentic Presence, your original nature, the Natural Buddha within.

FIVE WAYS TO BE REAL, THROUGH THE PRACTICE OF DZOGCHEN

- ***Naturalness and simplicity***
  Rely on the natural state. Be yourself, your true unaltered self. A meditation instruction to carry with you: Everything we need is within the natural mind – innately whole and complete. So relax.

- ***Authenticity, noncontrivance, nonfabrication***
  There is nirvanic peace in things left just as they are. Striving and struggle is extra. Leave it as it is and rest the weary heart and mind. See through everything, be through everything – and remain free, luminous, and complete.

- ***Openness and oneness***
  Stay open-minded and inclusive. Pure presence is a state of nonjudgmental, noninterfering choiceless awareness or panoramic attention to the 'is-ness' and 'now-ness' of all things. Be open to your experience. Let go and let things fall into place as they will. Perhaps wherever they fall *is* the right place.

- ***Awareness and wisdom***
  Present awareness knows and sees what is, as it is. Innate wakefulness is wise and effective in its own brand of insight and discernment combined with uncommon common sense.

- ***Spontaneous energy/flow***
  With freedom and decontraction, inexhaustible uninhibited energy is released, surging forth, bubbling up from within. When we let go and loosen our tight-fisted grasping, our repetitive holding patterns, we are buoyed up and become one with the flow. This is the natural flow, the sacred zone masters describe. You can access it at will.

Keep these principles in mind when practicing the following Natural Meditations. Remember to apply them also when you are going about your daily life, which is the natural meditation par excellence. Zen masters call it 'genjo-koan,' the riddle or challenge of realizing and manifesting with everyday life. This is Buddha's wisdom body of love.

Dzogchen Sky-Gazing Meditation

◆

When we were children, long before we heard the word 'meditation,' most of us spent at least a little time lying on our backs in the grass or on a rock watching the clouds go by. Were we day-dreaming or were we in heaven? Who knows. But those were precious moments that some of us still remember. As children, we didn't have a grand plan or program in mind. We weren't thinking about theology, mindfulness, or relaxation techniques; we probably weren't even escaping or avoiding anything. We were just little kids at play in the fields of the Lord, giving ourselves up to life and light, naturally relaxed and at ease.

Whether we knew it or not, we were intuitively returning to our true nature – the Buddha-nature that is our natural state. This is the nirvana within each of us. If we remember those moments clearly and can go there right now in our minds, we have already begun to master the Dzogchen practice of sky gazing. If we have no such memories, then we can go out and start practicing on the grass or on rooftops, lying down or in a lounge chair.

To begin the practice Sky-Gazing Meditation, we need simply look out into space, like a child looking up at heaven. Doing this, we free our minds of concepts, doubts, hesitation. All that is required is that we are happy enough just being in that place at that time. It doesn't even have to be a daytime sky. Look up at night and give yourself up to the infinite heaven of stars. Many who read Saint-Exupéry's *The Little Prince* remember the Little Prince listening to the tinkling of the stars, like little bells, over the vast Sahara desert. Sky gazing at night is a star-gazing meditation; what could be more natural for the little Buddha within each of us?

Be like an openhearted child. Look out into the sky and give yourself up to it. Offer your thoughts and feelings to the clouds. Cast your gaze into the skies and your cares into the wind.

More formally, Dzogchen Sky-Gazing Meditation is undertaken in a sitting posture.

> Get comfortable.
> Take a few breaths in and out and relax.
> Be present, receptive, and available.
> There is nothing to do, nowhere else to be.
> Nothing to accomplish, figure out, or achieve.
> Be as natural as a child dropping its body to the grass.
> Drop your mind.
> Let is rest in simplicity and awareness.
>
> With a big out breath, chant *Ahhhh*.
> Again, breathe in.
> Then chant with the exhalation: *Ah*, *ahh*, and *ahhhh*.
> Let the *Ahhh* take you beyond yourself. *Ahhh*.

Turn your mind inside out. *Ahhh.*
Raise your gaze.
Elevate the scope of your luminous sensitive awareness until it becomes like a global 360-degree sphere.
Be mindful. Be present.
Rest in that natural state of uncontrived wakefulness and presence of mind.
Like a child, lying in the grass watching the clouds roll by, allow everything to simply pass through the sky like the nature of infinite Buddha-mind.
Rest in that inclusive sky-like nature of mind, which has room for everything that momentarily comes up in the body or mind.
Unhindered, a sacred dance of phenomena and noumena, like floats in a divine parade.
Enjoy the procession of the Dharmakaya – absolute reality
Watch the Easter parade in your mind
pass by like waves in the sea,
and enjoy the spectacle.
There is room for everything.

The natural meditations of Dzogchen are sometimes known as non-meditations because they are mostly formless and effortless. Dzogchen stresses that everything in life could be contemplative by being recognized as a divine play of Buddha-mind, absolute reality.

To do sky-gazing meditation, for example, we don't really need the sky. We can gaze at the expansive inner sky space, the light behind our eyelids. We can mingle with that undifferentiated expanse, which reflects the empty, open, luminous, mirrorlike nature of mind.

Dzogchen meditators practice these meditations for hours at a time, but there is no reason why you can't practice natural Dzogchen meditations for ten or fifteen minutes, or for that matter five minutes, or even one minute. The question is: How long does it take to reconnect with that infinite expanse within? How long does it take to reaccess the View, the overarching bigger picture – the view from above?

We can use the same principles of Dzogchen Natural Meditation and apply them to a wide variety of natural meditations. We can, for example, practice earth gazing, fire gazing, water gazing, and even wind gazing. Most of us have gazed into bonfires or fireplaces. This can be a very heartwarming and calming, as well as a clarifying and centering, experience.

I personally like meditating by the ocean; I love the surfer's sense of throwing my mind out into the waves. The 'white noise' sound of the ocean is so pronounced and regular that it seems to synchronize with and take over the breathing process itself. When we practice earth gazing, we can look into any expanse that is vast and suggests the infinite or a sense of being lost in the earth. Deserts, mountains, canyons, and forests provide natural spots for earth gazing. The idea is to find spaces in which we can cast our small minds into the infinite so that our egoic small-self is awed and overtaken by a sacred sense of the infinite. A bonfire, for example, consumes everything; the ocean washes everything away; the Himalayas dwarf the largest mammal. A large wind gives the feeling of blowing everything away. Even seasons of the year can have this effect. The colors of autumn, for example, can overpower us with a sense of the beauty and grandeur of the natural world.

In the face of vastness such as this whatever is personally burdensome becomes smaller and less significant. The ocean, the fire, the earth, the wind takes over. We don't have to rely on natural phenomena for these meditations. We can use anything that naturally awes our wee little minds. Peering up at a skyscraper, the Parthenon, the Eiffel Tower, the Golden Gate Bridge, the pyramids of Egypt, or even a jumbo jet will do. The solidity, monumental scale, and hugeness of many manmade monuments can also serve as meditation objects providing the inspiration to draw us out of and beyond ourselves.

While doing these natural Dzogchen-style meditations, we breathe in and out in a regular, natural rhythm and let the natural experience of the infinite awe our finite sense of ourselves. These encounters with immensity can help us ground ourselves in reality; they can help us connect to what is and open up to the natural Buddha within.

Infinity can also be infinitely small. I have found a similar sense of sacred wonder and awe at the immensity of creation when viewing teeming anthills, or looking under a microscope and seeing the billions of creatures crowding every tiny drop of pond water, or peering into the face of a rose.

Henry Wadsworth Longfellow said it well in the following lines. This is a natural meditation instruction if there ever was one:

> ***Sit in reverie, and watch the changing***
> ***color of the waves that break upon the***
> ***ideal seashore of the mind.***

Conscious Drifting – Finding the Natural Meditations in Your Own Life

◆

Each of us needs to withdraw from the cares which will not withdraw from us. We need hours of aimless wandering, or spates of time sitting on park benches, observing the mysterious world of ants and the canopy of treetops.

MAYA ANGELOU

Natural mind or primordial intelligence informs those moments when we are most true to ourselves. These moments often occur when we are doing something I like to call 'conscious drifting.' Conscious drifting helps us get a glimpse of our natural Eden-like state. This is something we already are, not something we have to be injected with or acquire from anyone else.

Here are some examples of conscious drifting: staring at an ocean, lake, pond, river, waterfall, forest, or garden. Surprisingly enough, I think that fishing is for many people an instinctive expression of the human longing for peace, space, alone time, and a natural form of contemplative sweetness. One of my brother's mathematician friends spends a good part of each evening in the bathtub with a swiveling tray that holds papers filled with scrawled equations over his watery lap. Driving to my local post office, I often see a woman ambling along with her large dog. They both seem very happy. Conscious drifting has nothing to do with shirking responsibility, not to mention thinking or worrying. Quite the opposite. The symbol Thich Nhat Hanh chose for his hermitage at Plum Village in southern France is a hammock, which more than anything else expresses what 'drifting' means.

You can drift with others, 'Let's take a walk,' we say to a mate or a friend. Then without a real destination, we head off. 'I think there's a concert in the park. We could listen to some music. Or maybe ride the paddle-boats.' Drifting is letting things happen. Letting the mind drift. Sitting in the rocking chair and letting the clouds drift by. The secret inner aspect of this practice is relinquishing control by surrendering and trusting. Everything will be fine; what's the big deal?

Why is conscious drifting a spiritual practice? Because it helps us connect to our inner being. Our innate aliveness. Just being. To just be for a minute without trying to do anything; this is a spiritual discipline. It helps bring us more into the spirit of the moment – a spontaneous expression of oneness. We are in the right place at the right time. We can afford to just be there and enjoy it. Nothing special is required.

For Westerners it could be a leap to think of these unself-conscious moments as spiritual or connected to the sacred. And yet they are. About the truth that natural mind is Buddha-mind, Dzogchen master Kongtrul Rinpoche said, 'It seems too good to be true, so we don't believe it. It's so close that we overlook it.

It's so obvious that we don't notice it. It's not apart from ourselves so we can't obtain it.'

Dzogchen masters say that ordinariness and naturalness provide the most intimate approach to true being and the natural great perfection. Therefore it makes sense for each of us to find some natural, homegrown, conscious drifting meditations of our very own. This is the natural way to connect with the Buddha within.

At the end of a Dzogchen Foundation retreat in Santa Rosa, California, a student wrote the following poem about finding her own natural meditation. I think this poem eloquently reflects the innate wisdom in finding your own way to be through natural meditations.

I NEVER KNEW

Take off the backpack.
Lie down in long grass.
Pull up the blue sky-blanket.
Rest.

So many years of dharma practice, straight-spine diligence, straining toward enlightenment.
Today. This hillside. Just this.

Lie down in long grass
Let the earth take you.
Deer tracks and horse dung and the eye within the eye revolving and luminous
I never knew this.
Didn't someone tell me?

I remember my Zen Master in the interview room:
'Trust yourself,' he said. Just be yourself.'

I think his meaning was this:
Take off the backpack
Lie down in long grass.
Let the sky take you.
Rest.
Breathe space into space into space.

I never knew there was so much light.

DHARA GATLING-AUSTIN

Natural Walking Meditation

◆

Thoreau claimed that he needed no less than four hours a day of 'sauntering through the woods and over the hills and fields, absolutely free from all worldly engagements.' He wrote that he had met but one or two people in his life who understood 'the art of walking,' of what it means to just saunter and roam. I know two; one lives in Vermont, the other in Bhutan. Between the two of them, they must have touched most of the byways of this world with the love of their feet – and trod another firmer world as well.

Thoreau advised us to walk like a camel, which ruminates while slowly travelling. Thoreau likened this sauntering and wandering to the meandering of a river, which although seemingly willy-nilly in its course and progress is ineluctably finding the shortest course to the sea. He said, 'Every walk is a crusade.'

For most people, walking is an accessible and easy form of meditation. I think of my daily walk as a spiritual practice. I think of it – and these are the words I say to myself and hear in my head – as 'taking a walk with God.' No matter how deeply committed I may be to my nontheistic Buddhist practice, this ancient anachronistic theistic thought remains. It is probably ingrained in my Jewish gene pool, but never mind; it makes me happy. And I inevitably have the best possible walks in this best of all possible worlds. This is true. For 'one touch of nature makes the whole world kin,' as Shakespeare sang. I tell you, take a walk each day, and you too will be healed and whole again.

Whether or not I am with someone else – another person or my dog – the Eternal Companion accompanies me wherever I go. This is a gift I give myself. Like Thoreau, I find that I acquire rust if I stay in my 'chamber' for a single day without moving outside.

I don't think we need to be rigid about this and assume that the only walks that really count are walks in the woods or on a beach. Sometimes my walks are outside in the woods, but often I walk in city parks, on big boulevards as well as small streets, and even in airports or train stations. Even a walk in town, ambling along while looking at everything and nothing in particular, can be a very natural form of walking and drifting. In a pinch I've been known to walk up and down the aisles of trains or even planes, ships, and ferries. Sometimes I do slow-walking mindfulness meditation for an hour or so in whatever kind of terminal I might be waiting – along the platform or in the waiting room. Sometimes I just drift. After all, who is watching?

All you need is a comfortable pair of shoes. Or no shoes at all. This is *your* path. Your own feet will do.

Short Auto Meditation

◆

Paradise is where I am.
VOLTAIRE

Many of us spend long hours in the car. Since this is a natural part of our daily life, we should be able to integrate it into the spiritual path. Obviously we can never close our eyes to meditate while we are whizzing along the highway or even standing still in city traffic. Nonetheless we can effectively use meditative and mind-training techniques to improve our driving, calm down, and stay peaceful and focused even when we feel as though we are surrounded by automotive chaos.

Cultivate your own atmosphere of choice within your little spaceship, your automobile's interior. Remember my Zen master's koan, 'How to realize God while driving car?' Create your very own natural driving meditation to fit your particular frame of mind while driving. Here's one that I use:

Start with three breaths
Take a deep breath.
Inhale, exhale.
Pay attention
Inhale again, and let go.

Relax a little.
Release the tension,
the unnecessary hurrying and scurrying.
Sit in your own car seat.

Are your hands gripping the wheel?
That won't get you there any faster.
Is your back tense?
Shoulders bunched up?
How about your neck?
Stomach clenched perhaps?
Breath constricted, chest constricted?
Breathe, relax, smile.
You might as well enjoy the ride.

Settle back in your seat.
Relax
Fully inhabit your present experience
Here and now
Just sitting and driving the car.

Drive along the path
Driving home.
Be here now
at home and at ease
One with all.

You can bring the sacred into your life by creating the same kind of meditation to fit any activity that you do regularly.

Natural Light Energy Meditation

◆

The Sanskrit word 'prana' is usually defined as cosmic energy or the breath of life itself. Prana is found in the elements – fire, earth, air, and water. The sun, representing the element of fire, is a natural life-giving force, beaming warming light and energy on all of us.

In the East, the sun is often included in meditation practice. Everyone, for example, has seen pictures of the yogis in Benares facing the sun as they sit half naked on the wide old stone steps leading down to the Ganges River. Himalayan yogis have a similar tantric yoga practice of soaking up prana; it is called Light Energy Meditation.

To do this, we start by seating ourselves facing the sun. In the East, this is usually done early in the morning with the rising sun. We sit in a lotus or half-lotus position – or if this is uncomfortable, in a low beach chair. Place your hands on your knees, and your fingers in what is known as open mudra position. In this position your palms are facing up, the thumb and index finger of each of your hands touching gently, forming a little circle.

In this open asana (position), open yourself up to the sun's energy. As you breathe in and out, think of yourself taking in light and energy. Breathe it in through all the pores of your body. Let the outer energy vivify the inner light of spirit and awareness.

Breathe in the sun's energy through your arms, your legs, your face, your chest.

Breathe it in through your forehead and your fingertips.

Feel it soaking in through the soles of your feet and the palms of your hands.

Breathe in the light through your chakras, one by one, in ascending order – from your perineum, genitals, and navel up through your heart, throat, forehead, and out the top of your head.

Let the life-giving prana activate your inner energy, your natural wisdom, and your naturally loving heart.

Breathe in and out like a natural plant. As you do this, envision that your breath is being touched by the golden rays of the sun. Think of your breath going in and out, making a continuous circle. In Dzogchen, we call this the circle of luminosity that revolves continuously, day and night – that turns night into day.

Keep the breath going. Keep the energy flowing. Don't let it get stuck or become static.

You are receiving energy from an inexhaustible fountain. The universe is breathing through you so let it happen. If you feel like chanting, do so.

Himalayan yogis do this for fifteen or more minutes at a time. If you have a window facing the sun, try this practice for five or ten minutes in the morning to charge up. Or get to the park or beach early before the crowds, and use the gift of sunlight to help you find the sacred energy within.

As the golden sun rises on the eastern horizon, the golden inner light naturally rises within the temple of our bodies and within the heavens of our minds.

Embracing the Oceanic Goddess: A Natural Meditation

◆

Resting in water is an easy way to relax, heal, and return to the natural state. Try the following natural meditation to help put you more in touch with what it means to just Be.

Relax in bathtub, hot tub, Jacuzzi, lake, or pool.
Relax your head, your neck, and shoulders;
let all the tension drain away.

Lean back on something comfortable: a pillow,
  cushion, flotation device,
towel placed on edge of pool, or a soft warm lap.
Make yourself comfortable and safe.

Lie back in the warm, embryonic-fluidlike water.
Rest in the tub, float in the shallows,
or stretch out on a float.
Put your head back even more;
let go, surrender, relinquish control.
Open and vulnerable,
at home and at ease, space out a little.

Float. Drop your cares.
Let go and drop away body and mind.
Take rest. Relax. Breathe slowly
and quietly.
Let everything settle, in its own place,
in its own way,
in its own time.
Let it all go,
in natural flow.

Melt into the warm water.
Relax.
Dissolve.
Let all your cares melt
and flow away.

Now, look up
into the light—
light of sky,
of window, skylight,
or a white ceiling.
Raise your gaze,
elevate your awareness.
Look up into the infinite.

Watch your mind.
Watch all the mental events
and experiences
pass through like clouds.
Gaze into infinite space;
mingle mind with openness and awareness;
dissolve into luminous centerless openness,

the natural state
of pristine, primordial being – just being.

If there is a massage jet or hot water inlet flowing,
put the back of your neck against it
and let it gradually massage away all your cares
and preoccupations.
Return to the womb, prenatal,
before separation and individuation.

Bathe in that warmth, that love,
and light.
Lean back into it, in the water; lean forward into
it,
Rest in that feeling of wholeness and completeness.
Rest in the natural peace, simplicity, and buoyance
of natural meditation,
at home in this
innate great perfection.

Gardening and Other Naturally Grounding Practices

◆

Each one has his own most real thing.
Mine is the garden.
LOUISA YEOMANS KING

Ask yourself the following question: In the course of my daily life, what activities make me feel most grounded and alive – connected, and at home with myself and my surroundings?

Many men and women tell me that they feel connected to their center when they are cutting the grass, shoveling snow, chopping wood, or raking leaves. Some people tell me that they enjoy doing crossword puzzles because they find the process involving, grounding, and real. Dog walkers the world over know that walking with their canine pals can be a complete and natural meditative experience. What could be a more authentically satisfying way to spend twenty minutes than taking a walk with a dog? In the mornings I often see businessmen in suits walking the family dog before going to work; this is a ritual they can't leave home without.

I have a friend who feeds the birds in the winter. She has several feeders, and great flocks of chickadees, finches, and woodpeckers arrive in her yard every day to eat amazing quantities of birdseed. Once you make a commitment to feeding the birds, you have to stick with it because they count on the food being there. Every day she refills the feeders and cleans the ground around them. She hangs fresh suet in the trees, and throws down corn and peanuts for the squirrels. Most days it takes almost half an hour, but the time my friend spends filling the bird feeders gives her a natural sense of the lovely and sweet interconnectedness of all beings, large and small. She looks like a temple keeper while doing it.

When I return from a trip, I always find that I need to do some little activity that grounds me in the moment and helps me return naturally. There are dozens of activities that serve this purpose for me. I find it peaceful, for example, to wash and fold laundry. I have several friends who like to knit; others like to use their hands to work with tools.

I also like to sew. My mother taught me how when I was quite young and home sick from school. I think we made quilt covers. I even learned to use her sewing machine. Perhaps it was the continuous repetitions and meticulous regularity that I liked. It wasn't much of a guy thing, so as I approached adolescence, I quickly forgot that I ever knew how to do it. Then years later in Nepal, we needed to make instrument covers for the ritual bells and drums that we used in monastic ceremonies, and once again I found myself sewing and remembered that I enjoyed doing it. Once I even made a long robe.

Like many others, I sometimes find that cooking can be naturally grounding. Those who play musical instruments talk about the degree of total mindfulness and attention that is required. My cat-loving and -owning friends tell me that curling up on the couch with a furry feline creates a naturally meditative state. It must be true, since it's been scientifically shown that being around a cat can lower blood pressure!

An activity that most of us engage in, to one degree or another, is gardening. Your garden may be nothing more than a window box, a couple of potted geraniums, or some houseplants. Yet they need some small amount of care and attention. They need regular watering; the dead leaves need to be removed; they need a little bit of plant food every now and then. Taking care of even a few plants can turn into a natural loving meditation.

People who spend a great deal of time in their gardens attest to the natural mindfulness that gardening requires. What could be more naturally mindful than weeding? It requires a great deal of sustained attention. Weeds need to be taken up with care: Pull too hard, and the weed breaks in your fingers, leaving the root to grow and spread. Different weeds need different techniques and, sometimes, tools. When we weed our gardens, we have to pay attention to where and how we walk and bend. Move too far in one direction or another, and we'll squash growing things.

There is much joy and inner peace to be found in watching new flowers bloom. *Oh look*, we think, noticing new blooms and removing the ones that are about to go to seed. When we garden, we grow ourselves wisdom and understanding of the many interrelated forces that produce the miracle of growth. Gardening helps us love and care more. And what could be more soulful, prayerful, and spiritual than kneeling in a sunlit garden with our head bowed and our hands in the dirt as we try to cultivate the fruits of the earth?

There have been experiments that showed that plants and gardens grow most beautifully when they are talked to and prayed over. Years ago I met an Anglican bishop who was tending a garden in a spiritual community during the summer. He played music to his garden. If I remember correctly he said that the string beans liked Mozart, and the squash preferred rock and roll.

Of course, some gardens have no green growth at all and while they might like music, they definitely don't need water. When I took my parents to see the famous rock and sand gardens in the Zen temples in Kyoto, Japan, they both exclaimed in unison, 'Where's the garden, Jeffrey?' What they saw was a vast, perfectly raked expanse of white sand with four or five rocks clustered, almost randomly, in one section. The rocks stuck up like mountains in the sea of existence. This famous garden style was created by a Zen master some five hundred or more years ago; when we view it today, it makes a totally existential modern art statement as well as providing the visitor with a reminder that even the rocks are flowing in this mysterious universe that is sometimes called God's garden.

Walking in any garden reminds us of mankind's original garden. We can't go back in time to those mythological moments, but we can return to the Eden-like state that exists within our own being. A friend of mine has a son who is now grown, but when he was three years old, he told his family that when he grew up he intended to be a farmer so he could sit around and watch things grow. What could be more sacred, more naturally meditative? People in the Midwest say that on summer evenings you can hear the corn grow. How silent everything else must be.

What is the garden in your life? What do you want to watch grow and flower? It may be a standard garden with dirt and flowers, or it might be something else. Some people tiptoe into their children's bedrooms at night to watch them sleep. Their children clearly are the flowers they love best. We find our natural meditations in those places and ways of being that we love best. There is great peace in cultivating and gardening all the things that we hope to nurture in our lives, from our work to our families.

Gardening helps us realize somatically, viscerally, the laws of growth and gradual unfolding. We can't pull the plants up to make them grow, but we can help facilitate and midwife their blooming, each in its own way, time, and proper season. I have learned a little about patience and humility from my gardens. It's so obviously not something I'm doing that creates this miracle! I also like to reflect upon and appreciate the exquisitely evanescent, transitory, and poignant nature of things in the garden.

Growing a garden is one of the best ways to grow ourselves and cultivate our true selves. Then all the daily shit we go through can be transmuted into manure on the spiritual field of bodhi flowers – flowers of awakening. Everything becomes useful and has meaning and purpose regardless of how it seems to us at the time because it's all grist for the spiritual mill.

If you love the Dharma, you have to farm it.

Go to a garden
And just stand in it.
Breathe in the air, the fragrances,
the light, the temperature,
the music of the different plants, insects, birds, worms, caterpillars, grasshoppers, and butterflies.

Inhale the prana (cosmic energy) of all these abundantly growing things.
Recharge your inner batteries.
This is the joy of natural meditation.

Breathe, Smile, and Relax: Delivering Joy

◆

Your mindful breath and your smile will bring happiness to you and those around you. Even if you spend a lot of money on gifts for everyone . . . nothing you could buy them can give as much true happiness as your gift of awareness, breathing, and smiling, and these precious gifts cost nothing.

Zen master THICH NHAT HANH

Breathe, smile, and relax.
Breathe, smile, and relax.
Breathe, smile, and relax.
Breathe, smile, and relax.
Breathe, smile, and relax.

Such a simple natural practice. Breathe, smile, and relax. Let go. Try doing it five times. Ten. Twenty. Do it whenever you have a few seconds. Do it while you are walking to the water cooler or riding an elevator. Do it while you are standing in a crowded subway or walking home from work. Do it while you are stopped at a red light or waiting for the laundry to finish the last few minutes of the dry cycle. Instead of reading tabloid headlines while you are on a supermarket line, breathe, smile, relax, and let go.

This natural meditation can help us in countless ways. It's a quick technique to remind us to relax, be mindful, be authentic, be joyful, be present, and connect to others.

A Zen story I've always loved is about Hotei, a Chinese Zen master whom many call the Happy Buddha. We've all seen little statues of Hotei. He is typically depicted as a plump, smiling guy, carrying a large sack over his shoulder. In many ways, he can be described as Asia's Santa Claus.

During his lifetime, Hotei would walk through the streets carrying a huge sack of candy, fruit, and other goodies. Children would run up to him, and he would plop down his bag, reach in, and hand out his gifts to anyone who asked.

Although many considered Hotei a Zen master, he had no inclination to teach formally. Paul Reps tells the following story about Hotei in his wonderful collection of Zen stories, *Zen Flesh, Zen Bones*:

'Whenever he met a Zen devotee he would extend his hand and say: "Give me one penny." And if anyone asked him to return to a temple to teach others, again he would reply: "Give me one penny."

'Once as he was about his play-work, another Zen master happened along and inquired. "What is the significance of Zen?"

'Hotei immediately plopped his sack down on the ground in silent answer.

'"Then," asked the other, "what is the actualization of Zen?"

‘At once the Happy Chinese man swung the sack over his shoulder and continued on his way.’

Being happy and cheerful is a wonderful gift that we can give ourselves as well as those we meet. When I was first in India, one of the things that impressed me most about my spiritual teachers was how happy they looked. Many of them had experienced severe hardships, were refugees, or had serious illnesses, and yet they smiled, laughed, and had a keen sense of fun – all the time. Even today, when I look at the smile on the face of someone like the Dalai Lama, I automatically want to smile back. Here’s a meditation to help you smile like a Buddha.

LAUGHING BUDDHA/SMILING YOGA MEDITATION

Sit down, relax.
Breathe and smile.
Be happy, be peaceful
Let’s practice the smiling yoga.
Smile. Smile even more. Smile as if you were
enlightened.
Happy, blissful, delighted,
A happy camper on the shore of nirvana’s shining
sea.
Smile. Grin. Be silly
Breathing in. Relax your mind.
Breathing out, smile, smile,
And smile
Buddhas have more fun.
So try to look as enlightened as you can.

Why pretend to be unhappy, harried, and
miserable?
Since we all pretend anyway,
Why not pretend to be happy for a change?
See how that feels.
Try to look and act as if you are totally enlightened.
What would that look like?
Free, joyful, light, and buoyant.
Glorious, radiant, peaceful.
Perfectly content and fulfilled.
Fully evolved.
Awakened Buddha.
Be Buddha.
You too can do it.
Be Buddha. You-dha.
Become Buddhaful.
Smile wildly, turn your head upward, elevate your
spirit.
Let the mind unfurl and the heart soar.
Press your shining face up against the heavens,
Open to blessings, loving acceptance and
forgiveness.
Look as enlightened as you possibly can.
Smile happily.
Why not be happy?
Allow joy to happen.
Don't close yourself up.
Be 'there' now.
Be happy. Be peaceful. Be whole, complete,
luminous;
Be at home and at ease before your own hearth
An organic homegrown American Home-Buddha in

his or her own,
natural Buddha-field.
Smile, Home Buddha.
Enjoy yourself.
Be yourself, your true self.
Enjoy it. You deserve it.
Be happy.
Be Buddhaful
Be happy
Be beautiful
You are.

Write a Haiku

◆

In Zen Buddhism, poetry and practice always go together.
THICH NHAT HANH

I've always loved the simple spare form of poetry known as haiku. A Japanese haiku traditionally has three lines and seventeen syllables, and it usually invokes some aspect of nature or the physical world in the present moment. Many call it the world's most elegant form of poetry, and I agree.

When we write haiku we try not to add anything on to the word photograph we are creating. No emotion, no judgment, no interpretation. A haiku is a snapshot of a moment; in this way it captures a moment of reality. It is remarkable because it presents a picture of what is, just as it is.

The best known haiku poet is Basho, who lived in the seventeenth century. The following Basho haiku is arguably the best known in the world:

An old pond
Frog jumps in
Plop!

As we read this haiku, our mind creates an image of

the pond. It's expressive, beautiful, and simple. If we are standing by the pond, and if we are present in that moment, we will hear the sound of frog hitting water – nothing more and nothing less. If we stand by the pond, lost in our thoughts and the clutter of our lives, we will overlook the moment. We will miss the payoff; we will miss the 'plop.' Dr R. H. Blyth, an early British authority on haiku and Zen literature, described haiku in the following way:

'It is a way of returning to nature, to our moon nature, our cherry blossom nature, our falling leaf nature, in short, to our Buddha nature.' And that, of course, is the final definition of simplicity. Unalloyed, innate spiritual nature is the natural simplicity we each carry.

Haiku is a creative as well as natural and spontaneous way to simplify and essentialize your jumbled thought process. This is an enjoyable tried-and-true method that you can use to focus on the moment. Modern haiku poets, particularly in the West, typically retain the three-line structure, but they are far less stringent about the number of syllables that can be used. So when you write haiku, don't worry, nobody's counting syllables.

Right now, take three easy, deep breaths in and out. Center in the moment. What is taking place around you right now? Inhabit the moment by composing a haiku. For example, I'm in my house on a beautiful autumn day. Outside my window are a group of crows. Here's a spontaneous present-moment haiku:

From the treetops
Autumn crows
splashing mulberries on white car.

When asked, a friend gave me another present-moment haiku:

An orange cat walks
a straight line
to the sun.

Another friend calling from a car phone spontaneously provided me with another haiku that captured a moment of frustration in his life:

Cold day,
hot soup
Missing spoon

Once when camping in Nepal, I wrote the following haiku:

Toilet paper roll falling
down latrine hole
Eek!

Recently I've seen some very amusing haiku making the rounds on the Internet. As you can imagine, most of them are about computer stress. For example:

No power
No e-mail
What to do?

or

Work accidently deleted
lost yet again
A new beginning.

The great haiku masters wrote about the poetry of life in all its nitty-gritty aspects. They wrote about fleas, and flies, and horse droppings, not just about flowers. Issa, the great haiku master who lived from 1763 to 1827, wrote hundreds of haiku about insects. He was often quite funny and sometimes downright cynical. As a Buddhist, Issa respected the Buddha-nature in all beings. The following haiku shows his sensitivity to a small sparrow:

little bird
out of the way, out of the way!
The stallions are coming through.

Here's another example of a haiku by the humane Issa:

Don't worry, spiders
I clean the house
casually.

Haiku is like a natural form of meditation that helps you connect to the 'nowness' of life. You can use it to capture a moment of sadness, joy, beauty, or even utter banality. Try it right now and see how it grounds you to the moment. Describe this moment in a haiku. Let yourself open directly to the moment. Each moment is brief, but it includes within it the entire universe.

Children pretending to be cormorants
Even more marvelous
than cormorants.

ISSA

Dream Yoga

◆

In a dream we may initially feel that everything is concrete, but then suddenly remember that it is a dream. When you are aware in a dream, you know you are dreaming and that it is unreal. You know you are in a state of unreality. Once you have this experience, you can also make discoveries about your daily life such as about your major attachments.

NAMKHAI NORBU RINPOCHE

Have you ever had the experience of being awake enough in your dream to know that you are still asleep? In these experiences while we are dreaming, we are caught up in the melodrama of the dream, but just for a moment or longer, we might have a twofold vision of what is taking place. We are the dreamer, but we also have a God's-eye view of the dream, looking down on ourselves.

In Western psychology, this is called 'lucid dreaming,' and there are several practices and techniques for helping us awaken within our dreams. Carlos Castaneda wrote of his shaman mentor instructing him to practice trying to find his right hand in the dream so that he had a reference point to help him grasp that he was dreaming.

We tend to be aware that something is going on in our dreams that we can't quite explain. Some people have telepathic dreams in which they are aware of what loved ones are doing or thinking miles and miles away. I have a friend who says she received clear messages in her dreams, like 'Call your mother, she is feeling sick.' These messages are often accurate enough to make her pay attention.

Some people have predictive dreams about events that really take place. I remember reading that Lincoln had such a dream before he was shot. Quite a few people have told me about receiving messages from a dead relative that seemed very important. The Australian Aborigines actually have a concept of dream time, in which the dead get in touch with the living through their dreams.

Once in our monastery in France, I had many dreams about my late teacher, the Sixteenth Karmapa. Almost every night he visited me in my dreams, showing me his smiling face, and giving me teachings and initiations. One night he gave me an elaborate teaching on the eighty-one special secret oral instructions of the dakini, and he also gave me his bell and 'vajra' (diamond sceptre) from his hands into mine as a symbol of transferring wisdom and compassion in an initiatory manner. I held them in my hands, and he dissolved into me, and I experienced a great sense of bliss and oneness. It was a wonderful experience. In the dream I put the bell and sceptre down near my meditation seat where I meditated all day.

In the morning when I woke up, I was excited. I went to my teacher, Nyoshul Khenpo. Usually when I told him this kind of thing, he would say, 'Oh it was just a dream.' But in this case, I think he must have been affected by my excitement because he asked me to tell him every detail. And then he said, 'So what were the eighty-one secret oral teachings of the Dakini, and where is the Karmapa's bell and sceptre?'

And I had to say, 'I don't remember, and I don't have them.'

He put up his hands . . . so what to do? Later when Khenpo and I discussed it more, he said that there were stories of lamas discovering secret mystical teachings through their dreams. Sometimes they even had physical proof to support their claims of what they had received through their dreams and visions. In some instances lamas received sacred writings on old rice paper, as well as statues, or directions to a specific site that verified their claims.

These dreams in which we receive visitations in our sleep are blessed dreams. We are receiving love and support, usually from someone we care about or who cares about us. They feel real while they are happening, and perhaps they are. We tend to remember these dreams.

If we are going to bring the sacred and spiritual practice into every aspect of our lives, we have to consider how much of our life we spend asleep – roughly 30 percent for most people. Since the essence of Buddhism is awakening, what better time to practice doing it than when we are fast asleep? In Tibet we find the unique practice of dream yoga; in this way, practitioners use even sleep time to awaken. Tibetans call it 'seizing the dream.' By that we mean that we are becoming masters of the dream life; we are grasping the fact that we are dreaming while we are still asleep. We are masters of our projections, not victimized or deceived by them.

Here's how we do this.

Before going to sleep at night, settle down for a minute and crystallize your intention to 'seize' your dream. Affirm these intentions by chanting:

For the welfare and well-being of the world
And the sake of spiritual awakening
May I seize my dreams and awaken within them
And realize the true nature of mind and all things.

Chant this several times until you feel clear about this intention.

Then prepare yourself for sleep. Lie Down. Relax. Breathe in and out easily. Be peaceful. Be calm. Be joyous and happy. You are going to sleep. You are going to rest.

As you close your eyes, look into the shimmering dark or black light behind your eyelids.

Then visualize the syllable *Aah*.

In Dzogchen we visualize the symbol ཨ which is pronounced *Aah*.

Imagine that this *Aah* is written down in shining, glowing white letters, right there before your eyes.

Concentrate on the *Aah*.

Focus on it.

Then allow yourself to gradually go into that light.

As you fall asleep, dissolve gradually into the *Aah*.

Enter into the inner light and spontaneously awaken in the perfectly luminous, clear, dream light.

Row, row, row your boat, gently down the stream.
Merrily, merrily, merrily, merrily
Life is but a dream.

Finding a Deeper Silence

◆

There is no need to go to India or anywhere else to find peace. You will find that deep place of silence right in your room, your garden, or even your bathtub.

ELISABETH KÜBLER-ROSS

What could be more natural than silence? What could be more sacred? What could be more simple? Silence is the universal language of the soul. True inner silence is unpolluted by anxieties, habitual preoccupations and refrains, noisy internal static, innuendos, or agendas. Inner silence speaks directly to inner peace, which is beyond the dualism of noise and quiet. To question the purpose of silence is like asking about the purpose of fresh air, for no one can live without at least a modicum of it.

Many of the qualities we attribute to a divine spirit of love or sacred presence reflect the truest and most sacred silence. Divine silence is accepting, nonjudgmental, forgiving, openminded, and great-hearted. Divine silence implies the ability to listen, to hear, and to love. When we communicate with the sacred, whether we think of it as being an inner or outer presence, these are the qualities we take for granted. These are qualities we are seeking to nurture in ourselves as we cultivate the sacred within.

The Society of Friends, known as Quakers, believe that the silence holds all the answers. In silence they find God; in silence they find love, truth, community, and all the guidance and meaning they need. In silence they wait for divine wisdom. There is an old and true story about a group of Quakers who were gathered for their silent meeting of worship when America was still a group of colonies. Suddenly some irate Native Americans stormed into the meeting. No one in the congregation stirred, and the Quakers continued their silent meeting. The Native Americans were so impressed and moved by the spirit of silence that instead of confronting the group with hostility, they sat down and joined the Quakers in the sacred silence.

I have many students and friends who are Quakers. A couple of years ago some of them invited me to join them when they visited a group of inmates at a correctional institute in upstate New York. It is a part of the Quaker ministry to visit prisons and introduce the practice of silence to the prison population. When I have been with them I have been tremendously moved by the prisoners who spoke about the power of silence and its ability to bring about spiritual transformation and healing.

In Tibetan Buddhism, there is a well-known picture of the extraordinary yogi Milarepa, who lived many years in silent retreat. He is most often depicted sitting on the ground outside his Himalayan cave with his hand cupped to his ear. Milarepa, who wrote hundreds of songs of devotion, is listening to the celestial sound of silence from which his extemporaneous poems of enlightenment come forth. By becoming silent and listening, really listening, he became a channel-like flute through which these beautiful notes could be played. It reminds me of a lovely traditional hymn I've heard: 'Over my head, I hear music in the air, there must be a God somewhere.'

The late great Indian sage and teacher Meher Baba was silent for his entire adult life. He used a chalkboard and pointed at the letters. Even though he had taken a vow of silence, he did amazing work in Bombay's crowded mental institutions in the first half of the twentieth century. How was he able to communicate with people crowded together under the worst possible conditions? How could he make a difference without speaking? And yet he did.

Many Christian monks and nuns take vows of silence. I once went with the Dalai Lama to visit the Grand Chartreuse Monastery in France. It was the quietest place I've ever been. The abbot met the Dalai Lama at the gate, and only he was allowed to enter this monastery where cloistered monks lived in silence. Even standing outside the gates, the rest of us could sense the centuries of silence that lay over that sylvan valley. Contemplative silence seemed to invest and bless every molecule of the atmosphere.

Most of the time we are surrounded with sound. I know people who never turn off a television or radio. They keep their sets on for company. And we all talk so much of the time – to each other, to ourselves, to our nonverbal pets. We even talk in our sleep. Does the inner narrative ever stop? Wouldn't it be nice to have a reprieve or to bring one about intentionally? Wouldn't it be wonderful to be able to become so quiet, so still, so silent that we could hear the sacred presence?

Silence has always been a spiritual practice. In India there is an entire sect of silent yogis, called 'Mauni

Babas.' The word 'mauni' means silence, and for these yogis, this silence is their life practice. I once asked one of them, whose name was also Mauni Baba, why he kept silent. In reply, he pointed to his disciple, a teenage boy who had not yet undertaken the vow of silence.

The teenager told me that Mauni Baba communes only with God. I asked, 'What about people, what about birds, what about animals?' The boy said that Mauni Baba had so totally learned to speak to God that for him, talking to anybody was like talking to God . . . in silence. This reminded me of Surdas, the sixteenth-century blind poet of India, whose name I was given by my first guru, Neem Karoli Baba. Surdas' devotion was so complete that he was said to be blind to everything but God. He kept a silent vigil of inner vision.

Practices, like silence, help holy men and women focus more intensely on the spiritual path and the meaning to which they are dedicating their lives. When the Mauni Babas of India, for example, stop speaking, they are intentionally limiting their focus in order to intensify their devotional practice. They then later expand their focus so they can speak to God in everyone using the universal nonverbal language of the heart and soul. Prayers are heard in all languages. The divine spirit of love hears the silence of our sincerity and intentions, regardless of whatever noisemakers and party hats we may don.

The one quality that sets apart the great prophets of the ages is their ability to listen and hear divine or sacred presence. Rumi once wrote: 'God said of Muhammad: He is an ear.'

Silence is true; silence is grace,
silence is golden
Silence is medicinal,
Silence heals
Silence is real.
It is within you.

Silence is a natural mindfulness practice that has its roots in ancient monastic discipline. Silence, a form of inner fasting, is a time-honored way of hearing your own truth. Silence is not boring, and it's not lonely. So don't be afraid of it. Anyone who has ever lived or worked, even briefly, next to a construction site knows what a blessed relief it can be when the noise stops.

Silent practice helps us learn to stop our own noise. Fasting or depriving any of the senses makes them that much more sensitive and acute. I know that when I was in retreat, and we spent six months in silence, I became much more sensitive to the people around me. It felt as though it was possible to read people's moods just by the way they placed their sandals outside the door. I was struck by how much nonverbal language and communication there was. The practice of silence helps us learn to hear; it helps us develop awareness; it helps us see and feel. It can make us as sensitive as a tuning fork to the vibrations around us.

In Buddhism, the practice of intentional silence is called Noble Silence, and some monks and nuns practice Noble Silence for days, weeks, months, and even years at a time. You can begin to enjoy the benefits of Noble Silence by setting aside regular periods of time and engaging in your own silent retreats. Trust me, you can get many of the miraculous benefits of silence without committing yourself to very long periods of time. A silent lunch break or afternoon once a week, for example, can go a long way in helping you get in touch with your own deeper silence and inner peace.

When we take a vow of silence, for even a short period of time, we are agreeing to the following:

- no speaking
- no listening to the radio or television
- no gesticulating or sign language
- no eye contact in order to send messages
- no scribbling of notes, letter writing, or e-mail
- no reading

A general instruction for silent practice is: 'No input and no output.' There is, of course, a great deal of natural input and output around us that we can't stop, but Noble Silence limits the habitual input and output that we create ourselves. In this way, we can begin to listen and hear on a deeper level. Rumi said:

> *Close the language door, and open the love window,*
> *the moon won't use the door, only the window.*

Turn off the phone, and try taking a vow of silence for just an hour. It's a wonderfully contemplative practice to follow while you are taking a walk in the woods or along a beach. Start with an hour at first, then extend it to longer periods of time. Be silent for a morning, an afternoon, a day, or even a weekend.

I like to begin periods of silence by taking a shower or bath, or even just washing my face. This symbol of outer purification is a way to remind ourselves that we are engaging in a spiritual practice. During periods of Noble Silence, try to give your ego a rest. Don't feed your inner dialogues – the litanies of 'he said, she said' – or dissipate your sacred energy by telling yourself stories about life. Just relax and enjoy the present. Keep your thoughts positive. Relax and let your silence grow. Don't dwell on negative ideas or judgments about people or life.

Allow the silence to unfold. Trust the wisdom of your inner voice. Let the spotlight of awareness become deeper. Listen and be open to what is already there. Have faith and trust that there is much that is given around you – much beauty, much splendor, much music. We don't always have to create artificial stimulation. Listen to the sound of silence – the music of the celestial spheres.

> *Men cannot see their reflection in running water, but only in still water. Only that which is itself still can still the seekers of stillness.*
>
> CHUANG TZU

Live in the Now – Now, or Never

◆

Living in the now is a natural practice, because the present moment is the natural state. We're always in the now, even if we don't totally know it. If we are remembering the past, where does that take place except in the now through present awareness? If we are thinking about the future, we are doing our planning and thinking now. We are always in the present no matter how scattered and distracted we may be.

Returning to the now and maintaining that awareness is like coming home to ourselves. Of course, just as we've never been anyone else, we've never been anywhere else. But we lose touch, and we forget. Yet, it's always now. Now or never. This is our sane sanctuary in time called right now. It's where we really are no matter what stories we are telling ourselves. That's why it's such a relief to simply rest in the present, just as we are. Opening up to the miracle of the present moment is a gift we give ourselves.

I've always found it interesting and amusing that in Tibetan we use the same word for an aeon and an instant. Eternity, which is the sacred, is in this most fleeting moment. We experience the infinite in each finite thing, in each finite moment. The more free we become of the bonds of past and future, the better we are able to taste eternity in this instant.

Not that long ago, I visited Kathmandu for the first time in a dozen years. I found many changes had taken place. New urban development had reared its ugly head in the form of gray, square concrete tenements filled with Tibetan and Nepali refugees. The rice paddies around the Tibetan refugee camp of Bodhanath, formerly flooded with water and green rice shoots, were now filled with several dozen monasteries and countless small brick-and-concrete houses. The water pollution and air pollution was palpable. The noise level grated on me.

One day a French friend of mine and I took a break from the week-long monastery rituals we were involved in; we wanted to shop for Buddhas, silk, and other gifts to bring home. We decided to revisit the old Kathmandu town where we had both once spent so much time during the Seventies.

We passed by the tourist-thronged bazaar called Freak Street and headed for the river to see if it still looked the same. We found the old Hindu cremation site and riverside temple with a gnarled huge old tree still growing there, its tangled roots still sticking up out of the ground near where a hanging footbridge used to span the river. Kathmandu was still recognizable, but so intensely built up that we couldn't find some of the cheap old hotels and guest houses that we had frequented back then. The Pie and Chai Shop, the town's original hipster sweet shop destination, was still there but the Inn Eden was no longer to be found. In its place was a tall brick-and-concrete hotel, still under construction in its upper stories. The lobby and the lower floors, in the meantime, were already in business. Some things never change.

Walking near the river and then up the aptly named Pig Alley, where pigs used to be herded back and forth to the river for watering, sale, and slaughtering, we headed back toward the heart of Kathmandu. We passed near an old sunken spring and well where the sari-clad Nepalese women were still washing their clothes in the traditional manner, pounding them on the rocks and then hanging them out to dry in the sun on nearby stone walls, tree limbs, and fences. And then we stopped.

We were standing there, pop-eyed, craning our necks and looking around for the two- and three-story wood-mud-brick-and-thatch-roofed dwellings we used to stay in down on Pig Alley about a block from the river. We were reminiscing and joking when my French friend started crying, filled with longing for the good old days and our long-lost youth, along with the dreams she had had as a young woman of twenty. We must have been speaking loudly in order to hear each other above the usual Pig Street cacophony, for a shuttered window suddenly swung open from a second-story room in the five-story apartment building that now stood in the very place where our old digs used to be. A Buddhist monk in yellow robes poked his shaved head out the window and shouted at us, 'Live in the present!' He pulled his head back in, and the wooden shutters slammed shut with a bang. It was an appropriate reminder.

John Ruskin was a nineteenth-century social theorist who was so far ahead of his time that he proposed social reforms like retirement pensions and public education in 1865. On his desk he had a stone on which one word was carved: *Today*. Try creating a word, slogan, or mantra for yourself, one that helps bring you back to the joy of where you are right now. Place it where you will notice it regularly, as a reminder.

William Stafford was a well-known American poet and pacifist who died in 1993. On the morning he died, he wrote a poem that contained the line 'Be ready for what God sends.' I keep the following poem by William Stafford on the bulletin board in my study to remind me to remain attentive and awake, open to the miracle and sacredness of the present moment.

YES

It could happen any time, tornado,
earthquake, Armageddon. It could happen.
Or sunshine, love, salvation.

It could, you know. That's why we wake
and look out – no guarantees
in this life.

But some bonuses, like morning,
like right now, like noon,
like evening.

Epilogue

◆

For all that has been, thanks.
To all that shall be, yes.
DAG HAMMARSKJÖLD

When I first arrived in India in 1971 as a young college graduate, I was not alone in my search for the spiritual wisdom and teachings of the East. In fact, I was part of a wave; since the 1950s, many Westerners, women and men, old and young, have travelled back to the timeless East, back in place and time, seeking meaning and spiritual renewal.

The first time I walked into a Buddhist meditation center in India in 1971, it blew my mind. The feeling of peace and silence was awesome. I could have cut it with a knife – or so it seemed. The profundity of that sense of serenity within my own soul was undeniable; it was palpable. I knew it. I felt it. Nothing was more real for me.

I knew I wanted and needed that kind of inner peace. It was hardly a conscious decision. It was perfectly obvious to me at that time – a foregone conclusion that I had come home, spiritually speaking. There was nowhere else to go, nothing else to do. I had not yet met my guru, yet this was the beginning of my formal journey, my spiritual training. I had unconsciously, suddenly upgraded my desires. I wanted enlightenment; not just to get high, but to be free. This was the passion, the love of my life.

Back then I gave little thought to any part I or my fellow travellers would play in completing the circle by bringing these wisdom teachings back home to the West. Now this is something I think about all the time. I've come to realize that we are all seekers, spiritual wayfarers. We all have spiritual DNA; wisdom and truth is part of our genetic structure even if we don't always access it. We are all living, breathing spirit, embodied in mental form.

When we stop and think about it, we realize that some of our deepest spiritual roots are found in other parts of this planet. Our Western culture, as we now know it, started its journey to modern times from its native home in the Middle East. Our early ancestors began their travels, making their way westward around the Mediterranean up through northern Europe and across the Atlantic. Today, it seems appropriate that even as we move forward in time so many are reaching back to find ways of incorporating the timeless wisdom of the East into their lives, no matter what their chosen spiritual denomination or the religion of their family of origin.

We can all perceive that there is a great spiritual hunger today for meaning and humane values. It is estimated that 98 percent of all Americans believe in God; 90 percent pray regularly. The renewed public interest in spirituality of all kinds, wherever it may be found, is a natural expression of our shared longing for freedom and truth, for inner peace, joy, and fulfillment.

It is my prayer and wish that this public conversation, so pertinent in today's crazy, speedy, confusing times, may help transform the atmosphere of spirituality today by infusing it with the light, fresh breeze of timeless Buddhist wisdom coupled with heartfelt compassion and the spirit of unselfish service and altruism. I hope these teachings are able to help you, the reader, find your own inner truth and wisdom, awakening to the inexhaustible love and untrammelled inner incandescence that is your true spiritual nature.

I hope and pray that this style of post-denominational spiritual teaching and spiritual social activism can help our society, our young, and succeeding generations to find more spiritual and intellectual inspiration, moral guidance, wisdom, and divine blessings. I hope it may help facilitate and midwife their personal blossoming and spiritual awakening and contribute to a nonviolent and more peaceful, sane, and safe world.

SURYA DAS
Concord, Massachusetts
January 1999

◆

RECOMMENDED READING

Creating your own personal spiritual life from scratch means, among other things, that you get to decide for yourself what books, audios, CDs, and tapes speak directly to your spirit. Here are some that speak to me – like meeting the authors themselves. I find the company of these spiritual 'elders' so inspiring, edifying, and enjoyable that I can't resist referring you to their doorways. A good book – the right book in the right place at the right time – has transformed many a life.

Across the country, there are now a good number of bookstores that specialize in spiritual books. Take some time to browse in bookstores, or do it online. I have found that one of the best ways to research books that are available is by looking at catalogues from bookstores that specialize in spiritual material.

Books

(Many of the following titles are also available on audiotape.)

Peace Is Every Step: The Path of Mindfulness in Everyday Life. Thich Nhat Hanh. New York: Bantam Books, 1991.

The Long Road Turns to Joy: A Guide to Walking Meditation. Thich Nhat Hanh. Berkeley, CA: Parallex Press, 1996.

Insight Meditation: The Practice of Freedom. Joseph Goldstein. Boston: Shambhala Publications, 1993.

Zen Flesh, Zen Bones. Paul Reps, Nyogen Senzaki. Boston: Charles E. Tuttle, 1998.

The Healing Power of Mind. Tulku Thondup. Boston: Shambhala Publications, 1996.

Rainbow Painting. Tulku Urgyen Rinpoche. Boudhanath, Hong Kong: Rangjung Yeshe Publications, 1995.

The Tibetan Book of Living and Dying. Sogyal Rinpoche. San Francisco: Harper San Francisco, 1992.

Lovingkindness: The Revolutionary Art of Happiness. Sharon Salzberg. Boston: Shambhala Publications, 1995.

Zen Mind, Beginner's Mind. Shunryu Suzuki. New York: Weatherhill, 1994.

I Am That: Talks with Sri Nisargadatta. Maharaj Nisargadatta. New York: Aperture, 1990.

Going to Pieces Without Falling Apart: A Buddhist Perspective on Wholeness. Mark Epstein. New York: Broadway Books, 1998.

Nothing Special: Living Zen. Charlotte Joko Beck, Steve Smith (editor). San Francisco: Harper San Francisco, 1994.

When Things Fall Apart: Heart Advice for Difficult Times. Pema Chodron. Boston: Shambhala Publications, 1997.

It's Easier Than You Think: The Buddhist Way to Happiness. Sylvia Boorstein. San Francisco: Harper San Francisco, 1995.

Living Buddha, Living Christ. Thich Nhat Hanh. New York: Riverhead Books, 1995.

Natural Great Perfection: Dzogchen Teachings and Vajra Songs. Nyoshul Khenpo Rinpoche and Surya Das. Ithaca, NY: Snow Lion Publications, 1995.

Dzogchen, The Self-Perfected State. Chogyal Namkhai Norbu, Adriano Clemente (editor), John Shane (translator). Ithaca, NY: Snow Lion Publications, 1996.

Shambhala: The Sacred Path of the Warrior. Chogyam Trungpa Rinpoche. Boston: Shambhala Publications, 1988.

Gratefulness, The Heart of Prayer: An Approach to Life in Fullness. Brother David Steindl-Rast. New York: Paulist Press, 1984.

The Good Heart: A Buddhist Perspective on the Teachings of Jesus. Dalai Lama, Bstan-Dzin-Rgya-Mtsho, Robert Kiely (editor), Dom L. Freeman (illustrator). Boston: Wisdom Publications, 1998.

A Path with Heart: A Guide Through the Perils and Promises of Spiritual Life. Jack Kornfield. New York: Bantam Books, 1993.

Wherever You Go, There You Are: Mindfulness Meditation in Everyday Life. Jon Kabat-Zinn. New York: Hyperion, 1994.

Whole Heaven Catalog: A Resource Guide to Products, Services, Arts, Crafts, and Festivals of Religious, Spiritual and Cooperative Communities. Marcia M. Kelly, Jack Kelly. New York: Random House, 1998.

The Eye of the Spirit: An Integral Vision for a World Gone Slightly Mad. Ken Wilber. Boston: Shambhala Publications, 1998.

Heart Treasure of the Enlightened Ones: The Practice of View, Meditation, and Action. Patrul Rinpoche, Dilgo Khyentse. Boston: Shambhala Publications, 1993.

A Heart as Wide as the World. Sharon Salzberg. Boston: Shambhala Publications, 1997.

Meditation. Eknath Easwaran. Tomales, CA: Nilgiri Press, 1991.

Gandhi, the Man: The Story of His Transformation. Eknath Easwaran. Tomales, CA: Nilgiri Press, 1997.

The Art of Pilgrimage: The Seeker's Guide to Making Travel Sacred. Philip Cousineau. Emoryville, CA: Conari Press, 1998.

The Practice of the Presence of God, Brother Lawrence of the Resurrection. John Delaney, Henri J. M. Nouwen. Garden City, NY: Image Books, 1996.

A Year to Live: How to Live This Year As If It Were Your Last. Stephen Levine. New York: Three Rivers Press, 1998.

Centering Prayer in Daily Life and Ministry. Father Thomas Keating, Gustave Reininger (editor). New York: Continuum Publishing Group, 1998.

The Collected Works of Ramana Maharshi. Arthur Osborne (editor). New York: Samuel Weiser, 1997.

Contemplative Prayer. Thomas Merton (introduction by Thich Nhat Hanh). Garden City, NY: Image Books, 1971.

Autobiography of a Yogi. Paramahansa Yogananda. Los Angeles: Self Realization Fellowship, 1979.

The Way of a Pilgrim: And the Pilgrim Continues His Way. Reginald M. French (translator). San Francisco: Harper San Francisco, 1991.

Tao Te Ching. Lao-Tzu, Stephen Mitchell (translator). New York: HarperPerennial Library, 1992.

Jewish Renewal: A Path to Healing and Transformation. Michael Lerner. New York: HarperPerennial Library, 1995.

Kitchen Table Wisdom: Stories That Heal. Rachel Naomi Remen (foreword by Dean Ornish). New York: Riverhead Books, 1997.

Zen and the Art of Motorcycle Maintenance. Robert Pirsig. New York: William Morrow & Co., 1979.

Care of the Soul: A Guide for Cultivating Depth and Sacredness in Everyday Life. Thomas Moore. New York: HarperPerennial Library, 1994.

Buddhism Without Beliefs: A Contemporary Guide to Awakening. Stephen Batchelor. New York: Riverhead Books, 1997.

Stalking Elijah: Adventures with Today's Jewish Mystical Masters. Rodger Kamenetz. San Francisco: Harper San Francisco, 1997.

Freedom in Exile: The Autobiography of the Dalai Lama. His Holiness the Dalai Lama. New York: HarperPerennial Library, 1990.

How Can I Help? Ram Dass and Paul Gorman. New York: Alfred A. Knopf, 1985.

Fire in the Soul: A New Psychology of Spiritual Optimism. Joan Borysenko. New York: Warner Books, 1994.

The Kabir Book: Forty-Four of the Ecstatic Poems of Kabir. Robert W. Bly. Boston: Beacon Press, 1993.

Inner Revolution: Life, Liberty, and the Pursuit of Real Happiness. Robert Thurman. New York: Riverhead Books, 1998.

The Zen Teachings of Huang Po. Huang Po, John Blofield (translator). Boston: Shambhala Publications, 1994.

The Essential Rumi. Jalal Al-Din Rumi, Coleman Barks (translator), John Moyne (translator). San Francisco: Harper San Francisco, 1997.

Total Freedom: The Essential Krishnamurti. Jiddu Krishnamurti. San Francisco: Harper San Francisco, 1996.

Walking. Henry David Thoreau. San Francisco: Harper San Francisco, 1994.

Chanting: Discovering Spirit in Sound. Robert Gass, Kathleen Brehony. New York: Broadway Books, 1999.

How to Meditate: A Practical Guide. Kathleen McDonald. Boston: Wisdom Publications, 1984.

How We Die: Reflections on Life's Final Chapter. Sherwin B. Nuland. New York: Vintage Books, 1995.

The Work of This Moment. Toni Packer. Boston: Charles E. Tuttle, 1995.

Dharma Family Treasures: Sharing Buddhism with Children. Sandy Eastoak (editor). Berkeley, CA: North Atlantic Books, 1994.

The Healing of America. Marianne Williamson, Mary A. Naples (editor). New York: Simon & Schuster, 1997.

The Spirited Walker: Fitness Walking for Clarity, Balance and Spiritual Connection. Carolyn Scott Kortge. San Francisco: Harper San Francisco, 1998.

Spontaneous Healing: How to Discover and Enhance Your Body's Natural Ability to Maintain and Heal Itself. Andrew Weil. New York: Ballantine Books, 1996.

The Art of Breathing: Six Simple Lessons to Improve Performance, Health, and Well-Being. Nancy Zi. Glendale, CA: Vivi Company, 1997.

The Art of Doing Nothing. Veronique Vienne, Erica Lennard (photographer). New York: Clarkson Potter, 1998.

Chanting CDs

The Lama's Chant: Songs of Awakening. Lama Gyurme.

Tibet, Tibet. Yungchen Lhamo.

Cho. Choying Drolma, Steve Tibbetts.

A Pilgrim's Heart. Krishna Das.

One Track Heart. Krishna Das.

Chant I, Chant II. The Benedictine Monks of Santo Domingo De Silos.

Om Namaha Shivaya. Robert Gass.

Videos

Yoga for Meditators. John Friend.

Yoga Journal's Yoga Practice for Beginners. With Patricia Walden.

Sister Wendy in Conversation with Bill Moyers.

Sister Wendy's Story of Painting. Sister Wendy Beckett.

The Power of Myth. Vols. 1–6. Joseph Campbell.

Kundun. Martin Scorsese (director). Starring Tenzin Thutob Tsarong.

Book Clubs

One Spirit Book Club (1–800–348–7128)

Audio Catalogues

Sounds True/Prayer and Meditation Catalogue (1–800–333–9185)

SERVICE TO THE UNIVERSAL SANGHA

People who attend my lectures often say they want to volunteer to become more involved with service-oriented activities, but they don't know where to begin. Here are some suggestions:

Big Brothers Big Sisters
http://www.bbbsa.org
Phone: (215) 567-7000
Big Brothers Big Sisters of America, the oldest mentoring organization serving youth in the country, remains the leading expert in the field. BBBSA has provided one-to-one mentoring relationships between adult volunteers and children at risk since 1904. BBBSA currently serves over 100,000 children and youth in more than 500 agencies throughout all of the United States.

Greenpeace
http://www.greenpeace.org
Greenpeace USA Phone: (202) 462-1177
Greenpeace International Phone: 31 20 523 62 22
Greenpeace is an independent and nonpolitical international organization, dedicated to the protection of the environment by peaceful means. You can become a member on an international level, or join an organization in your own country.

Habitat for Humanity
http://www.habitat.org
Phone: (912) 924-6935

Habitat for Humanity International is dedicated to eliminating substandard housing and homelessness worldwide and to making adequate, affordable shelter a matter of conscience and action. Habitat invites people from all faiths and walks of life to work together in partnership, building houses for families in need. Through volunteer labor and tax-deductible donations of money and materials, Habitat builds and rehabilitates simple, decent houses with the help of the homeowner (partner) families. Habitat has built some 70,000 houses around the world, providing more than 300,000 people with safe, decent, affordable shelter.

Humane Society of the United States
http://www.hsus.org
Phone: (202) 452-1100
The HSUS was founded in 1954 to promote the humane treatment of animals and to foster respect, understanding, and compassion for all creatures. Today, their message of care and protection embraces not only the animal kingdom, but also the earth and its environment.

Literacy Volunteers of America, Inc.
http://literacyvolunteers.org
Phone: (315) 472-0001
Literacy Volunteers of America is a national, not-for-profit educational organization that delivers tutoring services through a network of more than 50,000 volunteers nationwide.

United Way
http://www.unitedway.org
Phone: (800) VOLUNTEER
United Way is a national system of volunteers, contributors, and local charities built on the proven effectiveness of local organizations helping people in their own communities.

Volunteer Match
http://www.volunteermatch.org
Phone: (650) 327-1389
Volunteer Match uses the power of the Internet to help individuals nationwide find volunteer opportunities posted by local nonprofit and public sector organizations. Volunteer Match's powerful online database allows volunteers to search thousands of one-time and ongoing opportunities by zip code, category, and date, and then sign up automatically by e-mail for those that fit their interests and schedule. Volunteer Match offers a variety of activities, including walk-a-thons, beach day cleanups, tutoring, home building, meal deliveries, and more.

Volunteers of America
http://www.voa.org
Phone: (800) 899-0089
From rural America to inner-city neighborhoods, Volunteers of America engages its professional staff and volunteers in designing and operating innovative programs that deal with today's most pressing social problems.

For more information about Lama Surya Das's schedule of lectures, workshops, retreats, tapes, CDs, and three-year integrated Dzogchen training program, please contact:

Lama Surya Das
Cambridge, Massachusetts
http://www.surya.org